ANCHORED GRACE PUBLISHING

Graceful grieving

without him

I0458997

5 MINUTE DAILY, 365 DAYS DEVOTIONAL JOURNAL FOR WOMEN NAVIGATING LOSS

The Grief Gift for Women Finding Comfort and Strength Through Writing and Reflection

© Copyright 2025
All rights reserved.
Anchored Grace Publishing
Binnovate Publishers

The content contained within this book may not be reproduced, duplicated or transmitted without direct written permission from the author or the publisher. Under no circumstances will any blame or legal responsibility be held against the publisher, or author, for any damages, reparation, or monetary loss due to the information contained within this book. Either directly or indirectly. You are responsible for your own choices, actions, and results.

A Gift for You

Thank you for choosing this devotional.

To support your journey of faith, we created a special gift bundle for our readers.

Inside the Anchored Grace Reader Gift Bundle, you will receive:

A free digital devotional

Printable prayer journal pages

Scripture reflection cards

Bonus devotionals for different seasons of life

Daily encouragement from Anchored Grace

Simply scan the QR code below or visit the link to receive your free bundle.

devo.anchoredgraces.com/griefgift

Scan the QR code with your phone camera or type the link into your browser.

We pray these resources continue to encourage your heart each day.

WHEN FAITH FEELS FRAGILE

*"So do not fear, for I am with you; do not be dismayed, for I am your God. I will strengthen you and help you; I will uphold you with my righteous right hand." **Isaiah 41:10***

DEVOTIONAL

There was a woman named Margaret who had spent years walking alongside her husband, sharing dreams and building a life together. After he passed, she found herself overwhelmed by grief, often questioning if she could carry on. One rainy afternoon, while sorting through their old photo albums, she stumbled upon a picture of them on their wedding day, laughing and radiant. As she traced her fingers over the image, a wave of warmth enveloped her, reminding her that while her faith felt fragile, the love they shared was a testament to God's unwavering presence in her life. In that moment, Margaret whispered a prayer for strength, feeling the gentle whisper of peace settle in her heart. *Even when faith feels fragile, there is a divine strength ready to uphold us through our deepest sorrow.*

DAILY REFLECTION

What does faith look like for you in this moment of uncertainty, and how can you nurture it even when it feels fragile?

PRAYER

Dear God, hold me close as I navigate this unfamiliar path. Help me find solace in Your love and strength in my moments of weakness. I trust that You are with me, even in my doubts.

'Even the smallest flicker of faith can ignite a light in the dark.'

TRUSTING GOD IN THE DARKNESS

"Weeping may endure for a night, but joy comes in the morning."
Psalm 30:5

DEVOTIONAL

When Linda lost her husband after years of shared joys and challenges, she often found herself sitting quietly with her Bible, searching for the right words to express her grief. One evening, she stumbled upon a passage that spoke of God collecting our tears in a bottle. This image of a tender-hearted God attending to her pain began to shift her perspective. Instead of feeling alone in her grief, she realized that her sorrow was known and cherished by the One who created her heart. Slowly, she began to allow the Scriptures to articulate her deepest feelings and guide her through the fog of loss.

In times of sorrow, allow the words of Scripture to voice your heart, providing both comfort and hope in your journey.

DAILY REFLECTION

What verses from Scripture have brought you comfort or strength during this time of loss, and how do they resonate with your current feelings?

PRAYER

Dear Lord, wrap your loving arms around this grieving heart. Help her find solace in your words and the strength to embrace each new day with hope.

'In the silence of grief, let His truth whisper healing into your soul.'

THE COMFORT OF SCRIPTURE

"Blessed are those who mourn, for they will be comforted."
Matthew 5:4

DEVOTIONAL

After losing her husband of forty years, Sarah often found herself wandering the aisles of the grocery store, her heart heavy and her eyes filled with tears. One day, amidst the familiar shelves, she stumbled upon a small bouquet of flowers that reminded her of the ones her husband used to bring home to her every Friday. In that moment, instead of overwhelming sorrow, she began to feel a gentle nudge of peace. As she stood there, she recalled Matthew 5:4, embracing the promise that her grief was acknowledged and that comfort was on the way. It was a reminder that even in the mundane moments of life, God shines a light on our pain, assuring us we are never alone.
In the depths of your mourning, remember that God sees your pain and offers a comforting embrace through His Word.

DAILY REFLECTION

What passages in Scripture have brought you comfort during this difficult time? How have they spoken to your heart and reminded you of God's presence?

PRAYER

Dear God, thank You for being our source of comfort and strength. Please wrap Your loving arms around my heart today, reminding me that I am never alone in this journey of grief.

"God's Word is a balm for the broken-hearted, offering solace in the midst of sorrow."

DIVINE STRENGTH IN WEAKNESS

"My grace is sufficient for you, for my power is made perfect in weakness."
2 Corinthians 12:9

DEVOTIONAL

After losing her husband of 40 years, Mary found herself sitting alone on their favorite park bench, feeling a heavy blanket of loneliness engulf her. One day, as she watched children playing and couples strolling, she noticed a young woman struggling to push her toddler's stroller up a steep hill. Without thinking, Mary rose and offered her assistance. As she helped, a surprising warmth filled her heart; in reaching out, she discovered that her own spirit had lifted. She learned that by being a source of support for others, she could also heal.
When we allow our weakness to open the door for others, we may find our own strength blooming in unexpected ways.

DAILY REFLECTION

What areas in your life feel most challenging right now? How can you invite God's strength into those moments of weakness?

PRAYER

Dear God, in my moments of deep sorrow and uncertainty, I ask for your strength to hold me close. Help me to feel your presence and find hope in the love that surrounds me.

"In the space where I feel weakest, your grace is made perfect."

FINDING PURPOSE THROUGH PAIN

*"Instead of your shame you will receive a double portion, and instead of disgrace you will rejoice in your inheritance; and so you will inherit a double portion in your land, and everlasting joy will be yours." **Isaiah 61:7***

DEVOTIONAL

After losing her beloved husband, Mary found herself adrift in a sea of loneliness. Every room in her home echoed with memories, and the silence became almost unbearable. However, as the months went by, she discovered a community of other widows who shared similar journeys. Together, they created a support group, where they could openly express their grief and find solace in each other. Through their shared stories of love and loss, Mary found a renewed sense of purpose, championing others to embrace joy amidst sorrow.

Your pain can become the very seed from which your purpose flourishes.

DAILY REFLECTION

What aspects of your life feel most empty right now, and how might those spaces be an invitation for new purpose to emerge?

PRAYER

Dear God, hold this precious woman in your embrace as she navigates through her pain. Grant her healing and the courage to seek new paths where she may find purpose once again.

"In the cracks of our brokenness, we often find the light of purpose shining through."

SURRENDERING THE "WHY"

*"Trust in the Lord with all your heart and lean not on your own understanding; in all your ways submit to Him, and He will make your paths straight." **Proverbs 3:5-6***

DEVOTIONAL

When Sarah lost her husband, she felt adrift in a sea of questions. Each day, the "why" of life without him echoed in her mind, sometimes loud enough to drown out the love and grace she once felt. One quiet evening, she found herself sitting in the garden they had tended together. The flowers were still blooming, a reminder that life continues even in the midst of pain. It was there, surrounded by beauty, that she felt a gentle nudge to let go of the need to understand every detail of her journey. In that moment, Sarah surrendered her questions and felt a peace envelop her, assuring her that her path could still be bright with possibilities.

Letting go of the "why" can lead to a deeper trust in the journey ahead, even when the way seems unclear.

DAILY REFLECTION

What questions do you find yourself asking in this season of loss, and how might releasing the "why" open your heart to new possibilities?

PRAYER

Dear Lord, in this tender moment of grief, help me to lay down my questions and trust in Your divine plan. Fill my heart with peace as I learn to embrace unanswered prayers and the unknown.

In surrendering the "why," we can begin to discover the beauty of the "what next."

WHEN HEAVEN FEELS CLOSER

*"In my Father's house are many rooms; if it were not so, would I have told you that I go to prepare a place for you? And if I go and prepare a place for you, I will come again and will take you to myself, that where I am you may be also." **John 14:2-3***

DEVOTIONAL

After twenty-five years of shared laughter and whispered dreams, Mary sat in her favorite chair, staring out of the window at the garden they had nurtured together. Each flower reminded her of him—his laughter during spring planting, his gentle hand guiding hers as they watered the blooms. On particularly lonely days, she felt a pull toward the memories of their life together, almost as if he was still present, guiding her through each moment. One evening, as the sun dipped below the horizon, casting a warm golden light over everything, she closed her eyes and inhaled deeply, realizing that while he was absent physically, the love they shared felt like a bridge connecting her to something deeper, reminding her that their love was eternal and that he was not truly gone.

Remember that love, once shared, still lingers and connects us to those we have lost, bringing a sense of closeness to heaven even in our heartache.

DAILY REFLECTION

What memories of your loved one bring you a sense of closeness to heaven? How do those moments shape your understanding of love and loss?

PRAYER

Dear God, as I journey through my grief, help me to feel your presence near and the comfort of those we've lost. Surround me with love and warmth as I seek to understand life and eternity.

In the silence of my heart, I sense the whispers of heaven,
guiding me toward peace and connection beyond this world.

PRAYING THROUGH THE PAIN

*"Do not be anxious about anything, but in every situation, by prayer and petition, with thanksgiving, present your requests to God. And the peace of God, which transcends all understanding, will guard your hearts and your minds in Christ Jesus." **Philippians 4:6-7***

DEVOTIONAL

After the passing of her husband, Margaret found herself wandering through the aisles of their favorite grocery store, her heart heavy with memories. Each familiar item sparked a flood of memories, and tears threatened to spill as she stood frozen, clutching a carton of their favorite ice cream. It was in that moment of deep sorrow that she whispered a simple prayer asking for guidance and a glimpse of peace. The very next moment, a friend unexpectedly appeared beside her, offering not only a warm hug but an invitation to share a meal together. In that little encounter, Margaret felt God reminding her that even in her hardest moments, He was sending help, love, and companionship her way.

The path of grief is marked by pain, but through prayer, we can open the door to God's comforting presence in our lives, allowing love and support to flow in unexpected ways.

DAILY REFLECTION

What specific pain are you feeling today, and how can you invite God into that space with you?

PRAYER

Dear God, in this moment of sorrow, I invite you into my heart. Please hold my pain gently and guide me through this journey of healing.

"Even in the valley of deepest sorrow, your presence is a light that guides me."

One Week Together

You've just completed your first week of devotionals.

If these reflections have brought peace or encouragement into your day, would you consider sharing a short Amazon review?

devo.anchoredgraces.com/grief

Your words help other women discover devotionals that may support them on their own faith journey.

Thank you for spending these moments in reflection.

HOLDING ONTO GOD'S PROMISES

"Fear not, for I have redeemed you; I have called you by name, you are mine."
Isaiah 43:1

DEVOTIONAL

When Martha lost her husband after many years together, she found herself lost in a world that felt foreign and cold. Every corner of their home echoed with memories, and the silence felt overwhelming at times. Yet, in her quiet moments of despair, she began to turn to her Bible, seeking solace in the promises that God made. It was there that she discovered verses that reminded her she was not alone; that she was still cherished, valued, and held by a love far beyond her earthly loss. Through her tears, she found strength in knowing God had a purpose still at work in her life.

In the midst of your grief, let each tear you shed be a reminder that you are embraced by God's unfailing love and that He will help you navigate this new chapter.

DAILY REFLECTION

How can you lean into God's promises during this difficult time, and which of His promises do you find most comforting right now?

PRAYER

Dear God, as I navigate this season of loss, help me to remember Your promises that bring hope and healing. Wrap me in Your love and remind me that I am never alone.

"Even in the valley of sorrow, God's promises shine like stars in the night sky."

JESUS, THE MAN OF SORROWS

"He was despised and rejected by men, a man of sorrows, and acquainted with grief."
Isaiah 53:3

DEVOTIONAL

Not long ago, a dear friend of mine lost her husband unexpectedly. In the days that followed, each passing moment felt like an eternity filled with silence and heartache. She found herself pouring over photo albums, reliving happy memories while grappling with a profound sense of loneliness. One evening, she sat in her garden, tears flowing freely, when unexpectedly, she felt a gentle breeze touch her cheek. In that moment, she sensed a presence beside her. It was as if Jesus Himself was sitting there, holding her hand, reminding her that she was not alone in her sorrows and that her pain had a companion.

In your grief, allow yourself to experience the presence of Jesus, who sits with you in your sorrow and whispers words of love and comfort.

DAILY REFLECTION

What feelings and memories does the phrase "Man of Sorrows" evoke in you, especially in this season of your life? How can knowing that Jesus understands your grief bring you comfort today?

PRAYER

Dear Lord, in your gentle embrace, I seek solace. Help me to feel your presence as I navigate this season of sorrow, and remind me that you walk alongside me in my pain.

"In our deepest sorrow, we find the deepest connection to Christ, who bears our burdens."

ANGELS WATCHING OVER

*"For He will command His angels concerning you to guard you in all your ways; they will lift you up in their hands." **Psalm 91:11-12***

DEVOTIONAL

After losing her husband, Mary often found herself feeling alone and overwhelmed by the silence in their once vibrant home. One evening, as she sat on the porch wrapped in a blanket, she gazed at the stars and felt a soft breeze caress her cheek. It felt as though a gentle presence had wrapped around her—a quiet assurance that her husband was watching over her, and that she was not truly alone. From that night on, she made it a habit to look to the sky for comfort, believing that love transcends even the boundaries of life and death.

Even in your grief, understand that you are cradled in divine care, and the love you shared continues to surround you, like angels watching over your heart.

DAILY REFLECTION

What comforts you in the quiet moments when you feel the absence of your loved one? Can you recall a memory where you felt an angel's presence guiding you?

PRAYER

Dear God, as I navigate this challenging season, please remind me that I am not alone. Fill my heart with your peace and the comfort of your loving presence.

"Even in the darkest nights, the stars shine bright, reminding us that light endures."

LET THE PSALMS SPEAK FOR YOU

"The Lord is close to the brokenhearted and saves those who are crushed in spirit."
Psalm 34:18

DEVOTIONAL

After losing her beloved husband, Margaret often found herself staring out the window, overwhelmed by the silence of her home. One day, she picked up her Bible and turned to the Psalms, allowing the ancient words of sorrow and hope to wash over her. As she read about the deep anguish of David and the comfort he found in God's presence, she felt a sense of solidarity emerge. Each verse seemed to echo the pain she carried inside, but also whispered gentle reminders of God's enduring love and unfailing support, helping her embrace the complexity of her grief.

In the midst of sorrow, the Psalms remind us that we are never truly alone—God sees our hearts and holds us close.

DAILY REFLECTION

What words are you longing to express during this tender time, and how can you invite the Psalms to give voice to your heart's deepest cries?

PRAYER

Lord, I lay my heart bare before You in this moment of sorrow. Help me to seek comfort and strength in Your Word as I navigate this journey of healing.

"In the midst of my pain, Your promises remind me that I am not alone."

WHEN WORSHIP IS A WHISPER

"Come to me, all you who are weary and burdened, and I will give you rest."
Matthew 11:28

DEVOTIONAL

After losing her husband, Clara found herself wandering through the quiet halls of her home, each room echoing the laughter and warmth they once shared. Some days, her spirit felt shattered, and the weight of her sorrow made it hard to articulate her prayers. In those moments, she would sit with a cup of tea, feeling the sun's gentle rays cast their warmth upon her. Instead of offering grand words, she would simply whisper her heart to God, sharing her fear, confusion, and longing. To her surprise, those hushed moments became the sweetest encounters, where she felt the Lord wrap His arms around her, holding her in her grief and inviting her to lean on Him.

Sometimes, the deepest worship happens in the quiet of our hearts, where whispers of longing and love for God become sacred conversations.

DAILY REFLECTION

What does it mean for you to offer a whisper of worship in your heart, especially when words feel too heavy to bear?

PRAYER

Dear God, in this quiet moment, I invite Your presence into my grief. Help me to find solace in the gentle whispers of worship, knowing You hear my heart even in silence.

"Worship is not about the volume of our praise, but the sincerity of our hearts."

A LEGACY OF LAUGHTER

"The Lord is close to the brokenhearted and saves those who are crushed in spirit."
Psalm 34:18

DEVOTIONAL

After losing her husband of over 30 years, Margaret felt a void that resonated in every corner of her home. One afternoon, while sifting through boxes of memories, she stumbled upon her old watercolor set. Encouraged by a flicker of nostalgia, she decided to paint again. As the colors danced on the canvas, she found herself expressing feelings she couldn't articulate with words. Each brushstroke became a step towards healing, transforming her grief into beauty. In sharing her art with friends, she discovered a community of fellow artists who also experienced loss, allowing her sorrow to connect her with others and ignite new friendships.

Embrace the healing power of creativity; it can turn your grief into a canvas of hope and connection.

DAILY REFLECTION

What crafts or artistic expressions bring you joy, and how might they serve as a pathway to healing in this season of your life? Consider a moment where the creative process allowed you to feel connected—to yourself, your memories, or your loved one.

PRAYER

Dear Lord, as I navigate this season of loss, may my hands find solace in the beauty of creation. Help me embrace the art that speaks to my heart and brings healing to my spirit. Amen.

"In creations, both tender and bold, we find threads of hope woven into the fabric of our grief."

THE PRESENCE OF GOD IN GRIEF

"Come to me, all you who are weary and burdened, and I will give you rest."
Matthew 11:28

DEVOTIONAL

When I lost my husband, the world felt like a heavy fog that I couldn't navigate. One evening, as I sat alone in our favorite spot, tears streaming down my face, I remembered the laughter and warmth he brought into my life. In that moment, a gentle whisper of peace wrapped around me, letting me know I was not alone. A soft breeze brushed against my cheek, and for the first time in many days, I felt the presence of God, not in grandeur but in the quiet comfort of that moment, assuring me that grief and love could exist side by side, and that His presence would carry me through the darkness.

In periods of intense grief, allow yourself to feel every emotion while also seeking the quiet reassurance of God's presence, who walks alongside you in love and understanding.

DAILY REFLECTION

What moments have you felt God's presence with you in your grief? How can you invite that presence into your daily life right now?

PRAYER

Dear God, in this time of sorrow, help me to feel Your comforting presence. Wrap me in Your love and guide me through each day with Your strength and peace. Amen.

"In the depths of sorrow, His love carries us gently forward."

ASKING GOD FOR HEALING

"Peace I leave with you; my peace I give you. I do not give to you as the world gives. Do not let your hearts be troubled and do not be afraid." **John 14:27**

DEVOTIONAL

In the wake of loss, it can feel as though the world is drenched in shadows, each day a daunting climb. There was a woman who, after losing her beloved husband, found herself pouring over old photographs late at night, tears flowing as memories replayed like a tender melody. In her quiet hours, she began to whisper her pain to God, asking for healing and peace amidst the storm of her grief. It wasn't instant, but gradually—like dawn softly breaking—the heaviness lifted, replaced by a gentle assurance of His presence. She discovered that healing was not about forgetting but about learning to carry her love with her, one day at a time.

Each moment spent in heartfelt prayer brings you closer to the healing you seek, reminding you that you are not alone on this journey.

DAILY REFLECTION

What does it mean for you to ask God for healing in this season of your life, and how can you invite Him into your pain and longing for restoration?

PRAYER

Heavenly Father, as I navigate this difficult time of grief, I ask for Your gentle healing in my heart. Wrap me in Your love and guide me toward the peace I seek in You.

"In the depths of sorrow, God's healing presence can spark a new beginning."

FINDING LIGHT IN SCRIPTURE

"But Ruth said, 'Do not urge me to leave you or to return from following you. For where you go, I will go, and where you lodge, I will lodge. Your people shall be my people, and your God my God.'" **Ruth 1:16-17**

DEVOTIONAL

After losing her husband of 45 years, Elaine felt the weight of loneliness more than she ever thought possible. One rainy afternoon, as she sorted through a box of old photos, she stumbled upon a snapshot of their last vacation together. It reminded her not only of her husband's warm smile but also of the love and faith they had built together. Amidst her grief, Elaine felt a stirring within her heart—a quiet nudge encouraging her to seek connection, both with her cherished memories and with her faith. Encouraged by the example of Ruth's unwavering commitment, she reached out to her church community, finding solace and encouragement in shared stories of love, loss, and hope.

In the midst of your sorrow, seek the connections that bring warmth to your spirit and allow God's light to shine through your darkness.

DAILY REFLECTION

What passages in Scripture have brought you comfort during this time of transition, and how can you allow those words to illuminate your path ahead?

PRAYER

Dear Lord, as I navigate this season of grief, help me to find solace in Your Word. Open my heart to the verses that speak light into my darkness, guiding me with Your love and peace.

"Even in the shadows, the light of His Word can guide your way."

LETTING GOD HOLD YOU

"God is our refuge and strength, a very present help in trouble. Therefore, we will not fear, though the earth gives way, though the mountains be moved into the heart of the sea."
Psalm 46:1-2

DEVOTIONAL

After losing her husband, Emma found herself navigating a world that felt both familiar and painfully different. Each empty chair at the dining table and each corner of their shared home echoed memories of love and laughter, now tinged with sorrow. One chilly morning, she wrapped herself in the shawl he used to wear as she brewed her coffee. It was during this moment of solitude that she heard a gentle whisper in her heart: "You are not alone. I am with you." It was as if God's arms were wrapping around her, tenderly inviting her to rest in His embrace amid her grief.

Letting God hold you means allowing Him to carry your sorrows and fill your heart with peace.

DAILY REFLECTION

What does it look like for you to let God hold you in this season of grief and uncertainty?

PRAYER

Dear God, as I navigate this tender time, help me to lean into Your embrace. May I find comfort in Your presence and strength in Your love.

"Even in the depths of sorrow, God's arms are open wide, inviting you to rest and heal."

GRACE FOR THE NEXT STEP

"Approach the throne of grace with confidence, so that we may receive mercy and find grace to help us in our time of need. In this season of profound loss, remember that God's grace is ever-present, offering strength for every daunting step ahead." **Hebrews 4:16**

DEVOTIONAL

After losing her husband, Sarah found herself standing at the threshold of her own home, the memories echoing around her like whispers of laughter and love. Each room held a story, yet each story now felt heavy with sorrow. On one particularly hard day, she decided to take just one small step—she planted flowers in the garden they had shared, envisioning how they would bloom anew. As she dug her hands into the earth, she felt a flicker of hope, a reminder that even in death, new life could emerge. With every seed she planted, she realized she could carry her husband's love into the future while embracing a new chapter of her journey.

Grace does not erase your pain, but equips you with the strength and courage to take the next step forward.

DAILY REFLECTION

What does taking the next step look like for you today, and where can you invite grace into that journey?

PRAYER

Heavenly Father, as you wrap your loving arms around her, grant her the strength to face today with courage and an open heart. May she feel your presence as she navigates each moment, finding peace in the unfolding path ahead.

"Grace opens the door to new beginnings, even when the past feels heavy."

ONE SMALL STEP AT A TIME

"The steps of a good man are ordered by the Lord, and he delights in his way. Though he may stumble, he will not fall, for the Lord upholds him with His hand." **Psalm 37:23-24**

DEVOTIONAL

After losing her husband, Clara found herself feeling lost in a world that seemed too big and overwhelming. The house felt emptier, the days longer, and even simple tasks felt insurmountable. One evening, after much contemplation, she decided to take a walk around her neighborhood. With each step, she breathed in the fresh air, letting nature's beauty soothe her aching heart. Clara noticed a blooming flower at the end of her street, a reminder that even in the midst of loss, life continued to flourish. Each small step turned into a journey of healing, helping her reclaim fragments of joy and hope.

Every small step you take is a testament to your resilience, reminding you that healing is a journey made one day at a time.

DAILY REFLECTION

What small step can you take today to honor your feelings and begin moving forward in your journey?

PRAYER

Dear God, grant me the courage to take each moment as it comes, trusting that Your love surrounds me. Help me to find comfort in the small steps I take toward healing.

"Each small step toward healing is a testament to your strength and resilience."

HOPE IS STILL HERE

*"But those who hope in the Lord will renew their strength. They will soar on wings like eagles; they will run and not grow weary, they will walk and not be faint." **Isaiah 40:31***

DEVOTIONAL

After losing her husband, Maria found herself at a crossroads. Days felt monotonous, and nights stretched endlessly. One gloomy afternoon, she decided to take a walk in the park where they used to spend time together. As she strolled, she saw a mother bird feeding its chicks, and she felt a flicker of warmth in her heart. This small yet powerful act of life reminded her that though her world had narrowed, beauty still existed around her. With every step, Maria discovered that hope could grow in her heart again, renewing her spirit gradually and teaching her to embrace each day as it came.

Hope doesn't just fade away; it can rise again, even amidst profound loss.

DAILY REFLECTION

What does hope look like for you in this season of your life? How can you nurture that hope even amid your grief?

PRAYER

Dear God, wrap your loving arms around this heart that hurts. Please whisper sweet promises of hope and healing, reminding her that she is never alone in this journey.

"Even in the midst of sorrow, hope can bloom gently like a flower breaking through the frost."

EMBRACING NEW ROUTINES

"See, I am doing a new thing! Now it springs up; do you not perceive it?"
Isaiah 43:19

DEVOTIONAL

After losing her husband, Sarah felt lost in a world that suddenly seemed foreign. Each day blended into the next as she trudged through routines that felt hollow without him. One afternoon, she decided to take a different route during her evening walk. As the sun dipped below the horizon, painting the sky in hues of orange and pink, she stumbled upon a quaint little café she had never noticed before. Inspired by its warmth, she ventured inside, where the aroma of fresh coffee and baked goods enveloped her in comfort. That small change ignited a spark in her spirit, reminding her that even in loss, new joys could be found in unexpected places.

Embracing new routines opens the door to healing and unexpectedly beautiful moments in your journey ahead.

DAILY REFLECTION

What new routines could you embrace in this season of change that might bring you peace and joy? How can you allow yourself to cherish memories while also welcoming the gift of fresh starts?

PRAYER

Dear God, as I navigate this new chapter of my life, help me to find comfort and strength in embracing new routines. May I feel Your presence guiding me through each day, bringing light and hope to my heart.

"Every day is a new page in the story of your life; make it one worth reading."

Three Weeks of Reflection

You've now spent several weeks walking through these devotionals.

If this book has encouraged your heart, a brief Amazon review helps other women find the same encouragement.

devo.anchoredgraces.com/grief

Your experience may guide someone else toward the hope they are searching for.

Thank you for being here.

HEALING DOESN'T MEAN FORGETTING

"Now faith is the assurance of things hoped for, the conviction of things not seen."
Hebrews 11:1

DEVOTIONAL

Once, a woman named Clara found herself walking through her quiet home, each room echoing with the laughter and love that once filled it. While the memories of her husband brought both joy and sorrow, she realized that preserving those moments kept him alive in her heart. With each passing day, Clara began to find ways to honor her husband's memory—not by dwelling in the shadows of grief but by embracing the light he brought into her life. She created a memory book filled with photographs and notes, a tangible piece of their journey together that she could revisit when the waves of longing washed over her.

Healing is not about forgetting; it is about weaving the memories of love into the fabric of your life as you move forward.

DAILY REFLECTION

What memories of your loved one bring you comfort, and how can you honor those moments as you continue to heal?

PRAYER

Dear God, wrap your comforting arms around her heart as she navigates her grief. May she find peace in remembering her loved one and strength to embrace the journey ahead.

Healing is not about erasing the memories;
it's about carrying them with grace and love as we move forward.

YOUR SOUL STILL SINGS

"He heals the brokenhearted and binds up their wounds."
Psalm 147:3

DEVOTIONAL

Marilyn found herself staring at the blank wall of her living room, a stark reminder of the love that once filled her home. For weeks, she avoided listening to music, convinced that it would only amplify her loneliness. One quiet afternoon, while dusting the shelves, she accidentally hit play on her old stereo. The sweet notes of a beloved song filled the space, catching her off guard. As the familiar melody washed over her, memories of happy dances and joyful laughter enveloped her. In that moment, Marilyn realized that while she was grieving, the essence of her love continued to sing within her soul, a testament to the life they shared.

Your heart may feel heavy, but know that even in this time of sorrow, your soul still has a melody, waiting to be sung anew.

DAILY REFLECTION

What melodies does your heart still long to sing, even in this season of loss? How can you honor the memory of your loved one while allowing your soul to express hope and joy once more?

PRAYER

Dear God, in this tender time of sorrow, embrace my heart with Your love. Help me to find the strength to let my soul sing, knowing that my loved one is in Your care.

Even in grief, your spirit is alive, and your soul still has songs to sing.

LEARNING TO COOK FOR ONE

"Those who look to Him are radiant; their faces are never covered with shame."
Psalm 34:5

DEVOTIONAL

When Clara's husband passed away, she found herself standing in their once lively kitchen, now echoing with silence. Cooking for two had always been a shared experience, filled with laughter and the warmth of companionship. The thought of preparing meals for just herself felt foreign and daunting. But one day, she found an old recipe book tucked away on the shelf. As she flipped through the pages, memories of cooking together flooded in. Inspired, Clara decided to try one of their favorite dishes. With each chop of the vegetables and sprinkle of seasoning, the memories intertwined with her present, reminding her that nurturing herself could be a way to keep their love alive.

Take heart, for cooking for yourself can be a beautiful act of self-love and remembrance, a way to honor your past while embracing the future.

DAILY REFLECTION

What does cooking for one mean to you, and how can it transform your moments of solitude into opportunities for nourishment and self-discovery?

PRAYER

Heavenly Father, guide me as I navigate this new chapter in my life. Help me find joy in cooking for myself, turning each meal into a comforting ritual that nurtures my spirit and body.

"Feeding your soul can be as essential as feeding your body."

REARRANGING THE HOUSE, GENTLY

"The name of the LORD is a strong tower; the righteous run to it and are safe."
Proverbs 18:10

DEVOTIONAL

After losing her husband, Mary felt as though she was standing on the edge of a cliff, unsure of what lay below. Every morning was a challenge as she navigated the world that felt changed forever. One day, she decided to take a step toward the unknown instead of away from it. She signed up for a painting class, knowing little about art but hoping to express the colors of her emotions. With each brushstroke, she felt a burden lift, revealing that trusting God didn't mean having all the answers but rather taking small steps into the beautiful uncertainty of life.

Trusting God means believing that even when the path is unclear, He is guiding your footsteps toward grace and healing.

DAILY REFLECTION

What unknowns are you facing in your life right now, and how might trusting God with those uncertainties bring you peace?

PRAYER

Dear God, as I navigate this unfamiliar path without my beloved, help me to lean on Your strength and wisdom. Wrap me in Your comforting presence and guide my steps into the unknown.

"Faith is taking the first step, even when you don't see the whole staircase."

THE GIFT OF SLEEP AGAIN

"Cast all your anxiety on Him because He cares for you."
1 Peter 5:7

DEVOTIONAL

When Mary lost her husband, the nights felt endless. Sleep eluded her as her mind raced with memories and unresolved questions. One evening, wrapped in a blanket, she decided to take a different approach. Instead of counting worries, she began counting the blessings she shared with him: laughter over shared meals, the warmth of his hug, the joy of building a life together. Gradually, peace settled in, and sleep finally enveloped her like a comforting embrace. Mary discovered that when she focused on gratitude, the gift of restful sleep returned, allowing her heart to heal.

Finding peace among the grief allows room for healing and the gentle return of restful sleep.

DAILY REFLECTION

What does resting in the stillness of night whisper to your heart and soul in this new chapter of your life?

PRAYER

Heavenly Father, wrap this dear woman in Your comforting embrace, granting her the peace and rest she needs. May her nights be filled with the tranquility that leads to rejuvenation and hope.

"Sleep is a gentle reminder that in the quiet moments, God is still working."

CREATING NEW MEMORIES

"Wisdom is the principal thing; therefore get wisdom, and with all your getting, get understanding." **Proverbs 4:7**

DEVOTIONAL

In the quiet moments after her husband's passing, Miriam found herself surrounded by memories—pictures, shared laughs, and dreams that felt as if they were etched in stone. One day, she discovered the old journal he had kept while they traveled together. Flipping through the pages, she was struck by his words about their adventures and small moments that brought joy. Inspired, Miriam decided to honor his memory by revisiting those places they had loved while also seeking new experiences to embrace life again. As she placed her foot on the path of one of their favorite hiking trails, she realized it felt different; it was almost as if he was there beside her, encouraging her to open her heart to new memories while cherishing the old.

Creating new memories does not mean leaving the past behind; it means carrying the love forward as you embrace life's new opportunities.

DAILY REFLECTION

What new memories could you begin to create today that honor both your past and your future?

PRAYER

Dear Lord, as I navigate this new chapter of my life, help me to find joy in the little moments and the strength to embrace fresh beginnings. May I feel your presence guiding me in all that lies ahead.

"Every new memory is a step towards healing and hope."

TINY JOYS, BIG HEALING

*"The steadfast love of the Lord never ceases; His mercies never come to an end; they are new every morning; great is Your faithfulness." **Lamentations 3:22-23***

DEVOTIONAL

In the days following her husband's passing, Linda found herself overwhelmed by the silence of her home. One morning, while sipping her coffee, she noticed a tiny bluebird at the feeder outside her window. For a brief moment, her heart lifted, and she smiled. Little by little, she began to notice other small gifts around her—flowers blooming in her garden, a friend's phone call, the warmth of the sun on her face—each one whispering of love and life despite her grief. These moments became like stitches, mending her broken heart with each tiny joy.

There is beauty in the delicate moments of life; they remind us that healing is often found in the smallest of joys.

DAILY REFLECTION

What tiny joys have you noticed in your daily life since your loss, and how do they make your heart feel? Reflect on how these moments of light can guide your path toward healing.

PRAYER

Dear God, in moments of sorrow, may I pause to recognize the small joys You place in my life. Help me to embrace each one as a step toward healing, finding comfort in the warmth of Your love.

"Even in the shadows, joy can bloom quietly, whispering hope to the heart."

WHEN YOU FINALLY BREATHE DEEP

*"I praise you because I am fearfully and wonderfully made; your works are wonderful, I know that full well." **Psalm 139:14***

DEVOTIONAL

When Sarah first found herself alone, the weight of her grief felt like an anchor pulling her under. Days turned into a blur, and nights were filled with memories that stung like fresh wounds. It wasn't until a quiet morning, surrounded by the gentle rustle of leaves and the soft light of dawn, that she took a deep breath — a real one. As she inhaled, she felt a flicker of hope in her chest, a reminder that life still held beauty. In that moment, she realized that even amidst her pain, God was inviting her to breathe deeply and embrace the journey ahead.

Breathe deeply; in your sorrow, there is room for renewal and the whisper of hope.

DAILY REFLECTION

What does it feel like to finally take a deep breath after feeling the weight of loss, and how can you allow yourself to embrace this moment of stillness?

PRAYER

Dear God, in the quiet moments, help her to feel Your presence wrapping around her like a warm blanket. Grant her peace and the strength to breathe deeply as she navigates this new chapter of her life.

In the stillness of sorrow, we often find the seeds of hope begin to bloom.

A NEW MORNING, A NEW MERCY

"To bestow on them a crown of beauty instead of ashes, the oil of joy instead of mourning, and a garment of praise instead of a spirit of despair."
Isaiah 61:3

DEVOTIONAL

Once, a woman named Clara found herself engulfed in silence after losing her husband. Every morning felt the same; the stillness of her home echoed the absence of his laughter. One day, as the sun began to rise, she stepped outside and felt the warmth on her face. The beauty of the dawn struck her, and with it, she realized that each day brings the chance for new experiences. Inspired, she started a gratitude journal, noting small joys that nudged her forward, from the first blooms of spring to the laughter of her grandchildren.

Embrace each new morning as an invitation to experience God's mercies and find beauty in unexpected places.

DAILY REFLECTION

What do you feel God is whispering to your heart this morning as you begin to navigate this new chapter in your life?

PRAYER

Dear Lord, I come to You with a heart that feels both heavy and hopeful. Grant me the strength to embrace each new day and the mercy to heal as I walk this journey of remembrance and renewal.

"Every new dawn is a gentle reminder that mercy is always waiting just beyond the horizon."

RECLAIMING YOUR PEACE

"And the peace of God, which transcends all understanding, will guard your hearts and your minds in Christ Jesus." **Philippians 4:7**

DEVOTIONAL

As Sarah sat alone in her quiet living room, the silence felt heavier than she had ever imagined. Each corner of the room held memories of laughter, love, and companionship, but now they echoed back to her only solitude. Overwhelmed by her grief, she noticed a small flower pot on the windowsill, a gift from her late husband. It was then that she remembered the way he used to say that even the smallest joys could bloom in the toughest seasons. Inspired, she decided to nurture that little flower and, in doing so, began to reclaim the whispers of peace that had long been overshadowed by sorrow. With every new leaf that unfurled, she felt a tiny piece of her heart mend.

Embrace the small joys that surround you; they are the first steps towards reclaiming your peace after loss.

DAILY REFLECTION

What does peace look like for you in this new chapter of your life, and how can you begin to embrace it amidst the uncertainty?

PRAYER

Dear God, as I navigate this journey of loss, please guide me toward the peace that surpasses all understanding. Help me to find solace in Your presence each day. Amen.

"Peace is not the absence of trouble but the presence of God amid the storms of life."

FINDING PURPOSE AFTER LOSS

"I will turn their mourning into joy, and I will comfort them and give them gladness for sorrow." **Jeremiah 31:13**

DEVOTIONAL

After losing her husband, Sarah often found herself drifting through days that felt heavy and unbearing. She spent countless evenings looking through photo albums, recounting sweet memories, and lamenting the loss of a partner who had been her rock. One day, while walking in her garden, she noticed how the flowers were blooming again after a long winter, bringing vibrant colors back into her life. Inspired by this, Sarah decided to plant a new flower bed dedicated to her husband's memory, realizing that while her grief was profound, she could still cultivate new beginnings. It became a space not only for remembrance but also for hope, laughter, and community as she invited friends over to help plant and share stories.

Embracing change, even amidst sorrow, can lead to unexpected joy and purpose.

DAILY REFLECTION

What dreams and passions have you set aside that you might revive as you seek a new purpose in this season of life? How can you take the first steps toward rediscovering what brings you joy?

PRAYER

Dear God, in this time of profound change, grant her the courage to embrace her new journey. May she feel your presence as she searches for meaning and purpose beyond her loss.

"Even in the shadows of sorrow, new beginnings can bloom like flowers in spring."

TRUSTING THE SLOW REBUILD

"Truly my soul finds rest in God; my salvation comes from him. Truly he is my rock and my salvation; he is my fortress, I will never be shaken." **Psalm 62:1-2**

DEVOTIONAL

When Anna found herself standing alone in the quiet home she had shared with her husband for decades, she felt the weight of an uncertain future. Each room seemed to echo memories of laughter and love, yet all she could feel was the silence that enveloped her. As the days turned into weeks, she began to notice small changes – the flowers she tended outside her window blossomed anew, and with each bloom, Anna found a flicker of hope. It wasn't a complete transformation, but rather a gentle reminder that even in sorrow, life continues, and healing, like spring, takes time. Slowly, she learned to embrace this process, allowing herself to grieve while also welcoming moments of joy back into her heart.

Trusting the slow rebuild of your life is an act of faith, knowing that joy will return in time, just as the seasons change.

DAILY REFLECTION

What does it mean for you to trust the process of rebuilding your life, step by step, in this season of change and uncertainty?

PRAYER

Dear God, hold this dear woman in your loving embrace as she navigates the slow journey of healing. Grant her patience and peace, reminding her that each small step forward is part of your greater plan for her life.

"Rebuilding takes time, but each day lays a new stone on the path of hope."

WHEN YOU LAUGH WITHOUT GUILT

"Strength and dignity are her clothing, and she laughs without fear of the future."
Proverbs 31:25

DEVOTIONAL

After losing her husband, Sarah felt lost in her sorrow. The days following his passing were heavy with grief, and laughter seemed like a memory from another life. One afternoon, however, while reminiscing with her friends over cups of tea and shared stories, a funny memory of her husband surfaced. In that moment, a genuine laugh erupted, surprising her with its brightness. It felt freeing, like a gentle reminder that joy could coexist with grief. As the laughter shared with her friends danced in the air, Sarah found comfort in knowing that it was okay to embrace moments of happiness amidst her sorrow.

It is perfectly natural to experience laughter and joy alongside your grief; allowing yourself to feel these emotions is an act of resilience and love.

DAILY REFLECTION

What memories make you smile when you think of your loved one? How can you embrace those moments of joy without feeling guilty?

PRAYER

Dear God, thank You for the laughter that still lightens our hearts. Help us to cherish the joyful memories while allowing ourselves to feel your peace and comfort in this new chapter.

"Laughter is the echo of love that remains in our hearts, a testament to the joy we once shared."

BUILDING A NEW IDENTITY

*"But now thus says the Lord, he who created you, O Jacob, he who formed you, O Israel:
'Fear not, for I have redeemed you; I have called you by name, you are mine.'"* **Isaiah 43:1**

DEVOTIONAL

After losing her husband, Linda felt as if she had lost not only her partner but a part of herself. Each day felt heavier, and the mirrors reflected a woman she barely recognized. However, during one quiet evening, she stumbled upon an old journal where she had written dreams and aspirations. In revisiting those pages, she realized that while the love of her life was gone, her dreams still remained. With every brave decision to rediscover herself —be it pursuing painting, joining a book club, or traveling to places she had talked about with her husband—Linda began to build a new identity, one that honored her past and embraced her future.

You are not defined by your loss, but by the strength you find in rediscovering who you are, even amidst the pain.

DAILY REFLECTION

What aspects of your identity have changed since your husband's passing, and how can you embrace this new chapter as an opportunity for growth and renewal?

PRAYER

Dear God, as I journey through this season of change, help me to find joy and strength in redefining my identity. May your love surround me as I take one step at a time towards this new path.

"From grief comes growth; in losing one part of ourselves,
we discover new dimensions waiting to be explored."

HEALING IN NATURE

"The heavens declare the glory of God; the skies proclaim the work of his hands."
Psalm 19:1

DEVOTIONAL

Last autumn, as the leaves turned brilliant shades of orange and gold, Susan found herself alone on a wooded path she once walked with her husband. With each step, she felt an ache in her heart, but the beauty of the vibrant foliage began to distract her from the heaviness of her loss. Suddenly, she spotted a lone tree still standing tall amid the shifting winds. It reminded her that, like that tree, she too could weather the storms. Nature provided her a glimpse of resilience, urging her to embrace life anew despite her overwhelming grief.

Nature has a way of soothing our souls, reminding us that healing can come in the soft whisper of the wind or the gentle warmth of the sun, guiding us through our darkest days.

DAILY REFLECTION

What specific moments in nature have brought you comfort or peace since your loss? How can you allow these moments to guide you toward healing?

PRAYER

Dear God, as I walk through your creation, open my heart to the healing that surrounds me. Help me to find solace and renewal in the beauty of nature.

"Nature whispers the promise of new beginnings
and the comfort of memories intertwined with the present."

PLANTING SEEDS OF JOY

*"Those who sow with tears will reap with songs of joy. Those who go out weeping, carrying seed to sow, will return with songs of joy, carrying sheaves with them." **Psalm 126:5-6***

DEVOTIONAL

After losing her husband, Linda often felt as if joy was an elusive dream, buried beneath layers of grief. Yet, one afternoon while tending her garden, she noticed how the soil, although dry and cracked, had tiny green shoots peeking through. With each passing day, those little plants grew stronger, a vibrant reminder that beauty can emerge from difficult circumstances. Inspired by this, Linda began to plant flowers—each blooming petal a symbol of the love she once shared, yet also an invitation to welcome joy back into her life in new forms.

Each moment of pain can also become a seed for new joys, reminding you that love and happiness can grow again, even from sorrow.

DAILY REFLECTION

What are some small moments today that could bring you joy, even amidst the shadows of your loss?

PRAYER

Dear Lord, as I navigate this season of change, help me to seek and recognize the seeds of joy that You plant in my life each day. May Your comfort guide me as I learn to nurture happiness within my heart.

"Even in the soil of sorrow, joy can bloom anew."

LETTING LOVE IN AGAIN

*"There is no fear in love. But perfect love drives out fear, because fear has to do with punishment. The one who fears is not made perfect in love." **1 John 4:18***

DEVOTIONAL

I once knew a woman who had lost her dearest friend and companion after many decades. In the days following her husband's passing, she found herself enveloped in a cocoon of memories, both comforting and painful. But one day, while tending to her garden, she noticed a tiny bud breaking through the soil. In that moment, she felt a gentle whisper: life is still unfolding, even amidst loss. As she tended to that bud, nurturing it with care, she felt warmth blooming in her heart, reminding her that love can find its way back, amid even the deepest sorrow.

Letting love in again may feel daunting, but it is an essential part of healing and renewal.

DAILY REFLECTION

What does the idea of opening your heart to love again stir within you? Can you identify the fears or hopes that surface when you think about allowing love back into your life?

PRAYER

Dear God, as I navigate this season of loss, help me to feel your warmth and encouragement. Grant me the courage to embrace the possibility of love once more, knowing that Your love surrounds me.

"Love is not a finite resource; it expands and grows when we allow it to."

THE LIFE YOU BUILT TOGETHER

"A wife of noble character who can find? She is worth far more than rubies."
Proverbs 31:10

DEVOTIONAL

When I think of my dear friend Martha, I am reminded of all the moments she and her husband, Tom, built together. From the laughter-filled dinners to quiet evenings spent just holding hands, their life was a tapestry woven with love, respect, and shared dreams. After Tom's passing, Martha often found herself wandering through their home, recalling the warmth of their years together—the echoes of shared stories, the familiar scent of his favorite coffee brewing in the mornings. Although the loss left a palpable emptiness, Martha discovered that the love they built not only remained in her heart but echoed in the lives of their children and friends, reminding her that their love story continues on in the memories they created together.

Cherish the memories you've built, for they are a testament to a love that continues to shape your journey even in his absence.

DAILY REFLECTION

What are some cherished memories you hold close that reflect the life you built together, and how can those memories bring you comfort today?

PRAYER

Dear God, as I navigate this time of loss, help me to lean into the love that surrounded my marriage. May I find peace in the memories and strength in Your embrace.

"Every corner of our home whispers the story of love; may I find solace in those echoes."

WHAT HE TAUGHT YOU

"Are not two sparrows sold for a penny? Yet not one of them will fall to the ground outside your Father's care. And even the hairs of your head are all numbered. So don't be afraid; you are worth more than many sparrows." **Matthew 10:29-31**

DEVOTIONAL

As you sit in the quietness of your home, memories of shared laughter and love may feel heavy on your heart. In the stillness, you might find yourself reflecting on the small moments that brought joy — a quiet cup of coffee together, the playful banter during a walk, or the warmth of a gentle handhold. These memories serve as a bittersweet reminder of what was, but they also illuminate the legacy of love and wisdom he instilled in you.

When faced with the uncertainty of each new day, remember that the lessons he left behind can guide you — just as the stars light the night sky, his love continues to illuminate your path.

Cherish the memories of love, for they are the gentle reminders that you are never alone in your journey.

DAILY REFLECTION

What lessons do you carry in your heart from your beloved, and how can they guide your steps forward in this new season of life?

PRAYER

Dear Lord, please wrap your loving arms around this heart in mourning. Help her to see the beauty in the lessons learned and to find strength in the memories shared.

"Every moment shared was a page written in the story of love, and the lessons learned will light the path ahead."

CARRYING ON HIS KINDNESS

*"Even in darkness light dawns for the upright, for those who are gracious and compassionate and righteous." **Psalm 112:4***

DEVOTIONAL

After losing her husband, Lena felt like she was navigating a storm without a compass. The house felt empty, and the silence echoed through the rooms where laughter once resided. One gray afternoon, she decided to take a walk in the nearby park, hoping the fresh air would lift her spirits. As she strolled, she noticed a frail woman sitting on a bench, tears streaming down her face. Lena hesitated but felt a gentle urging to approach. After a few moments of conversation, Lena found herself sharing kind words and a comforting smile. In that moment, she realized that even in her own grief, she had the power to extend kindness into the world—keeping a part of her husband's spirit alive through the love she gave to others.

In the midst of your sorrow, remember that your kindness can illuminate the darkness in someone else's life.

DAILY REFLECTION

What does it look like for you to carry on the kindness your loved one embodied in their life? How can you express that kindness to yourself and others in this new chapter?

PRAYER

Dear God, help me to find strength in my grief and the courage to share kindness in every interaction. May my heart be open to the warmth that surrounds me, and may I honor my loved one by spreading love to those around me.

"In every small act of kindness, we can keep our loved ones alive in our hearts."

HIS FAVORITE SAYINGS

"He gives strength to the weary and increases the power of the weak."
Isaiah 40:29

DEVOTIONAL

After the loss of her beloved husband, Ellen felt adrift, like a ship lost at sea. Nights were long and quiet, filled only with the echoes of memories that haunted her heart. One evening, as she sorted through old photographs, she stumbled upon a handwritten card where he had penned his favorite sayings. "Always look for the silver lining," it read, accompanied by a familiar drawing of a sunrise. In that moment, Ellen realized that these were more than just words; they were a gentle nudge from her late husband, encouraging her to seek hope amid despair. She decided to embrace his wisdom and look for those moments of light, even in the darkest of days.

Seek out the whispers of love that remind you of hope and strength in your journey forward.

DAILY REFLECTION

What is one saying of Christ that has brought you comfort or strength during this difficult time? How can you carry that saying in your heart as you navigate your grief?

PRAYER

Dear Lord, wrap your loving arms around this heart, bringing peace in the midst of sorrow. Help her find strength in Your words and comfort in Your presence each day.

"His words may be silent, but their echoes can carry us through the darkest valleys."

COOKING HIS FAVORITE MEAL

"The Lord is close to the brokenhearted and saves those who are crushed in spirit."
Psalm 34:18

DEVOTIONAL

In the quiet of my kitchen, I found myself stirred by memories of my beloved husband as I prepared his favorite meal. Each ingredient seemed to whisper stories of laughter, warmth, and love shared over the dinner table. As I chopped the vegetables, I recalled how his eyes would light up when he tasted that familiar dish, and the thought of bringing that joy back, even if just within my own heart, became a small comfort. This act of cooking became more than just a meal; it turned into a cherished ritual—a way to keep his spirit alive and to nurture my own heart amidst grief. Through this process, I realized that even in my sorrow, there were moments of connection and gratitude that could be found in the simplest of tasks.
Nourishing your body through familiar, loving practices can bring comfort and healing during your time of loss.

DAILY REFLECTION

What does cooking his favorite meal bring to mind for you? How does it feel to create a space where cherished memories can mingle with new beginnings?

PRAYER

Dear Lord, as I gather my memories in the kitchen, help me to feel your comforting presence. May the act of cooking bring warmth to my heart and remind me of the love we shared.

"Every meal cooked in love carries a piece of the heart that prepared it."

VALENTINE'S DAY IN GRIEF

"So also you have sorrow now, but I will see you again, and your hearts will rejoice, and no one will take your joy from you." **John 16:22**

DEVOTIONAL

As Valentine's Day approaches, a chill settles in the air, reminding you of the warmth you once shared. Memories of shared laughter, surprise dates, and whispered promises fill your heart, but this year feels different—tinged with an ache that's hard to shake. You find solace in knowing that while he may not be physically present, the love you shared remains eternal. Perhaps you light a candle and speak softly to the memories, letting the tears flow like a river, cleansing your soul while honoring the love that shaped you. On this day dedicated to love, allow yourself to grieve and celebrate, mingling the sorrow with sweet remembrances of your journey together.
In this season of grief, recognize that love transcends the physical and continues to knit your heart to his, a bond that grief cannot sever.

DAILY REFLECTION

What memories of love bring you both joy and sorrow as Valentine's Day approaches? Can you find space in your heart for both feelings to coexist today?

PRAYER

Lord, as I navigate this season of love and loss, help me to feel your embrace and remember the beauty of our shared moments. Grant me peace and comfort, reminding me that love endures beyond the physical presence.

"Grief is the price we pay for love, a testament to the depth of our connection."

HIS STRENGTH IN YOU

*"But he said to me, 'My grace is sufficient for you, for my power is made perfect in weakness.' Therefore I will boast all the more gladly about my weaknesses, so that Christ's power may rest on me." **2 Corinthians 12:9***

DEVOTIONAL

After losing her husband, Maria felt like a shadow of her former self. Every morning, she would sit in her favorite chair, staring out the window at the garden they had nurtured together, feeling as if she had been left behind. One day, as she sipped her tea, a small bird landed on the windowsill and began to sing. She listened, tears streaming down her face, realizing that in this moment of deep sorrow, there was beauty, love, and life still surrounding her. In her vulnerability, she sensed a warm whisper—God was reminding her that even in her weakness, He was pouring His strength into her heart, giving her the courage to embrace each new day.

In your moments of vulnerability, remember that God's strength is at work within you, providing hope and courage to face each day anew.

DAILY REFLECTION

What strengths have you discovered within yourself since the loss of your partner, and how can you lean into those as you move forward?

PRAYER

Dear Lord, please wrap Your comforting arms around her today and remind her of the strength You have placed within her. Guide her steps as she navigates this new chapter, filling her heart with peace and assurance.

"When we feel weak, His strength becomes our anchor."

WHAT HE'D WANT FOR YOU NOW

*"I waited patiently for the Lord; he turned to me and heard my cry. He lifted me out of the slimy pit, out of the mud and mire; he set my feet on a rock and gave me a firm place to stand. He put a new song in my mouth, a hymn of praise to our God. Many will see and fear the Lord and put their trust in him." **Psalm 40:1-3***

DEVOTIONAL

After her husband's passing, Clara felt a profound emptiness that echoed through her days. Each morning, the silence of the house was a stark reminder of her loss, and nights were often spent wrestling with memories that both comforted and stung. One afternoon, while sorting through some old photographs, she stumbled upon a picture of them laughing on the beach, arms around each other, smiles bright. In that moment, she remembered the joy they shared, and it became clear to her that he would not want her to live in sorrow but to honor their love by embracing life again. A small, determined flame ignited in her heart, and gradually, she began to find new joys and new passions, allowing the sweet memories to weave into her journey forward.

Your late husband would want you to find joy in the memories you shared and hope in the future ahead, knowing that it's possible to honor him while also allowing yourself to flourish anew.

DAILY REFLECTION

What is one thing you believe he would encourage you to embrace or pursue in this new chapter of your life?

PRAYER

Dear God, grant her the strength to navigate this season of change, filling her heart with comfort and hope. May she feel Your love surrounding her as she takes each step forward.

"Your journey doesn't end here; it evolves into something beautiful and new."

TELLING HIS STORY

*"We will not hide them from their children; we will tell the next generation the praiseworthy deeds of the Lord, his power, and the wonders he has done." **Psalm 78:4***

DEVOTIONAL

As I sat on the porch, the warm sun on my face felt like a gentle hug. It was difficult to imagine life without my husband, who had always shared stories of his childhood – the funny mishaps, the sweet moments with his family, and the faith that guided him. When I felt lost, those memories became a compass pointing me back to the love we built together. Sharing these stories with my children not only honors his memory but also reinforces the legacy of faith and resilience he left behind. In telling his story, I find healing, and surprisingly, it brings smiles and a sense of togetherness amidst the grief.

Your husband's story is a treasure that can bring healing to your heart and joy to those around you.

DAILY REFLECTION

What story of love and faith has your journey written so far, and how can you share that narrative with others as a way of honoring his memory?

PRAYER

Dear God, as I navigate this new chapter of my life, help me to find solace in the stories we've shared. May my heart be open to tell our journey, honoring the love that still lives within me.

"Every story of love leaves an imprint on our lives; yours is a testament to grace, resilience, and hope."

LIVING WITH HIS LOVE STILL

"For I am convinced that neither death nor life, neither angels nor demons, neither the present nor the future, nor any powers, neither height nor depth, nor anything else in all creation, will be able to separate us from the love of God that is in Christ Jesus our Lord."
Romans 8:38-39

DEVOTIONAL

After losing the love of her life, Sarah found herself wandering through an empty home filled with echoes of laughter and memories that felt both comforting and painful. On particularly quiet evenings, she would pour herself a cup of tea and sit on the porch, gazing at the stars. It was during these moments that she began to feel the warmth of love that transcended even her grief. On one such night, she closed her eyes and imagined her husband's voice whispering to her, reminding her that while he may no longer be by her side, the love they shared would carry on through the very fabric of her being. In that gentle breeze, she felt a new kind of companionship – one that exists even in absence.

You are never truly alone; God's love wraps around you, providing comfort and hope as you navigate this new chapter of your life.

DAILY REFLECTION

What are some ways you can feel and express your husband's love in your everyday life, even though he is no longer physically present?

PRAYER

Dear Lord, wrap Your loving arms around me as I navigate this new chapter. Help me to feel Your presence and the love my husband shared with me, filling my heart with comfort and peace.

"His love is a legacy that continues to shape my heart and guide my path."

CHERISHING THE WEDDING VOWS

"For better or for worse, in sickness and in health, we made our promises, we shared our dreams. Now, even in the silence of his absence, the words we spoke still echo in our hearts. 'Love is patient, love is kind; it does not envy, it does not boast, it is not proud.'
1 Corinthians 13:4

DEVOTIONAL

Maggie often found herself retracing the paths she walked with her husband, the places where laughter lingered in the air and happy memories were etched into every corner. One day, while sitting on a park bench where they used to enjoy ice cream together, she pulled out a tattered note from her purse. It was his handwritten promise to always cherish her. Tears streamed down her cheeks as she realized that those vows were not just words spoken long ago; they were a living testament to the bond they shared. In that moment, she felt both the weight of her loss and the warmth of his love, reminding her that even when he was gone, the essence of their relationship would always be a part of her journey.

In your journey of grief, remember that the essence of your wedding vows is a source of strength and comfort, allowing you to honor your love in every step forward.

DAILY REFLECTION

What do your wedding vows mean to you now, in this season of your life, and how can you carry those promises forward as a source of strength and love?

PRAYER

Heavenly Father, wrap your comforting arms around this heart that mourns. Help me to treasure the vows I made and to find peace in the love we shared.

"Vows are not just words spoken on a special day;
they are a testament of love that endures through every season."

WHAT HE LOVED ABOUT YOU

"How precious to me are your thoughts, God! How vast is the sum of them! Were I to count them, they would outnumber the grains of sand—when I awake, I am still with you."
Psalm 139:17-18

DEVOTIONAL

She sat on the edge of their bed, the sunlight streaming through the window, illuminating the room that once felt like a sanctuary of love and laughter. The void felt overwhelming without him, and yet, there remained a whisper of fond memories that would not fade. She picked up an old postcard he had sent her during their early days together, a simple note that expressed just how beautiful he found her spirit. "Every day, you inspire me," he had written. In that moment, she realized that even in his absence, his love still echoed through the gentle reminders of who she had always been to him.

You are cherished for the unique qualities that your partner admired, and even now, those fragments of love remind you of your worth and beauty.

DAILY REFLECTION

What are the unique qualities or moments that your loved one cherished about you, and how do they still resonate in your heart today?

PRAYER

Dear God, in this moment of grief, help me to remember the love that surrounded me and the joy I brought to my partner's life. May I find comfort in these memories and strength to carry their love within me.

"You were a reflection of their greatest joys and a light in their darkest days."

LESSONS FROM A LIFE TOGETHER

"This is my comfort in my affliction, that your promise gives me life."
Psalm 119:50

DEVOTIONAL

After losing the love of her life, Judy found herself spending countless hours in the garden they had tended together. As she pulled weeds, tears flowed freely, but with each blossom she discovered, a memory emerged—of laughter, shared dreams, and quiet moments in the sun. She realized that within each flower lay not just a reminder of her husband, but also the promise of new life. Over time, her garden transformed into a beautiful sanctuary, symbolizing both her grief and growing hope. In cultivating her garden, Judy learned that though the love they built together had changed form, it continued to nourish her spirit.

In grief, hold tightly to the beautiful lessons of love that remain, for they can bloom anew in your heart.

DAILY REFLECTION

What are some of the cherished memories you hold onto that bring both comfort and joy during this time of reflection?

PRAYER

Dear God, in this moment of quiet, help me to embrace the love I shared and to find peace in the memories that remain. May Your presence surround me as I navigate through this new chapter of my life.

"In remembering, we find love's enduring strength."

A MEMORY THAT WARMS YOU

"In the same way, let your light shine before others, that they may see your good deeds and glorify your Father in heaven." **Matthew 5:16**

DEVOTIONAL

As I sift through the memories of my own marriage, one picture stands out vividly—a quiet evening on our porch, bathed in the soft glow of candlelight. We would sit side by side, sharing laughter and stories, the world around us fading away. It felt like pure bliss, a sanctuary untouched by time's relentless march. Those moments were precious, where love was spoken in silence and solidified in shared glances. Since my husband's passing, I often find myself returning to that memory, allowing it to warm my heart amid the chill of loss. It reminds me that though he may be gone, the love we shared continues to illuminate my soul.

Treasure the memories that bring warmth to your heart; they are the gentle reminders that love endures beyond physical presence.

DAILY REFLECTION

What is a cherished memory of your loved one that brings you comfort and warmth in this challenging time?

PRAYER

Dear God, surround her with Your love and peace as she navigates her days. May the sweet memories fill her heart and guide her through moments of sorrow toward joy.

"Memories are the threads that weave our hearts together, reminding us of love that never fades."

SHARING HIS MEMORY WITH OTHERS

"Therefore encourage one another and build each other up, just as in fact you are doing."
1 Thessalonians 5:11

DEVOTIONAL

After my husband passed away, I felt inundated by a sense of loneliness that often left me unable to face the day. One afternoon, a neighbor stopped by. We began to reminisce about shared gatherings, laughter, and the kindness my husband extended to others. As I spoke, I noticed a lightness in my heart. Sharing these cherished memories not only kept his spirit alive for me; it also allowed my neighbor to see a glimpse of him. We laughed and shared tears, realizing that in sharing his memory, we both found solace.

Remember, sharing the precious moments you had with your loved one not only honors their life but also brings healing and connection to your own heart.

DAILY REFLECTION

What memories of your loved one bring you comfort, and how can you share those moments with others who may need encouragement today?

PRAYER

Dear Lord, thank you for the precious moments we shared with our loved ones. Help us to keep their memory alive in our hearts and through our actions as we reach out to others.

"Every memory shared is a thread in the tapestry of love that keeps us connected."

PASSING DOWN HIS VALUES

"One generation will commend your works to another; they will tell of your mighty acts."
Psalm 145:4

DEVOTIONAL

After losing her beloved husband, Margaret felt a profound emptiness, as if the fabric of her life had unraveled. Yet amidst the pain, she found herself surrounded by her children, who reminded her of the cherished values their father instilled in them. Sharing stories of love, kindness, and humility, they created a tapestry of memories that celebrated his spirit. Margaret realized that although her husband was gone, his essence lived on through their shared values, and she felt a renewed purpose in nurturing those teachings in their lives.

The strength and love of your late partner can continue to shine brightly through the values you pass down to your family.

DAILY REFLECTION

What values from your late husband's life do you wish to carry forward into yours and share with those around you? Think of his wisdom, kindness, or strength—how can these qualities continue to flourish in your life?

PRAYER

Dear Lord, as I navigate this new chapter, please help me to embrace and pass down the beautiful values my beloved husband showed me. May I find strength in his memory and share that love with those around me.

"Our loved ones live on through the values we uphold and share."

A TRIBUTE IN EVERYDAY LIVING

*"The Lord watches over the foreigner and sustains the fatherless and the widow, but he frustrates the ways of the wicked." **Psalm 146:9***

DEVOTIONAL

Once, there was a woman named Clara who had recently lost her husband. Every morning, she would step outside to water her garden, a space once filled with laughter and shared dreams. As she tended to each flower, she began to notice their resilience; despite the harsh weather, they always found a way to bloom. Inspired, Clara decided to cultivate her own strength, honoring her husband's memory in the small, daily acts of love, like preparing his favorite meals or sharing stories with her grandchildren. Through each act, she felt not just the weight of her loss but also the joy of a life well-lived, carrying her husband's legacy forward.

In the simplest moments of our daily lives, we can pay tribute to those we've lost while nurturing our own healing journey.

DAILY REFLECTION

What small act of kindness can you incorporate into your daily routine as a tribute to your loved one? How does it feel to imagine carrying their memory with you in these moments?

PRAYER

Dear Lord, grant me the strength to honor my beloved through the gentle acts I share with others each day. May your warm embrace fill my heart as I remember the love we built together.

'Every kindness we show is a whisper of love that echoes through time.'

HIS FAVORITE HYMN

*"Why, my soul, are you downcast? Why so disturbed within me? Put your hope in God, for I will yet praise Him, my Savior and my God." **Psalm 42:11***

DEVOTIONAL

Martha sat quietly in her living room, wrapped in a soft blanket, lost in thought. The sun was setting, casting a warm glow that reminded her of evenings spent with her late husband singing their favorite hymns together. As she sipped her tea, the melody of "It Is Well with My Soul" drifted into her mind, bringing both comfort and a sweet sense of nostalgia. Each note felt like a gentle reminder of God's presence, a promise that amidst her grief, her heart could still find peace. In this moment, she gathered strength from the lyrics, realizing that even in sorrow, her spirit could still rejoice.

Your heart has taken a deep hit, yet within the notes of your favorite hymn lies a message of hope and healing, reminding you that it is possible to find peace even as you navigate this journey of grief.

DAILY REFLECTION

What song brings you peace in this season of mourning? How does it speak to your heart and remind you of God's presence alongside you?

PRAYER

Dear Lord, as I navigate this journey of grief, remind me of Your unending love and comfort. Help me to find solace in the songs that lift my spirit and draw me closer to You.

"In the silence of loss, His melodies break through."

A LETTER TO HIM IN HEAVEN

"You keep track of all my sorrows. You have collected all my tears in your bottle. You have recorded each one in your book." **Psalm 56:8**

DEVOTIONAL

As I sit in the quiet of the evening, I often find myself writing letters to you, sharing the everyday moments and lingering memories that bring both joy and heartache. I recall the way you would laugh at my silly antics and how your presence filled our home with warmth and love. On days when the clouds seem too heavy, I imagine you smiling down, encouraging me to find solace in the little things: a blooming flower, a gentle breeze, or even the laughter of our grandchildren. These moments remind me that while you may no longer be here physically, your spirit is forever woven into the fabric of my life.

Cherish each memory and allow sorrow to flow, for every tear is a testament to the love shared.

DAILY REFLECTION

What memories come to mind when you think of your time together? How do those moments bring you comfort today?

PRAYER

Dear God, thank you for the love I shared with my husband. As I navigate this journey of loss, please wrap me in Your warmth and remind me of the joy that he brought to my life.

"Love never leaves; it just transforms."

YOU LOVED WELL

"I have loved you with an everlasting love; I have drawn you with unfailing kindness."
Jeremiah 31:3

DEVOTIONAL

As you navigate through the waves of sorrow that come after losing your beloved, remember that your capacity for love remains a precious gift, a testament to the bond you shared. When moments of solitude feel overwhelming, reflect on the beautiful memories you created together—the laughter, the quiet evenings spent side by side, the dreams nurtured in each other's hearts. Each moment was a thread woven into the fabric of your love story, and although the physical presence is gone, the essence of that love remains alive within you. Love transforms grief into a bittersweet reminder of a life well-lived together.

You loved well, and that love continues to shape your path forward.

DAILY REFLECTION

What do you cherish most about the love you shared, and how can those memories comfort you in this time of grief?

PRAYER

Dear God, please wrap your arms around this precious woman as she walks through her grief. May the beautiful memories of her loved one bring her peace and strength.

"You loved well, and that love remains, echoing through each tender memory."

ACCEPTING HELP WITH GRACE

"Bear one another's burdens, and so fulfill the law of Christ."
Galatians 6:2

DEVOTIONAL

When Sarah lost her husband, she felt an overwhelming wave of emotions. Grief wrapped around her like a heavy blanket, making even the simplest tasks feel monumental. Friends and family reached out, offering help, but accepting their kindness felt like an admission of weakness. One day, while sitting on her porch, an elderly neighbor brought over a batch of cookies, along with a warm smile. Instead of politely declining, Sarah accepted the gesture. As they talked, she realized that this small act of kindness forged a connection that not only lightened her heart but also let her feel the love of community surrounding her in this difficult time.

Accepting help is not a sign of weakness, but rather a beautiful acknowledgment of our shared humanity and the bonds that lift us up.

DAILY REFLECTION

What emotions come up for you when someone offers to help you? How can you allow yourself to receive support while honoring your need for independence?

PRAYER

Dear Lord, in this time of grief, help her to see that accepting help does not diminish her strength. Grant her the grace to receive kindness from others and find comfort in their presence. Amen.

"Grace often comes wrapped in the hands of others; allow yourself to be embraced."

WHEN YOU NEED A FRIEND

"One who has unreliable friends soon comes to ruin, but there is a friend who sticks closer than a brother." **Proverbs 18:24**

DEVOTIONAL

Some time ago, a woman named Clara found herself alone after the passing of her husband. In the early days of her grief, she would sit quietly in her garden, surrounded by memories, often feeling overwhelmed by an emptiness that seemed insurmountable. One afternoon, her neighbor, noticing Clara's solitude, brought over tea and sat with her in silence, allowing her to grieve while sharing the warmth of companionship. It was in that moment, amid shared tears and stories, that Clara realized she had friends who cared and would walk alongside her during this heavy journey.

Friendship is a gift that blossoms even in the midst of sorrow, reminding us that we are not alone in our pain.

DAILY REFLECTION

What does friendship mean to you in this season of change, and how can you cultivate those connections even in your moments of solitude?

PRAYER

Dear Lord, be with me in my loneliness. Help me to reach out and seek the companionship I need, and remind me of the love that still surrounds me, even when I feel alone.

"In the quietness of your heart,
remember that every new day brings the opportunity for friendship to bloom again."

SUPPORT GROUPS AND SACRED CIRCLES

"He heals the brokenhearted and binds up their wounds."
Psalm 147:3

DEVOTIONAL

After losing her husband of over thirty years, Linda felt utterly lost. One evening, while walking through a local park, she stumbled upon a support group meeting. Hesitant at first, she found the warmth of shared stories and empathetic hearts to be the light she needed. Women from various paths gathered to share their grief, and in that sacred circle, Linda learned she wasn't alone in her pain. Each voice became a thread, weaving together a tapestry of support and understanding, reminding her that healing doesn't come through isolation but through connection.

In the embrace of support groups and sacred circles, you discover that your grief is honored, your voice is heard, and your heart can begin to heal.

DAILY REFLECTION

What does true connection look like for you in this season of grief, and how can you open your heart to receive support from others who understand your journey?

PRAYER

Dear God, in this time of sorrow, gently surround her with loving hearts and understanding souls. May she find solace in shared stories and the strength of community.

"In the sacred circle of shared experiences, healing whispers softly in the silence between words."

FINDING COMFORT IN OTHERS' STORIES

"For where two or three gather in my name, there am I with them."
Matthew 18:20

DEVOTIONAL

After losing her husband, Marjorie felt like a solitary island in a vast ocean of grief. One day, she decided to join a support group for widows. As she listened to other women share their journeys, she found pieces of her own story woven in their words. Their laughter, tears, and shared memories of loss created an unbreakable bond. With each gathering, she realized that comfort resides not just in silence but in the wisdom and compassion that comes from shared experiences.

You may find that as you share and connect with others, healing blooms like new life after a long winter.

DAILY REFLECTION

What stories have you encountered recently that offered you comfort or a sense of connection? How have these narratives mirrored your own journey and provided insights into your healing process?

PRAYER

Dear God, as I navigate this new path, help me to find solace in the stories of others. May their experiences inspire and uplift me, reminding me that I am never alone in my grief.

"In the sharing of our stories, we find threads of hope that weave us together."

WHEN SOMEONE REALLY LISTENS

"The heartfelt counsel of a friend is as sweet as perfume and incense."
Proverbs 27:9

DEVOTIONAL

In a small café, I once sat with a dear friend who had recently lost her partner. As the aroma of coffee filled the air, she spoke softly, her words woven with heartache and memories. I listened, really listened, as she shared stories of laughter, love, and the emptiness that now lingered. Those moments were sacred, reminding us both that sometimes, the greatest gift we can offer each other is our full attention—a space where raw emotions can be expressed without fear of judgment. In that little café, her pain felt lighter, and our connection deepened, just because I chose to listen.

When someone really listens, it can help transform our grief into a journey of healing and connection.

DAILY REFLECTION

What does it mean to you to have someone truly listen to your heart during this time of grief?

PRAYER

Dear God, please send me listeners who can embrace my sorrows with compassion and understanding. Open my heart to their comfort, and let me also learn to listen to others in their times of need.

"In the silence of your sorrow, the gift of a listening heart can bring healing grace."

COFFEE WITH A KIND SOUL

"Let mutual love continue. Do not neglect to show hospitality to strangers, for thereby some have entertained angels unawares." **Hebrews 13:1**

DEVOTIONAL

After losing her husband, Mary felt an emptiness that surrounded her every morning with her coffee. One day, while sipping her daily brew in the local café, she noticed a woman at the next table, staring wistfully out the window. With a gentle smile, Mary reached out, "Mind if I join you?" This simple act began a beautiful conversation, where both shared their stories of love and loss. In that moment, sipping coffee and connecting with a kind soul, Mary realized that the warmth of human connection could soothe her aching heart, bringing with it a sense of community and hope.

In the midst of grief, reaching out to others can heal not just your own heart, but theirs as well.

DAILY REFLECTION

What does it mean to you to find kindness within yourself as you navigate this new chapter of your life? How can you invite moments of grace and compassion into your daily routine?

PRAYER

Dear Lord, as I sit with my coffee and reflect on the journey ahead, I ask for Your gentle guidance. Wrap me in Your love, help me to uncover kindness within myself, and remind me of the beauty life still holds.

"In the quiet spaces, kindness becomes a soothing balm for a weary heart."

SHARING A TEAR AND A LAUGH

"People of Zion, who live in Jerusalem, you will weep no more. How gracious He will be when you cry for help! As soon as He hears, He will answer you." **Isaiah 30:19**

DEVOTIONAL

After losing her beloved husband, Margaret often found herself torn between the cherished memories of their laughter and the heavy weight of her grief. One afternoon, while sorting through a box of old photographs, she stumbled upon a snapshot of them at a silly costume party, heads thrown back in laughter. In that moment, the tears flowed freely, yet a smile crept onto her face, reminding her of the joy they shared. She realized that in remembering the love and laughter, she could honor his memory while also embracing the tears that accompanied her healing journey.

Even amidst profound loss, it is possible to find joy and sorrow intertwined, allowing both tears and laughter to coexist as a testament to love.

DAILY REFLECTION

What brings a smile to your face even in moments of sadness? How have laughter and tears danced together in your journey recently?

PRAYER

Dear God, in this time of loss, help me to find comfort in laughter and solace in my tears. Remind me that both are gifts from You, guiding me through my healing.

"In the midst of sorrow, joy can still find a way to break through."

GRIEF SHARED IS GRIEF HALVED

"Come to me, all you who are weary and burdened, and I will give you rest. Take my yoke upon you and learn from me, for I am gentle and humble in heart, and you will find rest for your souls." **Matthew 11:28-29**

DEVOTIONAL

In the quiet hours of the night, when the darkness seemed to close in around her, Ellen found solace in the company of her friends. They gathered in her living room, sharing stories of laughter and tears, each memory a thread weaving through their grief. As they hugged and cried together, she felt the weight of her sorrow lift, if only a little. Their shared moments showed her that she was not alone; they were walking this path together, each offering comfort to one another. It was in this circle of friendship that Ellen realized grief, though deeply personal, could be lightened by a shared burden.

Grief shared is grief halved; there is strength in vulnerability and healing in community.

DAILY REFLECTION

What memories do you cherish most about your loved one, and how can sharing those stories with others bring comfort to your heart?

PRAYER

Dear Lord, wrap your loving arms around me as I journey through this time of grief. Help me to find solace in the company of others and to share my heart in a safe space. Amen.

In community, the burden of sorrow becomes lighter, and healing begins to bloom.

ENCOURAGEMENT FROM UNEXPECTED PLACES

*"I lift up my eyes to the mountains—where does my help come from? My help comes from the Lord, the Maker of heaven and earth." **Psalm 121:1-2***

DEVOTIONAL

During a particularly hard day after her husband passed, Sarah took a simple walk to clear her mind. As she sat on a park bench, watching children play, an elderly woman approached. With a gentle smile, the woman sat beside her and began to share stories of her late husband, how laughter had often emerged in their grief. Intrigued and moved, Sarah found a burgeoning sense of solace in their shared experience. In that moment, God's comfort came through the kindness of an unexpected friend, reminding her that connection often brings healing.

Encouragement can come from places we never expect; be open to moments of grace that remind you, you are not alone on this journey.

DAILY REFLECTION

What unexpected places in your life have offered you comfort or encouragement since your loss? How can you remain open to those moments today?

PRAYER

Dear God, as I navigate this new chapter of my life, help me to see Your presence in the unexpected places. Grant me the courage to embrace the moments of joy and hope that come my way.

"Sometimes, the sun breaks through the clouds when you least expect it."

NEW FRIENDSHIPS IN NEW SEASONS

*"Seek the peace and prosperity of the city to which I have carried you into exile. Pray to the Lord for it, because if it prospers, you too will prosper." **Jeremiah 29:7***

DEVOTIONAL

After losing her beloved husband, Emily found herself in a quiet home that seemed to echo with memories of laughter and love. Each day felt heavy, but she felt a gentle nudging to step outside. At the local community center, she stumbled upon a gardening class. Hesitant but hopeful, she joined and found herself surrounded by women who shared stories of loss and renewal. With each petal planted, new friendships began to blossom, reminding her that while life had changed, beauty could still be found in unexpected places.

In times of change, seek out new connections that can nourish your spirit and help you grow in this new chapter of life.

DAILY REFLECTION

What new friendships could God be guiding you toward in this season of your life? Are you open to exploring connections that may bring unexpected joy and support?

PRAYER

Dear Lord, as I navigate this new chapter, I ask for your guidance in building new relationships. Open my heart to those you place in my path and help me find comfort in these new connections.

"Every ending presents an opportunity for a new beginning."

LETTING OTHERS IN AGAIN

*"I no longer call you servants, because a servant does not know his master's business. Instead, I have called you friends, for everything that I learned from my Father I have made known to you." **John 15:15***

DEVOTIONAL

When Sarah lost her husband, she felt as though the walls around her heart had grown impenetrable. After many months of profound solitude, she hesitated at every invitation to gather with friends or meet new people, fearing the vulnerability that comes with sharing her pain. One evening, an old friend reached out, patiently encouraging Sarah to join a small group at church. The warmth of shared laughter and tears gradually melted her reservations. With each meeting, she began to find the strength to let love and companionship back into her life, discovering that opening her heart again was not a betrayal of her past but a celebration of her future.

Healing begins when we allow ourselves to be vulnerable and let others in, reminding us that love is a gift that continues to flourish, even in the wake of loss.

DAILY REFLECTION

What fears or hesitations do you feel when you think about letting others into your life again, and what steps might you take to gently overcome them?

PRAYER

Dear God, as I navigate this season of grief, help me to open my heart just a little more each day. Surround me with supportive friends and the warmth of Your love.

"Opening your heart again can be a gentle act of courage."

BUILDING SISTERHOOD IN SORROW

*"And let us consider how we may spur one another on toward love and good deeds, not giving up meeting together, as some are in the habit of doing, but encouraging one another." **Hebrews 10:24-25***

DEVOTIONAL

Once, a woman named Clara found herself feeling isolated after losing her beloved husband. One day, she decided to gather a few friends for tea and share her feelings of loss. As they talked and cried together, she realized that these women, too, had known heartache. Through their shared experiences, laughter and tears, they began to form a sisterhood rooted in a deep understanding of sorrow. This new bond breathed life into Clara, reminding her that she was not alone on her journey.

In the midst of sorrow, you are not meant to walk alone; reach out and build the sisterhood that will uplift your spirit.

DAILY REFLECTION

What does sisterhood mean to you in this season of sorrow, and how might you reach out to those who share a similar journey?

PRAYER

Dear God, as I navigate the waves of grief, help me to find comfort and connection in the sisterhood around me. May I be open to the love and support of others, allowing your light to shine through our shared experiences.

"In the embrace of shared grief, we discover the strength of sisterhood."

OFFERING SUPPORT TO ANOTHER WIDOW

"My flesh and my heart may fail, but God is the strength of my heart and my portion forever." **Psalm 73:26**

DEVOTIONAL

Maria sat quietly in her living room, the weight of widowhood heavy upon her shoulders. One chilly afternoon, she noticed Sarah, another widow from the neighborhood, sitting alone on a park bench. Maria felt a familiar ache of loneliness and thought back to her own moments of despair. Gathering her courage, she approached Sarah and offered a warm smile. Their conversation blossomed into shared stories—the memories of their late husbands and the silent battles they both faced. Deep down, Maria realized that in lifting Sarah's spirits, she found a healing comfort for her own heart.

In offering support to another widow, you may find a bond that soothes your own wounds.

DAILY REFLECTION

What small acts of kindness can you offer to another widow in your community this week? Reflect on how your own journey can become a source of comfort and strength for someone else.

PRAYER

Dear Lord, guide me to those who need support and help me to offer love and understanding in their time of grief. May I be a source of comfort and light, just as others have been for me.

'In lifting others, we find our own strength renewed.'

PHONE CALLS THAT SOOTHE

"The Lord is close to the brokenhearted and saves those who are crushed in spirit." **Psalm 34:18**

DEVOTIONAL

As the phone rang after a long, quiet day, I hesitated to pick it up. It was a dear friend calling, her voice a sweet balm for my aching heart. We talked about memories, shared laughter, and explored dreams I once thought had faded away. In those moments, I felt a gentle reminder from God that I am not alone, that connections can nurture resilience and provide comfort even amidst grief. Each conversation became a lifeline, offering hope and the assurance that love continues in our hearts.

Sometimes, it is through the simple act of reaching out that we find the strength to embrace tomorrow.

DAILY REFLECTION

What phone call have you received that brought you unexpected comfort during this challenging time? How did it make you feel?

PRAYER

Dear God, in this time of grief, I ask for your gentle presence. Surround me with voices of love and encouragement that remind me I am not alone.

'In the echoes of loving voices, we find the strength to heal.'

A HUG THAT HEALS

*"May the God of hope fill you with all joy and peace as you trust in Him, so that you may overflow with hope by the power of the Holy Spirit." **Romans 15:13***

DEVOTIONAL

After the loss of her beloved husband, Carol often found herself enveloped in a heavy silence, the house echoing the absence of laughter and companionship. One rainy afternoon, as she sat with a cup of tea, she noticed a small, tattered teddy bear sitting on the shelf. It had once belonged to her children, but today, it felt like a reminder that comfort could come in the most unexpected forms. She picked it up, hugged it close, and despite the tears streaming down her face, an inexplicable warmth enveloped her, as if her husband were holding her once again, whispering that it was okay to grieve and to welcome joy back into her life.

Allow yourself moments of tenderness, for even in grief, healing comes through accepting love in all its forms.

DAILY REFLECTION

What does a comforting embrace look like for you during this time of grief? How can you invite that sense of warmth into your daily life?

PRAYER

Dear God, wrap your loving arms around this heartache. May I feel your presence as a gentle hug that brings healing and solace to my soul.

Grief can feel isolating, yet the warmth of love can embrace us anew, reminding us we are never truly alone.

THE MINISTRY OF PRESENCE

"Rejoice with those who rejoice, and weep with those who weep."
Romans 12:15

DEVOTIONAL

In the midst of her sorrow, Julia found herself often sitting alone on her porch, reflecting on the life she shared with her husband. One afternoon, a neighbor, who had lost her husband years before, quietly joined her. They shared the silence, sitting close enough to hold hands but not forcing conversation. In that sacred space, they allowed each other to feel their deep sadness without judgment. Those moments of shared heartache deepened their connection and slowly began to heal their wounds.

Your presence, and the presence of others, can bridge the gap of loneliness; embrace the comfort found in simply being with one another.

DAILY REFLECTION

What does it mean for you to simply be present for those you love, especially in this season of your life?

PRAYER

Heavenly Father, wrap your loving arms around me as I navigate this new chapter. Help me to find peace in the moments of silence and to be a source of comfort for others, just as they have been for me.

"Sometimes, the greatest gift you can offer is simply your presence."

SAYING "YES" TO INVITATIONS

"A friend loves at all times, and a brother is born for a time of adversity."
Proverbs 17:17

DEVOTIONAL

After the passing of her husband, Clara felt adrift in a world that seemed unfamiliar. Days passed slowly, with an echo of silence in the home they once shared. One evening, she found an invitation on her kitchen table—a potluck dinner at a neighbor's house. Hesitant but yearning for connection, she decided to attend. That night, surrounded by laughter and shared stories, Clara realized that saying "yes" to an invitation didn't erase her grief but rather reminded her of the beauty and warmth of community, helping her to heal little by little.

Saying "yes" to invitations opens doors to new friendships and healing journeys.

DAILY REFLECTION

What invitations have you been hesitant to accept lately? How might saying "yes" to these opportunities help you heal and connect with others?

PRAYER

Dear God, grant me the courage to embrace new invitations as I navigate this season of my life. Help me find joy in the connections I make and the memories yet to come.

"Every invitation is an opportunity for a new beginning."

REBUILDING COMMUNITY

"For where two or three gather in my name, there am I with them."
Matthew 18:20

DEVOTIONAL

Once, a woman found herself alone in her favorite café, feeling the emptiness of her days post-loss. As she sipped her coffee, she noticed a small gathering of voices at a nearby table, laughter echoing in the air. Tentatively, she approached and introduced herself, sharing a piece of her story. To her surprise, those strangers welcomed her with open arms, and over time, she transformed from a solitary figure into a cherished part of a community that met regularly.

In rebuilding your community, remember that vulnerability can lead to connection and healing, both for you and for others who share in your journey.

DAILY REFLECTION

What does community mean to you now, and how can you invite others in to share your journey as you rebuild your life?

PRAYER

Dear God, wrap this woman in Your love as she navigates the profound changes in her life. Help her to find comfort in old connections and courage to forge new ones, embracing the beauty of community once again.

"Every ending is a new beginning waiting to unfold."

FINDING YOUR PEOPLE AGAIN

*"Do not fear; you will not be put to shame. Do not be discouraged; you will not be disgraced. You will forget the shame of your youth and remember no more the reproach of your widowhood." **Isaiah 54:4***

DEVOTIONAL

After losing her husband, Marie felt as if the weight of solitude was unbearable. The laughter and connections that once flooded her days seemed to vanish, leaving nothing but echoing silence. Yet, in her journey back into the world, she discovered a group of women at her local community center who, like her, were navigating the path of loss together. Sharing stories over cups of tea, they formed bonds that helped mend their broken hearts, reminding each other that even in grief, there is room for friendship and joy again.

True healing often comes when you open your heart to find and embrace those who share your journey.

DAILY REFLECTION

What brings you comfort and strength during this time of transition? Can you think of individuals or groups that have always lifted your spirit?

PRAYER

Dear God, as she walks through this new chapter, surround her with supportive hearts and warm connections. Help her to recognize the love that still exists and guide her gently toward finding her people again.

"Connection is the thread that weaves the fabric of our healing."

SPEAKING YOUR STORY ALOUD

*"Come and hear, all you who fear God; let me tell you what he has done for me." **Psalm 66:16***

DEVOTIONAL

There's a woman named Ellen who, after losing her husband, found herself drifting through days filled with silence. She often refrained from talking about her grief, feeling as though the weight of her sorrow was too heavy to share. One day, a friend invited her to a local grief support group where the theme was "Speaking Your Story Aloud." Initially hesitant, Ellen found that as she shared her journey, her heart began to lighten and new connections formed. Each story told was a thread weaving them closer together, and Ellen realized that sharing her struggles not only honored her husband's memory but also allowed others to acknowledge their own pain, creating a beautiful tapestry of understanding and hope.

In the act of sharing your story, you honor your loss while inviting the healing light of community into your life.

DAILY REFLECTION

What parts of your story are you holding inside that long to be shared? How might your voice bring healing to yourself and others?

PRAYER

Dear God, in this quiet moment, help her to find the courage to speak her truth. Wrap her in Your embrace, guiding her through each word with love and grace.

"Your story has the power to heal, both you and those who hear it."

PERMISSION TO REST

"And why do you worry about clothes? See how the flowers of the field grow. They do not labor or spin. Yet I tell you that not even Solomon in all his splendor was dressed like one of these." Matthew 6:28-30

DEVOTIONAL

After losing her beloved partner, Mary found herself in the whirlwind of tasks that came with managing everything alone. The mornings rushed by with endless to-do lists, and the evenings felt longer than the days. One quiet afternoon, she sat by her window with a comforting cup of tea in hand. As she watched the sunlight dance across the garden, she felt a gentle whisper urging her to rest. In that stillness, she remembered the joy and laughter they once shared and allowed herself to simply be in that moment, feeling the warmth of memories wash over her like a warm blanket.

Your heart deserves the same kindness you so readily offer to others; give yourself permission to rest.

DAILY REFLECTION

What does it feel like to grant yourself the grace to simply rest, without the weight of expectation or the need to fill every moment with activity?

PRAYER

Dear Lord, in this quiet moment, help her find peace in rest. May she feel Your comforting presence as she allows her heart to heal.

"Rest is not a luxury; it's a necessity for renewal and healing."

TAKING CARE OF YOU

"Come to me, all you who are weary and burdened, and I will give you rest." Matthew 11:28

DEVOTIONAL

As a recently widowed woman, the journey of healing can feel overwhelming. You might find yourself lost in a sea of emotions, reminiscing about shared laughter or quiet moments that are now just memories. One woman I know, Sarah, after losing her husband, spent her days lost in grief, neglecting her own needs. It wasn't until a friend gently encouraged her to take walks in the park and nurture her loves, from gardening to painting, that she began to rediscover herself. Each small act of self-care opened her heart to new joys, slowly helping her weave a new tapestry of life, stitched with both memories and hope.

Taking time for yourself is not a luxury; it is a necessity for healing and growth.

DAILY REFLECTION

What are some small, nurturing practices you can incorporate into your daily life to begin healing and rediscovering joy?

PRAYER

Dear God, as I navigate this journey of grief, help me to embrace the moments of self-care and allow Your love to guide my heart towards healing. Let each new day be a reminder of Your grace and strength within me.

"Caring for yourself is a beautiful testament to the love you have shared and the life waiting for you to embrace."

NOURISHING BODY AND SOUL

*"The Lord is my shepherd; I shall not want. He makes me lie down in green pastures. He leads me beside still waters. He restores my soul." **Psalm 23:1-3***

DEVOTIONAL

After losing her husband, Mary felt as if she had lost her purpose. Days blurred together in a haze of grief, and simple tasks became monumental challenges. One afternoon, while taking a walk, she stumbled upon a community garden. It was vibrant and full of life—a stark contrast to her own emotional state. Intrigued, she decided to help with planting and watering the flowers. Over time, as she nurtured the garden, she found pieces of herself slowly returning. The flowers began to bloom, and so did her spirit.

Nourishing your body and soul is not just about sustaining life; it's about rediscovering joy and purpose in each small moment.

DAILY REFLECTION

What activities or practices bring you nourishment and joy during this time of transition in your life? How can you honor your body and soul in the days ahead?

PRAYER

Dear God, as I walk this path of grief, help me to seek nourishment for both my body and my soul. May I find moments of peace and joy in Your presence, reminding me that I am cherished and never alone.

"Even in the midst of loss, I can cultivate compassion for myself, embracing the journey of healing one gentle step at a time."

WALKING FOR HEALING

"Therefore encourage one another and build one another up, just as you are doing."
1 Thessalonians 5:11

DEVOTIONAL

After losing her husband, Clara felt a void in every aspect of her life and struggled to envision her future without him. One day, she decided to take a walk in the local park, hoping the fresh air might lift her spirits. As she strolled along the paths, she noticed other widows, each carrying their own stories of love and loss. They exchanged knowing smiles and shared small moments of comfort, reminding Clara that she was not alone on this journey. With each step, she felt a little lighter, nurtured by the warmth of community and the realization that healing sometimes comes with the simple act of walking alongside others.

You don't have to walk through this journey of grief alone; seek connection and share your experience as part of your healing.

DAILY REFLECTION

What does walking in the fresh air and feeling the earth beneath your feet bring to your heart in this season of change and healing?

PRAYER

Dear God, as I take each step in this journey of healing, guide me with Your love and comfort. Help me to find peace in my memories and strength for the days ahead.

"Healing is found in the rhythm of each step, as your heart learns to embrace new beginnings."

A CUP OF TEA AND STILLNESS

"For God alone, my soul waits in silence; from Him comes my salvation."
Psalm 62:5

DEVOTIONAL

As the sun began to set, casting a warm, golden light through the window, Mary found herself sitting at her kitchen table, a fresh cup of tea cradled in her hands. It had been a few months since the world felt as if it had tilted on its axis with the loss of her husband. In the soft stillness of the evening, the familiar aroma of chamomile wrapped around her like a comforting hug. Instead of the chaos of life that had once filled her home, there was now a gentle quiet that whispered to her heart. In that sacred silence, she began to reflect on their many shared moments over tea, realizing that even in her solitude, love remained an eternal presence, guiding her toward hope and healing.

In stillness, we can rediscover the love that remains and find new paths to healing.

DAILY REFLECTION

What does stillness mean to you in this season of your life, and how can you invite moments of quiet reflection into your days?

PRAYER

Dear Lord, as I hold this cup of tea, may it warm my heart and bring me peace. Help me to embrace the stillness and find comfort in Your presence.

'Amidst the silence, we can hear the whispers of hope.'

JOURNALING FOR RELIEF

"A joyful heart makes a cheerful face, but by sorrow of heart the spirit is crushed."
Proverbs 15:13

DEVOTIONAL

As I sat alone one evening, a blank journal on my lap, I felt the weight of my solitude press heavy on my heart. I had spent the day quietly sifting through memories of laughter with my late husband, yet as night fell, an overwhelming wave of loneliness washed over me. In that stillness, I picked up a pen and began to write; each word poured from my heart like a gentle rain, washing away the ache, if only for a moment. My journal became a safe sanctuary where I could express my sorrow, gratitude, and the myriad emotions I had tucked away. Each entry was a conversation with my deeper self, helping me find relief amid the chaos of grief.

Our hearts can find solace in expressing our emotions, and through journaling, we can navigate the journey of healing one word at a time.

DAILY REFLECTION

What thoughts swirl in your heart right now, and how might writing them down bring you clarity or comfort?

PRAYER

Dear Lord, wrap your loving arms around this precious woman as she navigates her grief. Grant her peace in the chaos and the courage to express her heart's deepest longings through her journal.

'In the quiet pages of your journal, your heart finds its voice and your soul begins to heal.'

HEALING IN ART OR CRAFT

"He has sent me to bind up the brokenhearted."
Isaiah 61:1

DEVOTIONAL

After losing her beloved husband, Mary found herself wandering through the days like a ghost, her heart heavy with sorrow. One afternoon, she picked up a paintbrush that had long been collecting dust. As she splashed colors onto the canvas, something miraculous began to happen; with each stroke, it felt as if she was releasing a piece of her grief. The colors transformed not only the canvas but also her heart, reminding her of the joy, laughter, and love they had shared. The act of creating allowed her to reflect on beautiful memories while simultaneously finding solace in the process of creating something new.

In moments of sorrow, turning to art or craft can be a healing balm for your soul, providing a space to express and process your emotions.

DAILY REFLECTION

What emotions rise to the surface when you immerse yourself in creating something new? How might they guide you toward healing?

PRAYER

Dear God, as I navigate this season of loss, may Your gentle presence fill the spaces in my heart. Help me find solace and expression through the beauty of my creativity.

In the tapestry of grief, every thread of creation weaves a path toward renewal.

READING THAT RESTORES

"He heals the brokenhearted and binds up their wounds."
Psalm 147:3

DEVOTIONAL

After losing her husband, Sarah found herself wandering the aisles of her favorite bookstore, searching for solace in the written word. Leafing through novels and memoirs, she stumbled upon a book of comforting poetry filled with hope and healing. As she read, the words wrapped around her like a warm blanket, reminding her of love that endures and the possibility of joy rediscovered. In those pages, she encountered stories of resilience and faith that spoke directly to her heart, allowing her to dream again, albeit in a different way.

In the midst of sorrow, find refuge in the pages that uplift your spirit and connect you to God's whispers of hope.

DAILY REFLECTION

What words or stories can you turn to now that feel like a gentle embrace, offering you solace and understanding in this difficult time?

PRAYER

Dear God, envelop this woman in Your peace as she seeks comfort through the words she reads. May each page turn into a pathway that leads her closer to healing and hope.

"Within the pages of a book, we often find pieces of ourselves waiting to be rediscovered."

DECLUTTERING THE PAIN

"Let us hold unswervingly to the hope we profess, for he who promised is faithful."
Hebrews 10:23

DEVOTIONAL

When Sarah lost her husband, the world felt like a heavy blanket wrapped around her, stifling her ability to breathe. Her home, once a sanctuary of love and laughter, now felt cluttered with reminders of a life that was no more. Every corner held echoes of shared memories, leaving her with a heart full of pain and a home filled with reluctance. One day, she took a deep breath and slowly began to remove items that weighed heavily on her heart. With each box she filled, she felt a small piece of her sorrow lift, revealing a clearer path toward healing and hope. As she decluttered her physical space, she also began to declutter her emotional space, allowing herself to grieve while also cherishing the beautiful moments they shared. *It is through releasing the physical symbols of our pain that we give ourselves permission to heal and embrace new beginnings.*

DAILY REFLECTION

What pieces of emotional baggage are you ready to let go of today? As you reflect, consider how each memory or feeling serves you and what it might be time to release.

PRAYER

Dear God, as I navigate this journey of loss, help me find the strength to let go of the pain that weighs on my heart. May I embrace healing and welcome the new beginnings you have in store for me.

Healing often comes as we intentionally declutter our hearts, clearing space for new hope and joy.

MUSIC THAT SOOTHES THE HEART

"Make a joyful noise unto the Lord, all ye lands. Serve the Lord with gladness: come before his presence with singing." **Psalm 100:1-2**

DEVOTIONAL

Once, after losing her husband, a woman found solace in an old vinyl record collection they had enjoyed together. Each song brought back cherished memories, intertwining joy and sorrow, helping her feel closer to him. As she played their favorite tunes, she found herself singing softly, allowing each note to resonate with her heart. In this sacred space, she discovered a way to both honor her loss and embrace healing, recognizing that love endures through the music they had shared.
In the midst of your grief, remember that music has the power to soothe your heart and connect you to cherished memories, guiding you toward healing and hope.

DAILY REFLECTION

What songs bring you comfort in your moments of sadness or solitude? As you listen, reflect on how the melodies wrap around your heart, offering solace and peace.

PRAYER

Lord, as I navigate this challenging time, I thank You for the gift of music that soothes my weary heart. Help me find melodies that lift my spirit and remind me of Your everlasting love.

"Music has a unique way of speaking to our souls,
filling the spaces of grief with hope and healing."

GRATITUDE AS MEDICINE

"In everything give thanks; for this is the will of God in Christ Jesus for you."
1 Thessalonians 5:18

DEVOTIONAL

After losing her beloved husband, Mary found herself standing among the remnants of their life together, enveloped in a silence that felt heavy and suffocating. Days turned into weeks, and she often felt lost in her grief. On a particularly gloomy afternoon, she forced herself to go for a walk, hoping the fresh air would clear her mind. As she strolled through the park, a soft breeze brushed her cheek, and she noticed a group of children laughing as they played. In that moment, Mary felt a spark of warmth in her heart. It reminded her of the joyful moments she shared with her husband. She began to remember and recount the blessings they had in their years together. That simple act of gratitude began to lift her spirits, reinforcing the beauty within her memories while gradually allowing healing to unfold.

In the depths of your sorrow, remember that gratitude can gently unveil glimpses of joy and peace, acting as a soothing balm for your heart.

DAILY REFLECTION

What are the small blessings in your life today that you can choose to acknowledge and appreciate, even amidst your grief?

PRAYER

Dear God, thank you for the moments of light that still break through the clouds of sorrow. Help me to see and cherish these gifts, finding solace in gratitude as I navigate this new path.

"Gratitude is a gentle reminder that even in loss, there is beauty to be found."

A DAY OF NO EXPECTATIONS

"You will keep in perfect peace those whose minds are steadfast because they trust in you." **Isaiah 26:3**

DEVOTIONAL

One morning, after a particularly challenging week, Clara woke up and decided to have a "day of no expectations." Instead of diving into her to-do list or dwelling on memories of her late husband, she immersed herself in nature. She took a long walk, feeling the sun on her face and the gentle breeze in her hair. For the first time in a long while, she simply observed — the vibrant flowers dancing in the wind, the birds serenading her with song, and the laughter of children at play. In those moments, she realized that it was okay to let go of her burdens and just be present in the beauty surrounding her.

Embracing days with no expectations can lead you to unexpected moments of peace and joy, allowing your heart the space to heal.

DAILY REFLECTION

What does a day without expectations look like for you, and how might it offer space for healing and peace in your journey?

PRAYER

Lord, grant her the strength to embrace each moment without pressure or judgment. Fill her heart with peace as she takes this time to simply be, to rest in Your presence.

"Sometimes, the most profound growth happens when we release our expectations and open our hearts to experience life's gentle unfolding."

THE POWER OF TOUCH (MASSAGE SPA)

"See what great love the Father has lavished on us, that we should be called children of God! And that is what we are!" **1 John 3:1**

DEVOTIONAL

As she walked into the massage spa, the aroma of lavender and warm essential oils enveloped her like a gentle embrace. In that moment, she let out a breath, feeling the weight of her loneliness begin to lift with each step. It had been a few months since she lost her beloved, and every day seemed a little heavier than the last. This was her time to relax, to feel appreciated and cared for, if only for an hour. As the therapist's hands worked across her shoulders, she realized that touch not only heals the body, but also soothes the soul. Each stroke was a reminder that she was not alone in this journey, that love could still flow into her life in unexpected ways.

Cherish the power of touch to heal not only your body, but your spirit, reminding you that you are enveloped in love and care.

DAILY REFLECTION

What does touch mean to you in this season of your life? How can you invite gentle moments of care into your daily routine, allowing them to nurture your spirit and healing journey?

PRAYER

Dear Lord, in this tender moment, I ask for your comfort to envelop my heart. Help me find the soothing power of touch, whether through self-care or the warmth of a friend's hand. May I embrace each gentle moment as a step toward healing.

"Embrace the healing touch that reminds you of love and warmth still present in your life."

BREATHING THROUGH ANXIETY

*"Even though I walk through the darkest valley, I will fear no evil, for you are with me; your rod and your staff, they comfort me." **Psalm 23:4***

DEVOTIONAL

One woman shared how, after losing her husband, she found herself paralyzed by anxiety. Each breath felt heavy as thoughts of the future flooded her mind. Seeking solace, she began to take short walks each morning. During these walks, she would breathe deeply, whispering a prayer for strength and peace. Over time, she noticed that with every exhale, she felt a little lighter, and her heart grew more open to the possibility of new beginnings. Simple moments became her lifeline, reminding her that God was in each breath she took.

In the midst of your grief, find peace in simple acts of breathing, inviting God's presence to calm your heart as you step forward with courage and hope.

DAILY REFLECTION

What thoughts or emotions rise to the surface when you think about facing your anxieties, and how can you gently approach them with the love and support of those around you?

PRAYER

Dear God, in this moment of grief and transition, help me to breathe deeply and release my worries into Your hands. Surround me with Your peace as I navigate each day with courage and grace.

"Even in the midst of stormy seas, I can find moments of stillness within."

SETTING BOUNDARIES WITH GRACE

"I run in the path of your commands, for you have set my heart free."
Psalm 119:32

DEVOTIONAL

When I first found myself navigating life alone, I grappled with how to maintain my own space while still being there for family and friends who wanted to help. One day, I received a call from a dear friend asking if I could assist with a project at her church. Though I wanted to support her, I felt an overwhelming sense of fatigue. I realized that saying "no" was not an act of selfishness but a step towards nurturing my own healing. With a gentle heart, I explained my need for time to rest, and to my surprise, she graciously understood. This experience taught me that setting boundaries is not only beneficial for me but can also strengthen my relationships when approached with grace and honesty.

Setting boundaries with grace empowers you to care for your own heart while still valuing the connections around you.

DAILY REFLECTION

What boundaries do you feel you need to establish in your life right now to protect your heart and nurture your healing journey?

PRAYER

Dear God, grant me the wisdom to set healthy boundaries that honor both my heart and my memories. Help me to embrace this new chapter with grace and strength.

"Setting boundaries is not selfish; it's an act of love for yourself and those around you."

CHOOSING JOY WITHOUT PRESSURE

"The Lord your God is with you, the Mighty Warrior who saves. He will take great delight in you; in his love he will no longer rebuke you, but will rejoice over you with singing."
Zephaniah 3:17

DEVOTIONAL

After losing her husband of several decades, Laura found herself constantly feeling the weight of the world pressing down. Friends would say, "You must find joy again!" as if a flick of a switch could erase the pain. One afternoon, while sorting through old photographs, she came across a picture of them dancing at their favorite restaurant. A wave of bittersweet memories washed over her, and instead of feeling pressured to jump back into joy, she allowed herself to reminisce, savoring each moment. There, in her memories of love, she felt a tender reminder that joy could be found in moments of quiet reflection, not just in forced laughter or new beginnings.

Joy often comes softly and quietly, reminding us that it's okay to take our time in finding it again.

DAILY REFLECTION

What small moments today have brought you a sense of peace or happiness, even amidst your grief?

PRAYER

Dear God, as I navigate this new chapter of my life, help me to see the glimmers of joy each day brings. May I embrace those moments, free from pressure and filled with Your love.

"Joy can be found in the little things, often hidden between the layers of sorrow."

CRYING AS A CLEANSING RITUAL

"Yet you know me, Lord; you see me and test my thoughts about you. Drag me out of the net they have hidden me in, for you are my refuge." **Psalm 139:1-2**

DEVOTIONAL

In the quiet solitude of the night, after everyone had gone home, she sat alone on the edge of her bed, memories swirling around her like leaves in a brisk autumn wind. As tears streamed down her face, she felt a mixture of sorrow and relief, as if each drop was washing away not only her grief but also planting seeds of healing within her heart. Crying had never felt like a weakness; instead, it seemed sacred in that moment—a purging of sadness and a celebration of love lost. She whispered to herself, "It's okay to mourn; it's okay to feel deeply," allowing her tears to flow freely, recognizing them as a natural and necessary cleansing of her spirit.

Crying can be a powerful ritual, a way to release pain and give voice to the heart's unexpressed emotions, ultimately leading to a new season of healing and hope.

DAILY REFLECTION

What emotions are you holding onto today, and how might allowing yourself to cry bring you closer to healing?

PRAYER

Dear God, wrap your loving arms around me in my grief. Help me to embrace the tears as a healing journey, knowing you are with me every step of the way.

Tears can be a gentle reminder that love remains, even in sorrow.

WATER AS HEALING: BATH OR OCEAN

"He stilled the storm to a whisper; the waves of the sea were hushed."
Psalm 107:29

DEVOTIONAL

After my husband passed, the weight of loneliness felt like an ocean pulling me under. One day, I decided to take a long walk along the shore. As I dipped my feet into the cool water and let the waves lap around me, something miraculous happened. Each wave seemed to embrace me, lifting the heaviness in my heart just a little with each gentle surge. I found myself crying, but the ocean also brought a profound peace, as if the water itself understood my pain and was washing it away, one tide at a time.

In the midst of grief, remember that healing often comes through experiences that refresh your spirit, much like water soothes a weary soul.

DAILY REFLECTION

What does water represent for you in this season of your life? Can you envision the soothing qualities of a bath or the vastness of the ocean helping to heal your spirit as you navigate through your grief?

PRAYER

Dear God, as I seek peace in my heart, help me to feel your presence in the gentle waves and warm waters. May your love wash over me, bringing comfort and healing during this difficult time.

"Just as water flows and rejuvenates,
so too can my heart begin to heal and flow with new possibilities."

RELEASING THE NEED TO "BE STRONG"

"God is within her; she will not fall; God will help her at break of day."
Psalm 46:5

DEVOTIONAL

After losing her husband, Laura felt the weight of a thousand expectations pressing down on her. Everyone kept saying how strong she was, but inside, she felt anything but. On the outside, she wore a brave smile, but at night, in the quiet of her empty home, tears flowed freely as she grappled with her grief. It took time for her to realize that it was okay to let go of the need to "be strong" all the time. By allowing herself to be vulnerable, she discovered a deeper connection with God, who promised to be her strength when her own faltered.

Embracing vulnerability in your grief can open the door to profound healing and the presence of God's unwavering support.

DAILY REFLECTION

What does it mean for you to lean into your vulnerability during this tender time? How might releasing the need to "be strong" bring healing to your heart and soul?

PRAYER

Dear God, help me to embrace my feelings of loss and uncertainty. Grant me the courage to shed the pressure of always being strong and to find comfort in Your love and support.

"It's okay to feel weak; in surrendering, we find strength we never knew we had."

A DAY TO DO NOTHING

*"Be still, and know that I am God; I will be exalted among the nations, I will be exalted in the earth." **Psalm 46:10***

DEVOTIONAL

After the whirlwind of planning a life together, the silence can feel deafening. In the wake of your loss, it's easy to get swept up in the responsibilities left behind or consumed by what-ifs and maybes. Just yesterday, I decided to take a day where I would do nothing. I locked away my to-do list, turned off the phone, and simply allowed myself to sit in the stillness of my home. It reminded me of a quilt my husband made; with every patch and every thread speaking of love, stillness, and the warmth of precious memory. Sometimes, doing nothing allows us to reconnect with who we are, where we are, and who walks beside us in this journey.

In the quiet moments, you find the strength to feel, heal, and embrace the love that surrounds you still.

DAILY REFLECTION

What does it feel like for you to set aside a day without obligations, allowing space for rest and reflection? How might this intentional pause help you process your feelings and reconnect with yourself?

PRAYER

Dear God, as I seek rest and solitude in this day, grant me the peace to embrace stillness. Help me to find comfort in Your presence and clarity in my heart.

"In rest, we find renewal, and in stillness, we can hear the whispers of hope."

MY FAVORITE MEMORY OF US

"She is clothed with strength and dignity; she can laugh at the days to come."
Proverbs 31:25

DEVOTIONAL

As you remember the moments you shared with your beloved, it can be both joyful and bittersweet. Those simple afternoons spent in each other's company – cooking together, laughing over old stories, or basking in the comfort of silence – hold immense value. One particular memory that stands out might be a quiet evening, wrapped in a cozy blanket as you both watched the sunset, reflected in the silence of understanding and love. It's in these small yet profound moments that your love shone brightest, a testament to the bond that was unique and unshakeable. Though he may no longer be physically present, those memories remain as a source of warmth and comfort, weaving a tapestry of love that continues to inspire your spirit.

Every cherished memory is an anchor, reminding you of the love that will forever remain part of your journey.

DAILY REFLECTION

What is one cherished memory of your time together that brings a smile to your heart when you think about it? How does that moment reflect the love you shared?

PRAYER

Dear God, wrap this woman in Your comfort as she navigates her memories. Help her to cherish the joyful moments of love and connection, and may her heart find peace in those cherished times.

"Even in the silence, love still speaks through the memories we hold dear."

WHAT I MISS MOST TODAY

"You are the light of the world. A city set on a hill cannot be hidden. Nor do people light a lamp and put it under a basket, but on a stand, and it gives light to all in the house. In the same way, let your light shine before others, so that they may see your good works and give glory to your Father who is in heaven." **Matthew 5:14-16**

DEVOTIONAL

Today, like many days, I cannot help but reflect on what I miss most—his laughter, the warm embrace that made me feel safe, and the little moments we shared over morning coffee or quiet evenings. I remember one particular day when we sat on the porch watching the sunset, and he turned to me and said, "No matter what life throws our way, we've got each other." In that moment, I thought we'd always have time for more sunsets, more laughter. Now, as I watch the sun dip below the horizon alone, the space beside me is the most profound emptiness I've ever known.

Amidst the deep sorrow of loss, remember that your loved one would want you to embrace joy in the small moments and to shine your light brightly for others to see.

DAILY REFLECTION

What do you miss most about your loved one today, and how does that longing shape your heart in this moment?

PRAYER

Dear God, as I navigate this day without my beloved, help me to find comfort in your embrace. May I feel your presence in the moments of silence and longing, and remind me that love never truly leaves us.

"Grief is simply love with no place to go."

WHAT WOULD I SAY TO HIM?

"For your Maker is your husband, the Lord of hosts is His name; and the Holy One of Israel is your Redeemer, the God of the whole earth He is called." **Isaiah 54:5**

DEVOTIONAL

As you sit in the quietness of your home, memories wash over you like waves, each one heavier than the last. You remember his laugh, the way he held your hand, and the gentle strength he brought to your life. What would you say to him if he were here? Perhaps you'd thank him for the love, the shared dreams, or the small moments that turned into cherished memories. You might ask about his happiness now, hoping he feels your love even in this distance. In these moments of longing, remember that the conversations you shared on earthly grounds can continue through your heart's whispers to God, who understands every word you might say.

Cherish your memories, for they are the whispers of a love that transcends even the greatest sorrows.

DAILY REFLECTION

What would you say to him if you could sit down together for just one more moment? Would you share the little things, the memories you cherish, or the moments you wish you had spent differently?

PRAYER

Dear Lord, wrap your gentle arms around my heart. Help me to find peace in my sorrow and strength in my memories as I navigate this new chapter of life.

"Love doesn't end; it simply changes form."

THREE THINGS I'M GRATEFUL FOR

"Look at the birds of the air; they neither sow nor reap nor gather into barns, and yet your heavenly Father feeds them. Are you not of more value than they?" **Matthew 6:26**

DEVOTIONAL

In the quiet moments of the evening, as I sat on my back porch, I noticed a small bird diligently gathering twigs. It reminded me of the importance of gratitude amidst sorrow. This bird, though seemingly insignificant, was a powerful reminder that life continues and that provisions are made for each day. I recalled the simple joys—my favorite mug of warm tea, the beauty of a sunset, and the laughter of family that echoes in my heart. Each of these things felt like a small gift from God, encouraging me to find beauty in the mundane even during my grief.

Today, let gratitude unearth the light in the shadows of your heart, reminding you of the love that still surrounds you.

DAILY REFLECTION

What are three things in your life, no matter how small, that spark gratitude in your heart today?

PRAYER

Dear Lord, I thank You for the gift of life and the memories that bring warmth to my soul. Help me to see Your blessings even in the smallest moments and to embrace the journey ahead with hope.

Gratitude can be a gentle light, guiding us through the shadows of grief.

A PRAYER FROM MY HEART

"My life is consumed with grief and my years with sighing; my strength fails because of my affliction, and my bones grow weak. Because of all my enemies, I am the utter contempt of my neighbors and an object of dread to my closest friends—those who see me on the street flee from me. I am forgotten as though I were dead; I have become like broken pottery. For I hear many whispering, 'Terror on every side!' They conspire against me and plot to take my life. But I trust in you, Lord; I say, 'You are my God.'" **Psalm 31:10-14**

DEVOTIONAL

After years of sharing joys and sorrows, she found herself navigating life alone. Each morning felt heavier as the absence of his laughter echoed through their once-busy home. One day, while pruning the roses they had planted together, she noticed a small bud emerging from the seemingly lifeless stem—a symbol of hope amid her pain. This moment became a sacred reminder that even in her deepest sorrow, life could still bloom anew. Tears fell as she whispered a prayer, asking for strength to move forward, grateful for the love they had shared and the promise of tomorrow.

In the midst of grief, remember that your heart can still find a path toward healing and renewal.

DAILY REFLECTION

What is it that your heart truly seeks in this moment of quiet reflection?

PRAYER

Dear God, in my moments of sorrow and uncertainty, I seek Your presence to guide me. Help me to feel Your love surrounding me as I navigate this new path.

'Even in the depths of loss, there is the promise of new beginnings.'

A SCRIPTURE THAT SPEAKS TODAY

*"For I, the Lord your God, hold your right hand; it is I who say to you,
'Fear not, I am the one who helps you.'"* **Isaiah 41:13**

DEVOTIONAL

After losing her husband, Sarah felt like a shadow of her former self, floating through each day without purpose or direction. Every corner of her home echoed with memories that stung unexpectedly, reminding her of the joy they had shared. One quiet morning, as she sat in their favorite chair with a steaming cup of tea, she glanced around and began to recount the blessings she still held—the love of her children, the kindness of neighbors, and the warmth of friendships. She realized that while grief would always be part of her story, so too could joy exist alongside it, igniting a flicker of hope in her heart.

Embrace the small joys that remain in your life, for they are whispers of love amid the grief.

DAILY REFLECTION

What Scripture speaks to you in this season of your life, and how does it whisper comfort or guidance into your heart?

PRAYER

Dear God, please wrap your loving arms around this tender heart. Grant her peace and strength as she navigates the days ahead, and help her to trust in your perfect plan.

"In moments of sorrow, His grace flows abundantly."

WHAT I'VE LEARNED THROUGH GRIEF

"You turned my wailing into dancing; you removed my sackcloth and clothed me with joy, that my heart may sing your praises and not be silent. Lord my God, I will praise you forever." **Psalm 30:11-12**

DEVOTIONAL

After losing my beloved husband, I often found myself lost in the silence of our home. The echoes of laughter and love he left behind felt overwhelming. One evening, as I sat with a cup of tea by the window, I noticed the first blooms of spring pushing through the frost-covered ground. It struck me that life continues to unfold even in the most desolate times. I picked up a small flower and placed it in a vase, a living reminder of beauty springing forth amid my grief. Slowly, I began to embrace moments of joy, realizing that while sorrow was a part of my journey, it didn't have to define my story.

Grief teaches us to cherish fleeting moments and to allow ourselves to hold both sorrow and joy in our hearts simultaneously.

DAILY REFLECTION

What has this journey through grief taught you about yourself and your capacity to love?

PRAYER

Dear God, please hold this dear woman in Your gentle embrace, surrounding her with peace and comfort. Help her to find moments of grace amid the sorrow she carries.

"Grief reveals the depths of love that once thrived,
showing us that memories can be both a balm and a burden."

WHERE I FOUND COMFORT THIS WEEK

*"I waited patiently for the Lord; he turned to me and heard my cry. He lifted me out of the slimy pit, out of the mud and mire; he set my feet on a rock and gave me a firm place to stand." **Psalm 40:1-2***

DEVOTIONAL

This week was particularly heavy. I found myself sitting on my porch, the sun peeking through the clouds, reminding me of the warm memories spent with my husband. I closed my eyes and decided to listen to the gentle rustling of the leaves and the distant laughter of children playing. It was in that moment of solitude that I felt a sense of comfort wash over me, as if the very essence of my beloved was wrapped around me like a loving embrace. Nature became a refuge, a place where I could both mourn and find peace, allowing my heart to feel both heavy and light all at once.

Look for pockets of peace in the ordinary moments around you, as they often hold the most profound comfort during this journey of healing.

DAILY REFLECTION

What moments this week have brought you unexpected comfort, showing you that you are not alone in your journey?

PRAYER

Dear God, in these moments of sorrow, may I find solace in Your embrace. Show me the gentle reminders of love that surround me each day. Amen.

"Comfort often comes from the smallest acts of kindness and the loudest whispers of grace."

IF I COULD HAVE ONE MORE DAY

"I thank my God every time I remember you."
Philippians 1:3

DEVOTIONAL

There was a woman named Margaret, who had recently lost her husband after many wonderful years together. Each morning, she would wake with an ache in her heart, longing for just one more day with him—to hear his laughter, to share a cup of coffee, or to simply sit in comfortable silence. One evening, while going through old photographs, she found a note he had written her on their anniversary, filled with gratitude for their life together. In that moment, Margaret realized that, even though he was no longer with her, the love they had was a gift that would continue to shape her days. Inspired by his words, she began to honor his memory by sharing stories of their life with friends and family, allowing his spirit to live on in the bonds of love they had created together.

Your love story, though it continues in a new way, is forever etched in your heart.

DAILY REFLECTION

What would you say to him if you could have just one more day together, and how would you cherish those moments?

PRAYER

Dear God, in my grief, I long for comfort and connection. Please wrap your arms around me today and guide me to embrace the memories I hold dear.

"Love leaves an imprint that time cannot erase."

WHAT I NEED TO RELEASE

*"For I know the plans I have for you," declares the Lord, "plans to prosper you and not to harm you, plans to give you hope and a future." **Jeremiah 29:11***

DEVOTIONAL

As I sat alone in my favorite chair, gazing out the window, I felt a whirlwind of emotions surge through me. Memories of our life together flooded my thoughts, a bittersweet reminder of love lost. Yet, amidst the sorrow, I sensed a whisper calling me to release the burdens I had clung to tightly—fear, anger, and loneliness. In that moment, I began to understand that letting go didn't mean forgetting; rather, it was an invitation to allow myself to heal and step into a renewed hope for my future. Slowly, as I breathed deeply, I offered those burdens to God, trusting that He would transform my pain into purpose.

Embracing the journey of letting go is an essential step toward healing and discovering the new plans God has for your life.

DAILY REFLECTION

What emotions or memories do you feel holding on to, and how might releasing them create space for healing and renewal in your life?

PRAYER

Dear God, help me to find the strength to release what weighs on my heart, trusting in Your love and guidance as I walk through this season of change. Amen.

"Releasing what no longer serves me opens the door to new beginnings."

WHAT BRINGS ME PEACE

The Lord gives strength to his people; the Lord blesses his people with peace."
Psalm 29:11

DEVOTIONAL

After losing her beloved husband, Sarah often found herself sitting in the quiet of their home, surrounded by memories that both comforted and pained her. One rainy afternoon, as she watched the raindrops dance on the window, she remembered how her husband loved the rain. It was in that moment, wrapped in the gentle sound of the falling drops, that she felt a profound sense of peace wash over her. She began to consider that even in loss, there could be beauty, and perhaps, just perhaps, she could find a new rhythm of life filled with tender memories and unexpected moments of serenity. Sarah started a gratitude journal, noting things that brought her joy amidst her sorrow, discovering peace in her new journey.

Allow yourself to find moments of peace and beauty in your memories, letting them guide you gently toward healing.

DAILY REFLECTION

What brings you peace in this season of change? When you think about moments of stillness, what activities or memories comfort you the most?

PRAYER

Dear God, thank you for your presence in our lives, even in times of sorrow. Help me to find moments of peace amidst my grief, and remind me that you walk beside me every step of the way.

"In finding peace, we often discover strength we never knew we had."

WHO HAS SHOWN ME KINDNESS?

"The Lord bless him!" Naomi exclaimed.
*"He is a close relative, one of our family redeemers." **Ruth 2:20***

DEVOTIONAL

After losing her husband, Sarah felt adrift in a world that seemed too big and overwhelming. One day, while out shopping, she caught the eye of an elderly woman in the grocery aisle. The woman smiled warmly and offered her a genuine compliment about her scarf, causing Sarah to pause and realize that kindness, however small, could pierce through the heaviness of her heart. Over the following weeks, unexpected acts of kindness from neighbors, friends, and even strangers began to surface, creating a tapestry of hope in her life. With each gesture, Sarah found a flicker of joy igniting her spirit, reminding her that love continues in the most unexpected places.

There is profound beauty in recognizing and embracing the kindness that surrounds you, for even in your pain, you are woven into a community of love and support.

DAILY REFLECTION

Who in your life has offered you kindness during this challenging time? Can you think of specific moments or gestures that brought you comfort or a sense of connection?

PRAYER

Dear Lord, thank You for the kindness that surrounds us, even in our darkest hours. Help me to recognize and cherish those who show love and support in my journey of healing.

"Kindness is a language the deaf can hear and the blind can see."

MY HOPES FOR THE FUTURE

*"Know also that wisdom is like honey for you: If you find it, there is a future hope for you, and your hope will not be cut off." **Proverbs 24:14***

DEVOTIONAL

After losing her beloved husband, Mary found herself standing at a crossroads, unsure of what paths may lie ahead. Deep within, she harbored dreams and desires she'd often shelved in the name of love and support for her partner. As she embraced her solitude, she began to revisit those aspirations, creating a vision board filled with pictures of places she'd like to visit, hobbies she'd like to explore, and friendships she'd like to nurture. Through her journey of rediscovery, she learned that her hopes, once shadowed by grief, could take flight again, slowly transforming her quiet mornings into moments filled with possibilities.

Your future can still be filled with hope and purpose, reminding you that life holds new beginnings even after loss.

DAILY REFLECTION

What dreams or aspirations are waiting for you to embrace as you step forward into this new chapter of your life?

PRAYER

Dear God, in the quiet moments of my heart, I seek Your guidance and comfort as I envision my hopes for the future. May Your love fill the spaces of my grief and inspire me to dream anew.

"Hope is the gentle whisper that reminds us the future holds beauty yet to be discovered."

WHAT I'M AFRAID OF NOW

Psalm 56:3-4 (NIV): "When I am afraid, I put my trust in you, in God, whose word I praise; in God I trust and am not afraid. What can mere mortals do to me?" **Psalm 56:3-4**

DEVOTIONAL

When we lose a beloved partner, the world can feel overwhelmingly uncertain. I remember sitting at the kitchen table late one evening, grasping a cup of tea that had long gone cold, surrounded by silence that felt anything but comforting. The fear of being alone, of facing tomorrow without his steady presence, washed over me like a wave. Yet, as I looked at the empty chair across from me, I began to reflect on his love and encouragement to embrace life fully. It sparked a realization that even in my solitude, there is strength to be found in the memories we shared and the promise of each new day.

Embrace the fear, for it can lead you to a deeper trust in the love and support that surrounds you.

DAILY REFLECTION

What fears are creeping into your heart now that your world has changed? Take a moment to embrace those feelings and consider how they invite deeper understanding and connection with your inner self.

PRAYER

Dear God, I seek Your comfort in this time of uncertainty. Wrap me in Your peace as I navigate my fears and help me find hope in each new day.

"In the midst of fear, we often discover our hidden strength."

A LETTER TO GOD

"Cast your burden on the Lord, and He will sustain you; He will never permit the righteous to be moved." **Psalm 55:22**

DEVOTIONAL

There once was a woman named Mary, who after her husband passed, found herself enveloped in silence. The house felt emptier, the days longer. One evening, she decided to write a letter to God, pouring out her heart, sharing her fears and loneliness that echoed in every quiet room. As she penned her fears, a sense of relief washed over her, like an unburdening of her soul. It became a sacred ritual for her to write these letters, transforming her grief into conversations with the Lord, who always listened with love.

In your sorrow, remember that God welcomes your authentic feelings; allow yourself to express them freely.

DAILY REFLECTION

What are the thoughts and feelings you would pour out to God in a heartfelt letter, and how can you open your heart to His comfort today?

PRAYER

Dear God, in this tender and trying time, I seek Your presence and peace. Help me to express my sorrow and gratitude, knowing that You listen to every word I say.

"In the silence of your heart, God is waiting to read your letter."

WHAT STILL MAKES ME SMILE

"The Lord has anointed us to bring good news to the poor; he has sent us to bind up the brokenhearted, to proclaim freedom for the captives and release from darkness for the prisoners, to comfort all who mourn, and provide for those who grieve. In this season of mourning, may you find glimpses of hope that bring a smile to your heart again."

Isaiah 61:1-2

DEVOTIONAL

After losing her husband, Julia felt lost in a world that once seemed full and vibrant. Days stretched on, heavy with memory and grief, but one morning she decided to take a stroll through her neighborhood park. As she walked past the blooming flowers, their colors a stark contrast to her sorrow, a little girl giggled nearby, chasing butterflies. The sound stirred something within Julia—a realization that joy still existed. Smiling softly, she paused and took a moment to appreciate the simple beauty around her. It was a step toward healing, a reminder that even amidst pain, life still offered moments of delight.

Even in the depths of sorrow, seek out the small, joyful moments that can still bring a smile to your heart.

DAILY REFLECTION

What are the small joys or memories that bring a smile to your face, even in this difficult season?

PRAYER

Dear God, as I navigate this new chapter, help me to recognize the sparks of joy in my daily life. Thank you for the memories I've shared and the love that continues to surround me.

"In the cracks of sorrow, the light of joy still shines."

MOTHER'S DAY ALONE

"I have told you these things, so that in me you may have peace. In this world you will have trouble. But take heart! I have overcome the world." **John 16:33**

DEVOTIONAL

It was a rainy Mother's Day, and as the clouds matched her somber heart, she sat alone at the breakfast table, a single flower in a vase. Past memories flooded her mind—her husband's laughter, the warmth of his hand as they shared this day. Yet, as she watched raindrops trickle down the window, a small still voice reminded her of how they had always faced storms together. In this quiet moment, she decided to reach for her journal and write about her feelings, pouring out her grief as she had poured love into their life together. Through her tears, she felt a flicker of hope; she realized she could still celebrate the love they shared, even in his absence.

Grief may feel overwhelming, but even in loneliness, you can find peace by honoring the love that remains in your heart.

DAILY REFLECTION

What memories do you cherish about motherhood and your own journey as a mother, and how can you honor those moments this Mother's Day despite feeling alone?

PRAYER

Dear God, in this moment of solitude, wrap your loving arms around her. Grant her peace in her heart and joy in the memories of her loved ones as she navigates this special day.

"Even in solitude, love lingers and memories shine brightly."

WHAT I WANT MY KIDS TO KNOW

"Your word is a lamp to my feet and a light to my path."
Psalm 119:105

DEVOTIONAL

After losing my husband, I often find myself wandering through the memories of our life together. The night would sometimes feel lonelier, and the silence echoed the absence of his comforting voice. One evening, as I tidied up the bookshelf, I stumbled upon a note he wrote years ago. In it, he reminded me of the importance of love and resilience. With tears streaming down my face, I realized that while he was no longer physically beside me, his words still held the power to guide me, just like God's word lights our way in darkness.

Your strength to carry on will illuminate not just your path but also set an example of love and resilience for your children.

DAILY REFLECTION

What is one lesson from your journey that you hope to pass on to your children, knowing it can shape their futures in profound ways?

PRAYER

Dear God, in this time of reflection, please guide my heart and mind as I seek to share the love and wisdom I've gained. Let my words reach the hearts of my children, filling them with hope and strength.

"Love is a legacy that transcends time;
it is nurtured in the moments shared and the lessons imparted."

HIS VOICE IN MY HEART

"Do not fear, for I have redeemed you; I have summoned you by name; you are mine."
Isaiah 43:1

DEVOTIONAL

Maria sat in her favorite chair, the sun streaming through the window and warming her skin. Just days after her husband's funeral, she felt lost in a sea of memories, each one flooding her heart with both joy and sorrow. One morning, as she sipped her tea, she closed her eyes and took a deep breath, feeling an inexplicable sense of calm. In that stillness, she sensed a gentle voice within, reminding her that she was cherished and never abandoned. Even in her heartache, she found comfort in the knowledge that love endures, and that God was guiding her through each uncertain day.

You are held in divine love; even amid heartache, His voice will guide you through the whispers of grief towards the promise of healing.

DAILY REFLECTION

What does it feel like to hear His voice guiding you through this season of loss and change? Can you take a moment to listen for the gentle whisper amidst your heartache?

PRAYER

Dear Lord, as I navigate this challenging time, please help me hear Your voice and feel Your presence in my heart. Comfort me with Your love and guide my steps as I find my way forward.

"In my silence, I discover the whisper of His love."

ONE STEP FORWARD

*"You turned my mourning into dancing; you removed my sackcloth and clothed me with joy, that my heart may sing your praises and not be silent. Lord my God, I will praise you forever." **Psalm 30:11-12***

DEVOTIONAL

As I sat in my quiet living room, I found myself overwhelmed with memories. The chair beside me felt painfully empty, each corner of our home echoing laughter that now felt like a distant dream. It was during these moments of stillness that I realized I had a choice: to remain in the shadow of my sorrow or to take a brave step forward, even if that meant simply placing one foot in front of the other. I began to seek small joys—a flower blooming in the garden, the warmth of the sun on my face, and the sound of children playing outside. Each new day became a canvas, inviting me to fill it with colors of hope and renewal.

It's okay to grieve, but remember that taking one step forward, no matter how small, can lead to unexpected places of healing and new beginnings.

DAILY REFLECTION

What does taking one small step forward look like for you today, and how can you honor your grief while embracing the possibility of new beginnings?

PRAYER

Dear Lord, wrap your loving arms around this woman as she navigates her path of loss. Provide her with comfort in her sorrow and the courage to take each step forward, no matter how small.

"Every step, however small, is still progress toward healing."

YOU ARE STRONGER THAN YOU KNOW

"I can do all things through Christ who strengthens me."
Philippians 4:13

DEVOTIONAL

After losing her beloved husband, Anne felt as though a part of her had been ripped away. Days often blurred into one another, the weight of grief pressing down on her heart. One afternoon, while sorting through their shared memories, she stumbled upon a photograph of her wedding day, radiating joy and promise. In that moment, she remembered his words, "You are stronger than you think." With tears in her eyes, Anne realized that while her heart was heavy, she carried within her a reservoir of strength and resilience, gifted by love and faith.

Even in your deepest sorrow, you possess an inner strength that can guide you forward.

DAILY REFLECTION

What hidden strengths have you discovered within yourself since your loss, and how can you nurture them moving forward?

PRAYER

Dear God, hold me close in this tender moment of grief. Help me to see the strength you have placed within me and guide me as I navigate this new chapter of my life.

Strength often blooms in the cracks of our brokenness.

STRENGTH IN STILLNESS

*He makes me lie down in green pastures. He leads me beside still waters. He restores my soul." **Psalm 23:2-3 says***

DEVOTIONAL

After the loss of her husband, Martha found herself surrounded by silence that echoed the love that was once a vibrant presence in her life. One afternoon, sitting on the porch, she allowed herself to just breathe and be still. As she looked at the gentle sway of the trees and listened to the sweet chirping of birds, she realized that in the simplicity of these moments, her heart began to mend. Nature whispered to her, reminding her that solitude could also be a sacred space for healing.

In the stillness, you may discover a profound strength that will guide you through your journey of grief.

DAILY REFLECTION

What does it mean for you to find strength in the still moments of your day? Can you recall a time when quietness offered clarity or comfort?

PRAYER

Dear God, in these moments of transition, may I feel Your presence as I navigate my grief. Grant me peace in stillness, and help me discover the strength that resides within me. Amen.

"In the quiet, we often uncover the strength we didn't know we had."

GOD IS YOUR REFUGE

"The Lord is a refuge for the oppressed, a stronghold in times of trouble. Those who know your name trust in you, for you, Lord, have never forsaken those who seek you."
Psalm 9:9-10

DEVOTIONAL

As I sat alone in the quiet of my living room, the absence of my husband's laughter echoed in my heart. The soft glow of the lamp cast long shadows, reminding me of the many evenings we spent together. Life felt so heavy, and the weight of sorrow sometimes felt too much to bear. In those moments of longing and heartache, I whispered a simple prayer, seeking solace in the presence of God. Over time, I discovered that in my deepest sorrow, I found a refuge in Him, a stronghold that held my heart when it felt shattered. His comfort wrapped around me like a warm blanket, and though the road ahead seemed daunting, I learned to trust that I would never be alone.

God is your refuge, sustaining you through the painful journey of grief and opening pathways to healing and hope.

DAILY REFLECTION

What does it mean for you to find refuge in God during this time of grief? How can you open your heart to His presence and comfort each day?

PRAYER

Dear God, in this season of loss, help me to feel Your loving arms surrounding me. Grant me peace as I seek refuge in You, trusting that I am never alone in my sorrow.

"In your weakness, His strength will carry you."

WHEN COURAGE LOOKS LIKE GETTING OUT OF BED

*"If I take the wings of the morning and dwell in the uttermost parts of the sea, even there Your hand shall lead me, and Your right hand shall hold me." **Psalm 139:9-10***

DEVOTIONAL

When Miriam lost her husband, the weight of grief felt unbearable. Each morning was a mountain she didn't know how to climb, filled with shadows of memories and the silence that followed. Yet, one particularly gray morning, she realized that simply getting out of bed was, in itself, an act of courage. It was a decision to face the day, however daunting it felt. She took a breath, swung her legs over the side, and whispered a quiet prayer. With each small action, she began to reclaim moments of peace, remembering that even in her deepest sorrow, she was still held by a love beyond her understanding.

Courage isn't always loud; sometimes, it's just a gentle nudge to take one step out of the dark and into the light.

DAILY REFLECTION

What does it mean for you to find the strength to rise each day, even when the weight of grief feels heavy on your heart?

PRAYER

Dear God, please grant me the courage to face each new day, even when the burden feels overwhelming. Help me embrace the small victories, knowing that your love surrounds me and carries me through.

"Sometimes, the bravest step forward is simply stepping out of the shadows of yesterday."

BUILDING A NEW LIFE, BRICK BY BRICK

*"But now thus says the LORD, he who created you, O Jacob, he who formed you, O Israel: 'Fear not, for I have redeemed you; I have called you by name, you are mine.'" **Isaiah 43:1***

DEVOTIONAL

After losing her husband, Sarah found herself alone in a world that felt unfamiliar and daunting. Each room in their home echoed with memories, both sweet and painful. One day, while sorting through his old tools in the garage, she discovered a partially built birdhouse he'd started months before. Inspired, she decided to finish it, piece by piece, pouring her love and memories into the project. In the process, she began to envision her own life as something to be carefully constructed anew, building each day with purpose and intention, brick by brick, until she created a space that felt like home again.

Your life, though changed, can be rebuilt with beauty and purpose in each new day.

DAILY REFLECTION

What small steps can you take today to begin building the life you envision for yourself, and how can you honor the memories of your loved one in this journey?

PRAYER

Dear God, as I embark on this difficult yet hopeful journey of rebuilding, grant me strength and wisdom. Help me to see each day as an opportunity for growth and renewal in Your grace.

"Every brick laid in the structure of your new life
contributes to a foundation of hope and resilience."

GRIEF AND GRACE CAN COEXIST

*"He will cover you with his feathers, and under his wings, you will find refuge; his faithfulness will be your shield and rampart." **Psalm 91:4***

DEVOTIONAL

After losing her husband, Alice often felt a deep void, a silent ache that showed up in the quiet moments of her day. One evening, as she sorted through a box of his belongings, she discovered a handwritten note tucked between the pages of a book. It spoke of love and life's impermanence, reminding her that in the midst of sorrow, grace abounded in memories, laughter, and the warmth of shared moments. With wet eyes and a fragile heart, she realized the two could coexist—grief was not the absence of joy but rather a companion to her cherished memories. Each tear she shed was a testament to the beauty of their life together.

Even in deep grief, grace can provide comforting moments that remind us of the love and joy we once experienced.

DAILY REFLECTION

What does it feel like to hold both your grief and the grace of God in your heart right now? How can you allow both to coexist in your life today?

PRAYER

Dear Lord, wrap your loving arms around me as I navigate this time of grief. Help me to find your grace even amidst my sorrow, and remind me that I am never alone in this journey.

"Grief is not a wall that separates us from grace, but a bridge that brings us closer to it."

YOU CAN DO HARD THINGS

*"Is anyone among you in trouble? Let them pray. Is anyone happy? Let them sing songs of praise." **James 5:13***

DEVOTIONAL

As I sit on the porch, sipping tea and watching the leaves dance in the wind, I am reminded of the resilience found in nature. Just months ago, my world felt shattered after losing my husband. The heartache was unbearable, and the future seemed dim. Yet, as the seasons changed from winter to spring, something stirred within me. I began to realize that I had the strength to face each day, no matter how hard it felt. One morning, I decided to take a small step—planting flowers in the yard that we once shared. With each bloom that emerged, I felt a flicker of hope, reminding me that I, too, could bloom again despite the trials.

Remember, dear one, you can do hard things. Your strength will bloom in the presence of love and memories, guiding you toward brighter days ahead.

DAILY REFLECTION

What hard things have you faced since your loss, and how have you found strength in the moments of struggle?

PRAYER

Dear God, as I navigate this new chapter of my life, grant me the courage to embrace the challenges ahead. Help me to see my inner strength and to lean on You when I feel weak.

"Each step forward, no matter how small, is a testament to your resilience and courage."

GOD IS STILL WRITING YOUR STORY

"Many, O Lord my God, are the wonders you have done, the things you planned for us no one can recount to you; were I to speak and tell of them, they would be too many to declare."
Psalm 40:5

DEVOTIONAL

After losing her husband, Mary found herself in a fog of grief, struggling to find meaning in her once vibrant life. One day, while sorting through old photographs, she stumbled upon a picture of the two of them on a joyful trip they had taken together. As tears streamed down her face, Mary's heart began to feel lighter; memories flooded back, reminding her of the laughter and love they shared. But it also struck her that their journey had not ended—those beautiful moments were part of a greater story that was still being written. Encouraged by this realization, she began writing down her thoughts, prayers, and dreams, slowly seeing glimpses of hope unfolding in unexpected ways.

In the midst of your grief, remember that God is still penning beautiful chapters in the story of your life, inviting you to be open to new beginnings.

DAILY REFLECTION

What stories of your past do you cherish, and how might those stories be woven into the new chapter God is writing for you now?

PRAYER

Heavenly Father, hold this dear woman in your gentle embrace as she navigates her new path. Fill her heart with your peace and guide her with your wisdom, reminding her that you are always present in her journey.

Every ending invites a fresh beginning, and God's pen never leaves your hand.

THE POWER OF ENDURANCE

"But those who hope in the Lord will renew their strength. They will soar on wings like eagles; they will run and not grow weary, they will walk and not be faint." **Isaiah 40:31**

DEVOTIONAL

Once, there was a woman who, after losing her beloved partner, found herself wandering through days that felt endless and heavy. The memories of laughter lingered, intertwining with the silence that felt unbearable at times. As she journeyed through her grief, she discovered that while the days were sometimes filled with pain, they also held small moments of joy that reminded her of the love they shared. Each day, she allowed herself to cry, to remember, and to embrace the beauty of a life still worth living. Slowly, she learned that endurance wasn't merely about pushing through; it was also about honoring her spouse's memory and finding strength in each tender moment that came her way.
Endurance is not just surviving the storm; it is finding the light within its depths as you honor the love that brought you here.

DAILY REFLECTION

What does endurance look like for you in this season of your life? Can you identify moments where you've felt God's strength carrying you through your pain and uncertainty?

PRAYER

Dear Lord, in this time of loss, grant her the strength to endure each day with hope. May she feel Your loving presence as she navigates this difficult journey.

'Endurance is not the absence of struggle, but the quiet resolve to move forward, one step at a time.'

WHEN YOU FEEL BRAVE AGAIN

*"Beauty is fleeting, but a woman who fears the Lord is to be praised. In this challenging season of loss, your strength may feel hidden beneath layers of grief. Yet, with each passing day, as you turn your heart toward God, you can rediscover the courageous spirit He has placed within you. Allow His presence to draw out your inner bravery, giving you wings to rise above the sorrows that weigh you down." **Proverbs 31:30***

DEVOTIONAL

After my husband passed, I found myself standing at the crossroads of despair and determination. One evening, while sorting through our cherished memories, I stumbled upon a photograph of our favorite hike. In that moment, I felt a whisper in my heart: "It's time to step back into the beauty of life." Though the fear of facing the world alone loomed large, I found the tiny flicker of bravery within me that propelled me to take that walk. Each step I took reminded me that while my journey was altered, it was still a journey worth embracing.

Bravery is not the absence of fear, but the decision to move forward in faith, even when your heart feels hesitant.

DAILY REFLECTION

What small step can you take today that would help you feel a little braver than you did yesterday?

PRAYER

Dear Lord, guide this gentle heart through her grief. May she find the courage within to embrace new beginnings and trust in Your love and grace.

"Bravery is not the absence of fear, but the determination to move forward despite it."

FINDING STABILITY IN CHANGE

*"In the midst of your grief, remember that the Lord is unchanging. "Of old you laid the foundation of the earth, and the heavens are the work of your hands. They will perish, but you will remain; they will all wear out like a garment. You change them like clothing, and they will be changed. But you are the same, and your years have no end." **Psalm 102:25-27***

DEVOTIONAL

When I lost my husband, the world seemed to crumble around me. The routines we cherished together felt meaningless, and the once-familiar landscape of my life transformed into an unrecognizable terrain of sorrow. In those quiet moments, I found solace in visiting our favorite places, where memories lingered like a warm embrace. It was there, amidst the soft rustle of leaves and the gentle warmth of the sun, that I began to see God's hand guiding me toward new beginnings. Each day became an invitation to discover new strength within myself, reminding me that while life changes, God's love remains an anchor in every storm.

Even in the throes of profound change and loss, trust that God's unchanging love is your anchor, providing the stability you need to navigate each new day.

DAILY REFLECTION

What changes have been the most challenging for you since your loss, and how can you invite God into those moments of uncertainty?

PRAYER

Dear God, in this time of transition, help me to feel your presence in every moment of change. Grant me the strength to embrace new beginnings, knowing you are always by my side.

"Just as the seasons change, so too can our hearts learn to blossom anew in the midst of loss."

A DAY WITHOUT PANIC

"When anxiety was great within me, your consolation brought me joy."
Psalm 94:19

DEVOTIONAL

After losing her husband, Mary often felt overwhelmed by the quiet of her home. Each room seemed to whisper memories that unfolded like the pages of a fragile book. One afternoon, as she prepared tea, a sudden pang of panic washed over her, igniting thoughts of loneliness and uncertainty. But in that moment, she took a deep breath, recalling a cherished memory of laughter shared over similar cups. She closed her eyes and allowed the warmth of those moments to envelop her, reminding her that even in solitude, joy and peace could still coexist. It became a small practice for her—a way to turn a day that threatened panic into one filled with gentle reassurance.

Remember that even amidst your sorrow, you can find moments of peace and joy, drawing strength from the love that remains in your heart.

DAILY REFLECTION

What simple act can you take today to bring a sense of peace and calm into your life?

PRAYER

Dear God, help me to feel your presence in moments of uncertainty. May I find strength and solace in each breath I take today.

"Even in the shadow of loss, peace can be a gentle companion."

RESTING IN GOD'S PROTECTION

"He will cover you with His feathers, and under His wings, you will find refuge; His faithfulness will be your shield and rampart." **Psalm 91:4**

DEVOTIONAL

In the quiet moments of her new reality, Sarah often felt a wave of loneliness wash over her, making the world seem dark and heavy. One day, as she sorted through her late husband's belongings, she found a small feather tucked into his favorite book, a reminder of a cherished trip they took together. As she held it, she felt a warmth envelop her, as if she were wrapped in the gentle embrace of God's protection. Every time anxiety crept in, she would recall that feather and the peace promised in Psalm 91:4, reminding her that she was never alone. God was watching over her, longing to provide her with the refuge she so desperately needed.

In the stillness of your heartache, lean into the protective embrace of God, for He is your safe haven.

DAILY REFLECTION

What does resting in God's protection look like for you in this season of your life? Can you envision a safe place where your heart can find solace amidst the pain and uncertainty?

PRAYER

Heavenly Father, wrap your loving arms around this precious woman today. Help her to feel your presence and assurance as she navigates this difficult journey, trusting in your protection and care.

"Even in the midst of stormy seas, God's peace can be the anchor for our weary souls."

RESILIENCE THROUGH FAITH

"Wait for the Lord; be strong, and let your heart take courage; wait for the Lord."
Psalm 27:14

DEVOTIONAL

When Sarah lost her husband after 40 years of marriage, the world felt heavy and gray. Each day was a battle not only against sorrow but also the overwhelming silence of an empty home. One evening, while flipping through their old photo albums, she stumbled upon a photo of them on their wedding day, both smiling with dreams in their eyes. In that moment, the warmth of love wrapped around her, reminding her that while loss was painful, the memories they built together could also be a source of strength. It was in that nostalgia that Sarah learned she could honor her husband's memory while still forging her own path forward, discovering resilience in each step taken.

You are not alone in your grief; allow your faith to be your anchor as you courageously take each step forward.

DAILY REFLECTION

What does resilience look like for you in this season of your life, and how can you lean into your faith to navigate the challenges ahead?

PRAYER

Dear God, wrap your loving arms around those who are grieving and feeling lost. Grant them the strength to embrace each day with hope and the assurance of your unwavering presence. Help them to find comfort in their faith and the promise of new beginnings.

"In the quiet moments of sorrow, faith can be the gentle whisper that guides us forward."

HOLDING ON AND LETTING GO

"Fear not, for I am with you; be not dismayed, for I am your God; I will strengthen you, I will help you, I will uphold you with my righteous right hand." **Isaiah 41:10**

DEVOTIONAL

When I first lost my husband, I felt as if I was holding on to thin air, grasping for the familiar memories that comforted me. Each night, the silence in our home echoed louder than my sobs. I remember one particular evening, wrapped in my blanket, I found a letter he wrote to me years ago. Reading his words felt like he was right there with me, and in that moment, I learned to hold onto love, but also to begin letting go of the weight of sorrow. As I cherished his memory, I discovered a path forward where my grief could coexist with gratitude for the life we shared.

Always know that it is okay to hold onto cherished memories while letting go of the sorrow that weighs you down.

DAILY REFLECTION

What are the things you find yourself holding on to in this season of change, and what might you be invited to gently let go of? Reflect on how these elements impact your daily life and emotional well-being.

PRAYER

Dear God, embrace her heart in this time of transition. Surround her with Your love, guiding her through both the memories she cherishes and the new beginnings You have in store. May she find peace in Your presence as she navigates what it means to hold on and let go.

"Sometimes, letting go makes room for new hope to grow."

THE WOMAN YOU'RE BECOMING

"Delight yourself in the Lord, and He will give you the desires of your heart."
Psalm 37:4

DEVOTIONAL

There was a woman named Emily, who after losing her beloved husband, felt adrift in a world that seemed to have lost its color. Days blended into nights as she struggled to find meaning in her new life. One afternoon, while sorting through memories in the attic, she stumbled upon a journal filled with dreams and aspirations she had penned years ago. In that moment, she realized that those dreams had not vanished with her husband; they were still there, waiting to be rekindled. As she began to engage with her passions once more, she discovered a renewed sense of self and purpose, revealing the vibrant woman she was still becoming.

In this season of transformation, embrace the truth that your dreams still matter and you have the strength to pursue them.

DAILY REFLECTION

What aspects of yourself have emerged during this challenging season, and how can you nurture these new facets of your identity?

PRAYER

Dear Lord, as I navigate this new life, I seek your gentle guidance. Help me to embrace the woman I am becoming and to trust in your plans for my future.

"From grief comes growth, and in this transformation, you will find strength and beauty."

SMALL VICTORIES, BIG GROWTH

"Commit your way to the LORD; trust in Him and He will do this."
Psalm 37:5

DEVOTIONAL

After losing her husband, Sarah found herself overwhelmed with tasks she had never done alone. One day, as she sat in her kitchen staring at a pile of unopened mail, she decided to tackle just one envelope. As she pulled it open, she discovered a long-forgotten gift card. That small victory—noticing a bright spot amid the grief—led her to take a little time for herself that week. It was a simple lunch with a friend, which turned into laughter and shared memories. Each small step shifted her perspective just a bit, reminding her that joy and companionship still existed in her life.

Even the smallest victories can lead to profound growth in your heart and spirit as you navigate this new journey.

DAILY REFLECTION

What small victories have you experienced in your journey since your loss, and how have they contributed to your growth in faith and strength?

PRAYER

Dear God, as I navigate this new chapter of my life, help me recognize the small victories each day brings. Thank you for your constant presence and support in my healing journey.

"Every small step you take is a testament to your resilience and a foundation for your renewed self."

THE VOICE OF STRENGTH WITHIN

"Can a mother forget the baby at her breast and have no compassion on the child she has borne? Though she may forget, I will not forget you. See, I have engraved you on the palms of my hands; your walls are ever before me." **Isaiah 49:15-16**

DEVOTIONAL

As she sat in the quiet corner of her home, memories flooded in like a gentle tide, reminding her of laughter shared and days filled with love. Each time the door creaked, her heart leapt with hope, only to settle back into a hollow ache. But in this stillness, she began to uncover a strength she didn't know resided within her—a voice that whispered comfort and promise during the lonely hours. Just as the psalmist declared, "The Lord is a refuge for the oppressed, a stronghold in times of trouble," she slowly realized that even in her grief, she could lean into the reassurance of the divine presence surrounding her, guiding her steps one day at a time.

The voice of strength within you can guide you even through the darkest valleys—trust it, for it is a gift meant to lead you toward healing and hope.

DAILY REFLECTION

What does the voice of strength within you sound like, and how can you listen to it more closely during this time of transition?

PRAYER

Dear God, as I navigate this journey of loss, help me to hear the whispers of strength within me. Surround me with Your love and comfort, guiding my steps as I move forward.

"In the silence of sorrow, your spirit begins to unveil its deepest strength."

BLOOMING THROUGH BROKENNESS

"Every plant is to be called by its unique name."
Genesis 2:19

DEVOTIONAL

Anna sat on the porch, clutching a faded sweater that still held the scent of her late husband's cologne. As she watched the garden bloom around her, she recalled the countless afternoons they had spent planting flowers together, each one a testament to love and shared dreams. Now, much of it felt overwhelming, and the vibrant colors seemed to mock her grief. Yet, as a single tear fell onto a patch of soil, she was reminded that even in her brokenness, there could be beauty. Like seedlings breaking through the winter frost, she realized it was possible to flourish despite the ache in her heart, and that each tender bloom symbolized the enduring love they shared.

In the face of profound loss, remember that blooming can happen in the cracks of your heart, leading to a new chapter of growth even amidst the brokenness.

DAILY REFLECTION

What does it mean for you to embrace the beauty of blooming in this season of loss and change? How can you seek out the moments that nurture your spirit?

PRAYER

Dear God, in this time of sorrow, help me to find hope amidst my grief. May I feel Your love surrounding me and guide me to discover new beginnings, even in the pain.

"Even in the darkest moments, flowers can still find their way to the sun."

BRAVE ENOUGH TO BEGIN AGAIN

*"Forget the former things; do not dwell on the past. See, I am doing a new thing! Now it springs up; do you not perceive it? I am making a way in the wilderness and streams in the wasteland." **Isaiah 43:18-19***

DEVOTIONAL

After losing her husband, Sarah felt as if she were walking through a fog that would never lift. Each day seemed to blend into the next, a reminder of someone who used to be at her side. One afternoon, a friend invited her to a local art class. Hesitant but brave, Sarah picked up a brush and dipped it into color for the first time since her loss. As she painted, she released her grief onto the canvas and discovered that within the strokes, she could also find joy and hope for the future. Little by little, these moments of creativity allowed her to see that life, though different, could still be beautiful.

Every ending can also be a new beginning; embrace the journey ahead with an open heart.

DAILY REFLECTION

What in your heart is calling you to begin anew, and how can you honor that desire today?

PRAYER

Dear Lord, wrap her in Your comfort as she steps into this new chapter. Give her the courage to embrace change and the wisdom to see the beauty in fresh beginnings.

"Every ending is a chance to create a new beginning."

HOPE IS A HOLY THING

"Be strong and take heart, all you who hope in the Lord."
Psalm 31:24

DEVOTIONAL

After losing her husband, Clara found herself starting each day with an overwhelming sense of emptiness. One gloomy morning, while sitting on the porch, she spotted a tiny bird perched nearby, singing its heart out. Despite its fragile appearance, the bird seemed to radiate joy and hope-filled melodies that pierce through the stillness of her grief. Clara realized that this little creature was not allowing its circumstances to dictate its spirit. In that moment, she understood that even in her darkest hour, hope was like that song — a holy thing that could fill her heart if she chose to listen.

In the face of heartache, remember that hope can bloom quietly like a flower through the cracks of your pain, offering you a way to embrace each new day.

DAILY REFLECTION

What does hope feel like for you today, and how can you nurture it in the small moments of your life?

PRAYER

Dear God, in my sorrow, I long for Your light to guide me. Help me to find the whispers of hope in my heart and to trust in Your promises. Amen.

"Hope is the gentle dawn that follows the darkest night."

LOOKING FOR THE LIGHT

"Arise, shine, for your light has come, and the glory of the Lord has risen upon you."
Isaiah 60:1

DEVOTIONAL

In the wake of losing her beloved husband, Mary found herself enveloped in darkness. Each morning felt like an uphill battle, with the weight of her grief pressing heavily on her heart. One afternoon, as she sorted through their shared memories, she discovered a small, framed verse tucked away—"His mercies are new every morning." That night, as tears flowed, she whispered a prayer for strength. It wasn't an instant relief, but in time, the dawn broke through, reminding her that light could indeed shine through the cracks of her brokenness if only she would keep looking for it.

Every day may not feel easy, but seeking the light in your heart can bring moments of hope and healing amidst your sorrow.

DAILY REFLECTION

What small moments of light have you noticed in your day today, even amid the shadows of loss?

PRAYER

Dear God, as I navigate through this season of change and grief, I ask for your gentle guidance. Help me to open my heart to the light that still surrounds me, reminding me of the love and memories that will forever shine bright.

"Even in the darkest of nights, stars remain steadfastly present."

YOUR FUTURE IS NOT OVER

"You make known to me the path of life; in your presence there is fullness of joy; at your right hand are pleasures forevermore." **Psalm 16:11**

DEVOTIONAL

After losing my husband, I felt a profound void and questioned what my future held. One evening, I stumbled upon a small garden near my home. It was wild and overgrown yet bursting with unexpected blooms. As I tended to it, a realization washed over me: just like this garden, life could still produce beauty, even from the ruins of loss. With each flower that blossomed, I began to understand that my story was not finished; it was merely transforming into something new.

Your future is not over; it is a canvas yet to be painted, and God invites you to fill it with hope and new beginnings.

DAILY REFLECTION

What dreams or passions have you set aside, believing it was too late to pursue them?

PRAYER

Dear Lord, as I navigate this challenging season, help me to trust that my future is filled with possibility. May I find strength in Your love and guidance as I take my next steps.

"Grief has the power to close chapters, but it also opens doors to new beginnings."

JOY WILL RETURN

"You turned my wailing into dancing; you removed my sackcloth and clothed me with joy."
Psalm 30:11

DEVOTIONAL

After losing my beloved husband, I found myself enveloped in a darkness I never thought I could escape. Days turned into weeks, and I often felt lost, drifting through a world that had lost its vibrancy. One afternoon, I stumbled upon an old box of photographs. As I sorted through the memories, laughter erupted uncontrollably from deep within me, surprising even myself. Those glimpses of a joyful past reminded me that even in the midst of sorrow, love remains and can still spark moments of happiness. It was a gentle nudge from God, assuring me that joy, too, would find its way back to my heart.

In the midst of your grief, choose to hold on to the hope that joy will return, even in the smallest of moments.

DAILY REFLECTION

What small moments of joy have you experienced this week, even amid your sorrow? Can you see God's hand gently lifting your spirit in unexpected ways?

PRAYER

Dear God, wrap this dear heart in Your comfort, reminding her that joy will bloom again in her life. Help her to feel Your presence and to trust in Your timing. Amen.

"Just as the sun sets to rise again, so too does joy return to the heart that mourns."

TOMORROW CAN BE BEAUTIFUL

"To appoint unto them that mourn in Zion, to give unto them beauty for ashes, the oil of joy for mourning, the garment of praise for the spirit of heaviness; that they might be called trees of righteousness, the planting of the Lord, that he might be glorified."
Isaiah 61:3

DEVOTIONAL

After losing her husband of many years, Mary often found herself wandering through the quiet house, lost in memories. Each room held echoes of laughter, love, and shared dreams that felt painfully out of reach. One rainy afternoon, she decided to take a walk in the garden he had lovingly tended. As she observed the blooming flowers pushing through the damp earth, she felt a flicker of hope ignite within her. Nature's resilience began to mirror her own journey—reshaping her grief into a new narrative of beauty and growth. With each blossom, she realized that tomorrow could indeed be beautiful if she allowed the warmth of new possibilities to enter her heart.

Embrace the hope that tomorrow can bring new beauty and joy, even amid sorrow.

DAILY REFLECTION

What dreams or hopes have you tucked away since your husband's passing, waiting for the right time to revisit them?

PRAYER

Dear Lord, guide her gently as she steps into each new day. Fill her heart with hope and remind her that beauty still exists in the world around her.

Every sunset brings the promise of a new dawn,
and with it, the possibility of beauty yet to be discovered.

NEW CHAPTERS, NEW GRACE

"Therefore, if anyone is in Christ, the new creation has come:
The old has gone, the new is here!" **2 Corinthians 5:17**

DEVOTIONAL

After losing her husband, Sarah found herself adrift in a world that felt unfamiliar and daunting. It was one rainy afternoon while sorting through old photographs that she stumbled upon a picture of them hiking in the mountains. In that moment, she realized that the joy they shared could live on in her memories but did not have to define her future. She began to explore new interests, joining a local book club and volunteering in her community. Each small step filled her heart with renewed hope and the gentle reminder that life could still hold beautiful moments, all while cherishing the love she had experienced.

Grief may feel like a heavy burden, but within it, God offers fresh grace and the chance to discover joy anew.

DAILY REFLECTION

What new chapters are unfolding in your life today, and how can you invite God's grace into each step you take?

PRAYER

Dear God, hold this heart of mine as I navigate these new seasons. Grant me the strength to embrace change and the courage to see Your grace in each moment.

"Every ending is the beginning of something beautiful, orchestrated by God's loving hands."

THE NEXT SEASON

"Even the young may grow weary,
but those who hope in the Lord will renew their strength.." **Isaiah 40:30-31**

DEVOTIONAL

Lila had walked through the shadow of grief since her husband's passing, feeling as though the colors of her life had faded to gray. One morning, as she tended her garden, she noticed a stubborn bud pushing through the soil, reaching for the sun, despite the chill of the morning air. Inspired, Lila realized that grief, like winter, has its place and time, but it does not have the final say. With each flower that bloomed, she felt a flicker of hope, a whisper from God that said, "This season may be hard, but I am preparing you for new growth."

As you navigate this difficult time, remember that each day is an opportunity for renewal, and God has beautiful plans for the next season of your life.

DAILY REFLECTION

What dreams or passions have been set aside that you might want to revisit in this new season of your life?

PRAYER

Dear Lord, as I step into this new chapter, fill my heart with hope and clarity. Help me to embrace the opportunities ahead and know that I am never alone in this journey.

"Every ending is a new beginning wrapped in the gift of possibility."

THE PROMISE OF SPRING

"But the angel said to the women, 'Do not be afraid, for I know that you seek Jesus who was crucified. He is not here; for He has risen, as He said.'" **Matthew 28:5-6**

DEVOTIONAL

In the still of a quiet morning, Sarah sat by her window with tears gently tracing her cheeks. It had been just a few months since her beloved husband had passed, and the world felt cold and uninviting. As she watched the vibrant colors of spring bursting through the barren trees, she recalled the joys they had shared beneath those same branches. With each bloom, she felt a subtle whisper filling her heart, assuring her that life could bring beauty again. Just as the flowers were returning, so too would laughter and warmth, and Sarah began to let her heart open to the possibility of new beginnings.

The promise of spring reminds us that, even amidst profound loss, there is always potential for renewal and growth in our lives.

DAILY REFLECTION

What are the new beginnings that God might be inviting you to embrace in this season of your life?

PRAYER

Dear God, as I navigate this time of change, help me to open my heart to the new life blooming around me. Grant me peace and hope as I reflect on the beauty of your promises.

"Just as spring breaks forth from winter, so too can my heart find renewal after loss."

UNEXPECTED JOY

"For the Lord will comfort Zion; He will comfort all her waste places, and He will make her wilderness like Eden, and her desert like the garden of the Lord. Joy and gladness will be found in her, thanksgiving and the voice of song." **Isaiah 51:3**

DEVOTIONAL

After losing her beloved partner, Susan often found herself lost in memories of their life together. Each day blended into the next, filled with quiet rooms that echoed with silence. Yet, one sunny afternoon, while tidying up his old study, she stumbled upon a box overflowing with letters they had written to each other over the years. As she read each note, laughter broke through her tears, igniting unexpected joy that reminded her of their love and shared dreams. In that moment, she realized that while grieving was necessary, there was also room for the light of cherished memories to shine through the darkness.

Even amidst the sorrow of loss, joy can emerge from the beauty of shared memories that remind us of love's enduring presence.

DAILY REFLECTION

What small moments of joy have you experienced this week that lifted your spirits unexpectedly? How can you nurture those feelings amid your grief?

PRAYER

Dear God, as I navigate this new chapter of my life, help me to recognize and embrace the unexpected joys you place in my path. Fill my heart with gratitude and peace as I learn to find happiness again.

"Joy can be found even in the cracks of our broken hearts."

WHEN THE FOG BEGINS TO LIFT

*"Therefore, we do not lose heart. Though outwardly we are wasting away, yet inwardly we are being renewed day by day." **2 Corinthians 4:16***

DEVOTIONAL

After losing her husband, Sarah found herself in a haze of grief that felt like an unending fog. Each day seemed alike as she navigated through memories that both comforted and pained her. Yet, as time passed, she began to notice moments when laughter replaced tears—a shared joke with her daughter or a sunrise that brought her peace. Little by little, the fog began to lift. With each passing day, Sarah discovered that her heart was being renewed; the love she had shared was transforming into strength, hope, and the promise of new beginnings.

In the journey of grief, don't underestimate the gentle power of renewal that comes, even when it feels impossible.

DAILY REFLECTION

What small moments or memories can you cherish today that remind you of the love you shared, and how might they guide you towards healing?

PRAYER

Dear God, as I navigate this new path, please fill my heart with comfort and peace. Help me to embrace the memories while also finding hope for the future.

"Out of the fog, light begins to gather; each day reveals the beauty still woven into the fabric of life."

ANTICIPATING NEW JOY

*"The Lord Himself goes before you and will be with you; He will never leave you nor forsake you. Do not be afraid; do not be discouraged." **Deuteronomy 31:8***

DEVOTIONAL

There was a woman named Ellen who had recently lost her husband. In the quiet moments of the morning, she would sip her tea while gazing out the window, feeling the weight of her sorrow. One day, as the sun broke through the clouds, she saw new buds on her garden plants that she had thought were dead. In that moment, she felt a flicker of hope, a reminder that even after deep sorrow, new life and joy can emerge. With each passing day, she began to tend her garden again, discovering in each bloom a reflection of the joy that awaited her in the future.

Each day brings the potential for new joy, even when it feels impossible.

DAILY REFLECTION

What dreams or joys have you put on hold, and how might you start nurturing them again?

PRAYER

Dear Lord, as I navigate this new chapter of my life, help me to open my heart to the joys yet to come. Remind me that You are always with me, guiding my steps toward brighter days.

"New beginnings often bloom from the ashes of what has been."

HOPE IN THE MORNING

"In the morning, O Lord, You hear my voice; in the morning I lay my requests before You and wait in expectation." **Psalm 5:3**

DEVOTIONAL

After losing her husband, Sarah found herself lost in a haze of sorrow and loneliness. The mornings felt like a cruel reminder of her new reality, yet one day as she gazed out the window, she noticed the sun rising over the trees. It dawned on her that while her heart ached, each new day also brought a flicker of hope—a reminder that life still held whispers of beauty. With a deep breath, she whispered her heartbreak to God, and in that moment of vulnerability, she felt a gentle assurance that the Lord was with her, turning her mourning into dawn's embrace.

Even in your deepest sorrow, the dawn carries the promise of hope; lean in and let each morning become a sacred space where you meet the Lord and find renewed strength.

DAILY REFLECTION

What does hope look like for you in the quiet moments of the morning as you begin a new day without your loved one?

PRAYER

Dear God, please surround her with Your comforting presence each morning. Help her to find pieces of joy and hope in the light of a new day, reminding her that she is never alone.

"Every dawn brings a new opportunity to embrace hope and heal."

ROOM FOR SOMETHING NEW

*"Therefore, if anyone is in Christ, the new creation has come: The old has gone, the new is here!" **2 Corinthians 5:17***

DEVOTIONAL

When Elaine lost her husband after decades of being together, she felt like she had lost part of her very soul. Each room felt empty, every laugh echoed with memories, and the future seemed dim. One day, as she sorted through his belongings, she discovered a small journal filled with his dreams for their future, dreams he had never shared with her. As she read his hopes for family trips, simple joys, and personal growth, something stirred within her—a flicker of hope and a realization that life was still waiting for her to embrace it. Just like the spring flowers that bloom after a harsh winter, Elaine found the courage to create new memories while cherishing the love that had shaped her past.

This season, although heavy with grief, has room for the unexpected and the beautiful—a reminder that God provides space for new beginnings, even when we least expect it.

DAILY REFLECTION

What is one new thing you've always wanted to explore that could bring light and joy into your life right now?

PRAYER

Dear God, as I navigate this new chapter, help me to embrace the opportunities You lay before me. May my heart remain open to the possibilities that await, filled with Your comfort and love.

"Every ending paves the way for a new beginning."

TRUSTING GOD WITH THE UNKNOWN

*"Trust in the Lord with all your heart and lean not on your own understanding; in all your ways acknowledge Him, and He will make your paths straight." **Proverbs 3:5-6***

DEVOTIONAL

Last week, I met a woman named Mary at a local support group for widows. She shared her story of waking up to an empty house and feeling utterly lost for the first time in decades. One day, she found an old photo album that sparked beautiful memories of joy and laughter with her spouse. As she flipped through the pages, tears streamed down her face, but amidst those tears, she felt a sudden warmth in her heart—a reminder that love never truly leaves us. Through her grief, Mary discovered that even in the unknown, God's presence remained with her, guiding her to a place of healing.

Trusting God with the unknown means believing that He is crafting a beautiful story from our pain, even when we cannot see the final chapters.

DAILY REFLECTION

What fears or uncertainties are you holding onto today that you can surrender to God?

PRAYER

Dear Lord, I come to you with a heavy heart, seeking your comfort and guidance in this uncertain season. Help me to trust in Your plan, even when I can't see the path ahead.

"Even in the midst of change, His love remains a steady anchor."

PLANTING HOPE DAILY

"Hope deferred makes the heart sick, but a longing fulfilled is a tree of life."
Proverbs 13:12

DEVOTIONAL

There was a woman named Clara who recently lost her beloved husband. Each morning, she would stare at her garden, now overgrown and neglected. One day, she picked up her tools and began to clear the weeds, allowing the sun to shine in once again. As she worked, she recalled the summer garden they tended together, filled with vibrant flowers. Through her tears, she realized that by nurturing her garden, she was also nurturing her heart, choosing to plant seeds of hope for the future. Her daily ritual brought life back to her surroundings and her spirit, reminding her that healing takes time but is achievable.

Planting hope daily means allowing room for new beginnings, even amid overwhelming sorrow.

DAILY REFLECTION

What small seeds of hope can you plant in your heart today, even amid the heaviness of loss?

PRAYER

Dear God, in this moment of quiet, I ask for your gentle presence to fill the spaces where grief feels overwhelming. Help me to find small glimmers of hope to nurture as I learn to move forward.

"Hope is the quiet, persistent whisper that assures us we are not alone in our journey."

THE ANNIVERSARY THAT HURTS

"Blessed are those who mourn, for they shall be comforted."
Matthew 5:4

DEVOTIONAL

The first anniversary after losing her husband felt like an insurmountable wave of sorrow for Linda. Each corner of the house echoed memories of love and laughter that now filled her heart with longing. As she sat alone in the living room, she picked up his favorite photo and recalled the way he used to hold her close, his laughter lighting up even the darkest days. The tears flowed freely, and yet, as she remembered their times together, she felt a warmth envelop her—a gentle reminder that love doesn't dissipate with loss. It transforms and remains—a sacred bond that even time cannot erase.

In the pain of remembrance, recognize that love endures beyond separation, allowing you to carry cherished memories like a soft light guiding your path forward.

DAILY REFLECTION

What emotions surface for you as you approach the anniversary of your husband's passing? How can you honor his memory in a way that brings you peace?

PRAYER

Dear God, as I approach this challenging anniversary, help me to feel Your comforting presence beside me. Please grant me the strength to remember the love we shared while finding solace in Your embrace.

"Grief is a journey, not a destination; let each painful step be a testament to the love that remains."

HIS BIRTHDAY WITHOUT HIM

"Cast all your anxiety on him because he cares for you."
1 Peter 5:7

DEVOTIONAL

Sitting at the kitchen table, Mary sipped her morning tea, glancing at the empty chair across from her. It was the small rituals they had shared that echoed in her heart—the way he always added an extra spoonful of sugar to her cup or how they'd linger over a crossword puzzle on lazy Sundays. Each quiet moment felt like a reminder of what she lost, yet it also whispered of the love they had built together. One day, as she poured her tea, she remembered how he would say, "Let's make life sweet, one cup at a time." Inspired, she began to honor him by inviting friends for tea, sharing stories, and allowing laughter to fill the space that once held profound silence.
Every small act of love and connection you cultivate can become a tribute to the legacy of your beloved.

DAILY REFLECTION

What are some simple moments in your daily life where you can intentionally remember and celebrate the love you shared with your husband?

PRAYER

Dear God, as I navigate life without my beloved, help me to embrace the memories that bring me joy and comfort. May I find in each day opportunities to honor his legacy through love and kindness.

"Every small act of love carries the essence of those we cherish."

WHEN FRIENDS DON'T UNDERSTAND

"He heals the brokenhearted and binds up their wounds."
Psalm 147:3

DEVOTIONAL

After the loss of her beloved husband, Sarah found herself in a whirlpool of grief, especially when her friends tried to offer comfort. Some said, "You'll be okay in time," as if her heart could simply switch off its pain. Others seemed to gloss over her sorrow, distracted by their own lives and joys. In those moments, Sarah felt more isolated than ever, longing for someone to truly understand her heartache. One evening, as she sat alone, she opened her Bible for solace and was reassured by the gentle reminder that God sees her pain and walks alongside her. It was a simple truth, but one that filled the empty spaces around her heart with the warmth of divine companionship.
You are not alone; God is your constant companion, even when friends don't fully understand your journey.

DAILY REFLECTION

What do you wish your friends understood about your journey right now, and how can you gently express that to them?

PRAYER

Dear God, wrap your arms around this heart that feels so heavy right now. Help me to find understanding and patience as I navigate through this challenging time.

"You are not alone in your feelings; your heart is seen and understood by the One who created it."

A NEW DREAM BEGINS

*"Behold, I am doing a new thing; now it springs forth, do you not perceive it? I will make a way in the wilderness and rivers in the desert." **Isaiah 43:19***

DEVOTIONAL

When Sarah's husband passed away, the world seemed to dim around her. Grief wrapped itself around her like a heavy cloak, suffocating her dreams. As she navigated the first few months on her own, she began to find solace in the small things—a blooming flower in the garden, a cherished photograph, or a warm cup of tea. One afternoon, while cleaning out a drawer, she stumbled upon a travel brochure they never used. Instead of sadness, a flicker of hope ignited within her. She realized that while one chapter had closed, another was waiting to be written—a chapter filled with new adventures, friendships, and dreams yet to be discovered.

Just as a river can cut through rock over time, your grief may carve out new paths for unexpected joy and renewed purpose.

DAILY REFLECTION

What new dreams or passions are stirring within you, waiting to be discovered in this new chapter of your life?

PRAYER

Dear God, as she navigates this journey of loss and renewal, embrace her with Your love and guide her to new beginnings filled with hope and joy.

'In every ending, God whispers of new beginnings.'

LOSS IN THE QUIET MOMENTS

*"He will gently lead those that have young, comforting them in their grief and walking beside them in their pain. He knows the weight of your heart." **Isaiah 40:11***

DEVOTIONAL

In the stillness of the early morning, as the sun's first rays spill softly across the room, emptiness often fills the air where shared laughter once echoed. You find yourself reaching for the familiar scent of his favorite coffee, only to remember that the quiet moments now belong to you alone. Just as the coffee brews, memories wash over you—flashes of love interspersed with pangs of longing, reminding you of a life once vibrant. It is in these hushed instances that the heart wrestles with the paradox of cherishing the past and facing a future unknown. And yet, in this sacred silence, a gentle whisper emerges, offering consolation and strength to navigate each day anew.

In the quiet moments of loss, allow yourself to feel, for it is in this vulnerability that you will discover a deeper sense of healing.

DAILY REFLECTION

What are the small moments of stillness that remind you of your loved one, and how can you honor those memories in your daily life?

PRAYER

Dear God, in these quiet moments, envelop her with your love and comfort. May she feel your presence so profoundly that it brings her peace in her sorrowful times. Hold her heart gently as she navigates this path of loss.

'In the stillness, we find echoes of love that never truly fade away.'

WHEN MEMORIES TRIGGER PAIN

"Surely he took up our pain and bore our suffering."
Isaiah 53:4

DEVOTIONAL

After losing her husband, Sarah found herself surrounded by memories that seemed to pierce her heart. The soft hum of his favorite song, the familiar scent of his cologne lingering in the air, even the sight of their favorite coffee shop brought overwhelming waves of sorrow. Each trigger felt like a reminder of the love she had lost, and the pain often felt unbearable. However, in her darkest moments, Sarah would close her eyes and whisper a prayer, inviting the Lord into her grief. Through this invitation, she slowly began to understand that the joy of those memories could coexist with her pain. Healing was not about forgetting; it was about cherishing what was, while allowing herself to embrace the love that still surrounds her.

Memories may trigger pain, but they also remind us of the love we've shared and the strength we carry forward.

DAILY REFLECTION

What memories surface for you when you think of your loved one, and how do these memories make you feel today?

PRAYER

Dear God, as I navigate through the memories of my loved one, gently heal my heart and help me find comfort in Your presence. Wrap me in Your love and guide me through the emotions that arise.

"Memories may bring pain, but they also carry the love that will always remain."

CARRYING THE GRIEF WITH GRACE

*"He makes me lie down in green pastures.
He leads me beside quiet waters. He refreshes my soul."* **Psalm 23:2-3**

DEVOTIONAL

After losing her husband, Clara found solace in the little rituals that filled her day. Each afternoon, she would brew a cup of her favorite chamomile tea, letting its warmth seep into her hands while she sat in her sunlit kitchen, gazing out at the garden he used to tend. The stillness enveloped her; the gentle steam rising from her cup carried away the weight of sorrow, even if just momentarily. It was in those quiet moments she began to hear the whispers of hope, recognizing that her journey, while marked by loss, still contained flickers of beauty and remembrance.

Take a moment each day to create your own space of stillness, where you can listen for God's quiet encouragement and allow your heart to be refreshed in His presence.

DAILY REFLECTION

What does your heart whisper to you during your quiet walks, and how might those whispers guide you toward healing?

PRAYER

Dear God, as I take this journey of healing, help me feel Your presence with each step I take. Grant me peace and comfort as I navigate through this new chapter, reminding me that I am never alone.

"Every step on this path is a step toward discovering new strength within you."

THE COMFORT OF SCRIPTURE

"Comfort, comfort my people, says your God. Speak tenderly to Jerusalem and cry to her that her warfare is ended, that her iniquity is pardoned, that she has received from the Lord's hand double for all her sins." **Isaiah 40**

DEVOTIONAL

In the quiet stillness of her home, Sarah sat with a cup of tea, staring at the empty chair across the table where her husband used to sit. The silence felt heavy, a stark contrast to the laughter and love that once filled their lives. One evening, as she turned to her Bible for solace, her eyes fell upon the comforting words of Isaiah 40. They whispered secrets of hope and promise, reminding her that while her heart was aching, God saw her pain and longed to bring her peace. In that moment, she clung to the truth that her grief, like a storm, would eventually give way to the gentle whispers of healing and restoration.

Even in your deep sorrow, remember that God's love surrounds you, offering comfort and strength for each new day.

DAILY REFLECTION

What passages from the Bible have brought you comfort during this time, and how can you invite those words to speak to your heart more deeply today?

PRAYER

Dear Lord, as I grieve the loss of my beloved, I ask for Your gentle presence to surround me. Help me to find solace in Your Word and continuous strength in Your love. Amen.

"In the stillness of His embrace, His Word becomes a balm for my wounded spirit."

JOY THAT FINDS YOU IN SORROW

"Very truly I tell you, you will weep and mourn while the world rejoices. You will grieve, but your grief will turn to joy." **John 16:20**

DEVOTIONAL

When my dear friend lost her husband, she felt as if the world had dimmed around her. Every shadow held memories—and every memory was a bittersweet reminder of her love and loss. As she navigated those early days of grief, she discovered something unexpected; amidst the sorrow, little moments of joy began to break through—catching sight of a blooming flower in her garden, receiving a heartfelt letter from a friend, or sharing laughter while reminiscing with family about her husband's quirks. Each of these tiny sparks of joy felt like whispers of hope, reminding her that grief and joy could coexist, just like two sides of the same coin. It was in embracing those moments that she realized joy can find you, even when the heart is heavy.

In the depths of sorrow, remain open to the small joys that life still offers, for they are reflections of love that continues to surround you.

DAILY REFLECTION

What small moments of joy have you recently noticed, even amidst your sorrow? How can you embrace these moments and let them uplift your spirit?

PRAYER

Dear God, in this time of loss, help me to see the glimpses of joy that still surround me. May Your love shine through the shadows of my heart, reminding me that I am never alone.

"Joy can be a gentle whisper, softly inviting you to embrace the beauty of life, even in the midst of heartache."

LETTING GO OF GUILT

"As far as the east is from the west, so far has He removed our transgressions from us."
Psalm 103:12

DEVOTIONAL

After losing her beloved husband, Maria found it difficult to let go of the guilt that lingered in her heart. Each day held echoes of 'what ifs' and 'if onlys'—the conversations left unfinished and the moments they cherished that now felt bittersweet. One evening, as she sat with a cup of tea, Maria opened an old photo album filled with smiles and adventures. As laughter filled the room in her memories, a gentle warmth enveloped her, a reminder that those moments were gifts, not burdens. In that stillness, Maria began to uncover a profound truth: love remains, even in loss, and guilt has no place where love dwells.

Let go of guilt, for it serves only to hinder your healing; embrace the love you shared, for that is your greatest treasure.

DAILY REFLECTION

What lingering guilt do you hold onto, and how might releasing it bring you peace and healing?

PRAYER

Dear God, help me to release the burdens of guilt I carry. May Your love surround me, guiding me toward forgiveness for myself and others. Lift my heart as I lean into Your grace.

"Sometimes letting go is the bravest thing we can do."

SAYING GOODBYE AGAIN AND AGAIN

"You know when I sit and when I rise; you perceive my thoughts from afar."
Psalm 139:2

DEVOTIONAL

After losing my beloved husband, I found myself saying goodbye again and again—not just to him, but to the dreams we shared, the routines we built, and those simple moments that once felt so secure. One evening, as I sat on our porch where we used to watch the sunset, I felt the weight of my grief wash over me. I thought about the dinners that would never happen again and the laughter that felt foreign in the stillness. But then, in that silence, I heard a whisper: "I am with you in every goodbye, carrying you through each one." It reminded me that each farewell was not the end, but a step toward healing and new beginnings.

Every goodbye is an opportunity for a new hello, for God walks alongside us, transforming our sorrow into strength.

DAILY REFLECTION

What is one memory that brings both joy and sadness, and how can you honor that memory today?

PRAYER

Dear God, in this time of loss, help me to find comfort in your embrace and the memories of love. Guide my heart as I learn to say goodbye while cherishing the moments we shared.

"Every goodbye carries the weight of love, even as it beckons us toward new beginnings."

WHEN TEARS COME UNEXPECTEDLY

"He will wipe away every tear from their eyes, and death shall be no more, neither shall there be mourning, nor crying, nor pain anymore, for the former things have passed away." **Revelation 21:4**

DEVOTIONAL

In the quiet moments following her husband's death, Sarah found herself in an unexpected wave of tears. Each one seemed to come unbidden, washing over her as she sat alone in their favorite chair, holding a photo of their wedding day. Memories spilled from her heart without warning—the laughter, the shared dreams, the simple presence of a partner who understood her soul. With every tear, she felt both the weight of her grief and the gentle reminder that it was okay to cry. In those moments, she clung to the hope that somewhere beyond this pain, restoration awaited.

Your tears are a reminder of the love you shared and the healing journey ahead; embrace them as part of your sacred process.

DAILY REFLECTION

What are the moments that catch you off guard, leading to tears that feel both familiar and foreign? How can you allow yourself to simply feel in those times?

PRAYER

Dear God, in these moments of unexpected tears, remind me that you are near. Help me to embrace my emotions as part of my healing journey, trusting in your gentle presence.

"Wounds may be visible, but God's love can mend the unseen scars."

HONORING THE LOVE THAT REMAINS

"I will never leave you nor forsake you."
Hebrews 13:5

DEVOTIONAL

In a small town, a woman found herself alone after her husband's passing. Each morning, she would sit at their favorite coffee shop, sipping tea and reminiscing. One day, she noticed an elderly couple sharing stories and laughter at the next table. A warmth enveloped her, reminding her that love, albeit changed, still lingers. Gradually, she began to share her own stories with others, creating connections that not only honored her husband's memory but also welcomed new friendships into her life.

Cherish the love that remains; it can inspire new beginnings and connections even amidst the pain of loss.

DAILY REFLECTION

What memories do you cherish that remind you of the love you shared, and how can you honor that love in your daily life moving forward?

PRAYER

Dear God, as I navigate this journey of loss, help me to feel the warmth of love that remains. May I find peace in the memories and strength in the knowledge that love never truly leaves us.

"Love is a bond that transcends distance and time;
it continues to inspire and guide us, even from afar."

GOD SEES YOUR BROKENNESS

"The Lord is close to the brokenhearted and saves those who are crushed in spirit."
Psalm 34:18

DEVOTIONAL

Amelia felt as if her heart had splintered into countless pieces after the loss of her husband. Each room in their home echoed with memories, and loneliness wrapped around her like a heavy shroud. One rainy afternoon, while sorting through old photographs, she discovered a note he had written her on their anniversary. It simply read, "You have my heart, no matter where life takes us." In that moment, amidst her tears, she felt an overwhelming sense that love transcends even death, and she sensed God's gentle embrace wrapping around her in her brokenness.

Know that your brokenness is seen by God, and in His love, you are never truly alone.

DAILY REFLECTION

What broken pieces of your heart or daily life is God inviting you to bring before Him today? How can you recognize His presence in your feelings of loss?

PRAYER

Dear God, in moments of deep sorrow, comfort me with Your everlasting love. Help me to feel your presence in my brokenness and trust that You see every tear I've shed.

"In your vulnerability, God finds a space to heal, mend, and restore."

WHEN FAITH FEELS FRAGILE

"For the arms of the wicked shall be broken, but the Lord upholds the righteous."
Psalm 37:17

DEVOTIONAL

Not long after I lost my husband, I found myself sitting in our favorite coffee shop, surrounded by couples sharing laughter and stories. My heart felt like a fragile glass cup, surrounded by the chaos of life yet desperately longing for comfort. I sipped my tea, tears welling up, reflecting on memories that felt both joyful and painfully distant. As I looked through the window, I spotted a single flower pushing through the cracks of the sidewalk. It stood tall and hopeful despite its rocky surroundings, a gentle reminder from God of resilience and beauty amidst brokenness. Life can certainly feel fragile, but like that flower, our faith can bloom anew, even in the harshest conditions.

Even when your heart feels heavy, trust that God is nurturing your faith, helping it grow stronger day by day.

DAILY REFLECTION

What does your heart whisper to you in these quiet moments of uncertainty? Can you identify the small remnants of faith that still light your path?

PRAYER

Dear Lord, in this season of sorrow, help me to find comfort in Your presence. Wrap Your loving arms around me as I navigate this journey, reminding me that even in weariness, Your faithfulness remains.

"In the midst of brokenness, faith can flicker like a candle, illuminating the darkest corners of our hearts."

TRUSTING GOD IN THE DARKNESS

"Go, my people, enter your rooms and shut the doors behind you; hide yourselves for a little while until his anger has passed. See, the Lord is coming out of his dwelling to punish the people of the earth for their sins; the earth will disclose the blood shed on it; the earth will conceal its slain no longer." **Isaiah 26:20-21**

DEVOTIONAL

There was a woman named Clara who, after losing her husband, found herself enveloped in a deep solitude that felt insurmountable. Days became a blur; the laughter they once shared now echoed with silence that weighed heavily on her heart. One evening, as she gazed out the window into the darkened sky, she remembered the stars sparkling above, each one a reminder that, even in the darkest nights, light still exists. Taking a breath, she decided to pick up her knitting, a hobby her husband had always encouraged her to pursue, and in those quiet moments, she let her fingers weave hope back into her heart. With time, Clara discovered that God was present in her darkness, nurturing her with strength and gentle comfort.

Even in darkness, trust that God is crafting something beautiful within your heart, allowing hope to emerge once more.

DAILY REFLECTION

What does trusting God in your darkest moments look like for you? Can you recall a time when you felt His presence guiding you even when the path ahead seemed uncertain?

PRAYER

Dear God, in this time of deep sorrow and confusion, I ask for Your comfort and guidance. Help me to lean on You, trusting that You are with me in every moment of pain and uncertainty.

"Even in the shadows, there is a light that can guide our way."

DIVINE STRENGTH IN WEAKNESS

"The eternal God is your refuge, and underneath are the everlasting arms."
Deuteronomy 33:27

DEVOTIONAL

As I sat on the porch, the evening sun casting long shadows, I felt an overwhelming sense of loneliness wash over me. It was the little things that reminded me of my husband—the way he would have chuckled at the antics of the neighborhood children or how he always knew just the right words to comfort me when I was feeling low. One particular evening, the breeze rustled through the trees, and I found myself whispering a prayer, asking for strength I neither had nor understood. In that moment of vulnerability, a deep peace enveloped me, reminding me that even in my weakness, God was close, holding my heart as I learned to navigate this new chapter of my life.

In your moments of deep sorrow, remember that your weakness is an invitation for God's strength to fill the spaces you feel most empty.

DAILY REFLECTION

What are the moments in your day when you feel your weakness the most, and how can you invite God into those spaces to experience His strength?

PRAYER

Dear God, in this time of loss and heartache, help me to lean into Your presence. Surround me with Your love and remind me that even in my weakness, Your strength is made perfect.

"In surrendering our weakness, we often uncover the depth of His strength."

SURRENDERING THE "WHY"

"O Lord my God, I cried to You for help, and You restored my health."
Psalm 30:2

DEVOTIONAL

In the wake of loss, there was a woman named Grace who often found herself walking through the empty rooms of her home, the echo of laughter now replaced by silence. Every corner held a memory that spoke of her husband's love, and every question of "why" felt like a weight on her heart. One evening, as she curled up with a cup of tea, she opened a book of prayers and stumbled upon one that simply said, "Lord, hold my questions; I trust You have the answers." In that moment, she felt a shift—a tiny flicker of peace that settled in her heart. Instead of being overwhelmed by the unknown, she found strength in surrender, which began to soften her grief.

Trust that in surrendering the "why," you will rediscover hope and experience God's unending love in unexpected ways.

DAILY REFLECTION

What questions linger in your heart? How might surrendering the "why" be a step toward healing for you?

PRAYER

Dear God, in this moment of heartache and confusion, help me to trust that I don't need all the answers. Open my heart to peace as I release my need to understand.

"Sometimes, the answers we seek are found in the silence of our surrender."

WHEN HEAVEN FEELS CLOSER

"For behold, I create new heavens and a new earth, and the former things shall not be remembered or come to mind." **Isaiah 65:17**

DEVOTIONAL

In the quiet of the evening, Sarah found herself sipping tea on the porch, gazing at the stars. It was a time she once shared with her husband, whose laughter echoed in her memory. One specific evening, a shooting star streaked across the sky, igniting a flood of warm memories. She felt an unexpected wave of comfort wash over her; it was as if he nudged her from the heavens to remind her that love transcends even death. In that moment, Sarah understood that while the pain of loss was heavy, the presence of her husband lingered, wrapping her in a gentle embrace.

Love does not end with loss; it transforms into beautiful memories that guide us through our grief.

DAILY REFLECTION

What moments have made you feel the presence of your loved one close to you recently?

PRAYER

Dear Lord, carry this grieving heart as I seek Your comfort. Help me to feel the closeness of heaven in each precious memory and moment, reminding me that love never truly fades.

"In the silence, Heaven whispers."

PRAYING THROUGH THE PAIN

*"Finally, sisters, whatever is true, whatever is noble, whatever is right, whatever is pure, whatever is lovely, whatever is admirable—if anything is excellent or praiseworthy—think about such things." **Philippians 4:8***

DEVOTIONAL

As Mary cleaned out the attic after her husband passed, she stumbled upon a weathered box filled with letters and photographs. Each piece told the story of their shared adventures, laughter, and dreams. Inspired, she began to incorporate little bits of their history into her daily routine—she brewed his favorite coffee each morning, wore a necklace he had gifted her, and volunteered at their community garden where he had loved to spend his weekends. Through these small acts, Mary felt a flicker of his spirit, a gentle reminder of the love that never left her, even in the silence.

Honor his legacy by weaving moments of remembrance into your everyday life, allowing those cherished memories to fill your heart with peace and joy.

DAILY REFLECTION

What are some simple moments in your daily life where you can intentionally remember and celebrate the love you shared with your husband?

PRAYER

Dear God, as I navigate life without my beloved, help me to embrace the memories that bring me joy and comfort. May I find in each day opportunities to honor his legacy through love and kindness.

"Every small act of love carries the essence of those we cherish."

HOLDING ONTO GOD'S PROMISES

*"I remain confident of this: I will see the goodness of the Lord in the land of the living. Wait for the Lord; be strong and take heart and wait for the Lord." **Psalm 27:13-14***

DEVOTIONAL

In the quiet days after losing her husband, Sarah often wandered through the garden they had nurtured together. Each flower reminded her of shared laughter, love, and moments now tinged with absence. One day, she discovered a small bud pushing through the soil—delicate yet determined. It struck her that, just as that bud reached for the sun, she too could reach for God's promises. In her grief, she whispered prayers, and the Father met her in her sorrow, slowly transforming her pain into a hope that she never thought possible.

Amid grief, holding tightly to God's promises can nurture renewed hope and strength as you journey through this difficult season.

DAILY REFLECTION

What does it mean for you to hold onto God's promises during this challenging time in your life? How can you begin to see His faithfulness in your journey of grief and healing?

PRAYER

Dear God, in this moment of heartache, help me to cling to Your promises. Fill my heart with hope and remind me that You are always with me, even in the darkest hours.

"Even in the quiet moments of sorrow, His promises radiate like a beacon of light."

FINDING COMFORT IN CHRIST'S SUFFERING

*"Then he said to them, 'My soul is overwhelmed with sorrow to the point of death. Stay here and keep watch with me.'" **Matthew 26:38***

DEVOTIONAL

One evening, Martha sat alone, staring at a photograph of her husband on the shelf, a smirk frozen in time. She felt the ache of his absence like a heavy blanket that suffocated her joy. However, as she knelt by her bed in prayer, she sensed a presence wrapping around her, comforting her turmoil. That night, she opened her Bible, and through the pages, she found His whispers of solace. In her mourning, she felt the arms of Christ enveloping her — a gentle reminder that she was never truly alone.

Transformation and healing can come even in the darkest valleys when we seek comfort in Christ's willingness to suffer alongside us.

DAILY REFLECTION

What emotions rise to the surface for you when you think of Christ's suffering? How can remembering His pain offer you solace in your own journey of grief?

PRAYER

Lord, in the silence of my heart, I seek Your comfort. Help me to feel Your presence alongside me in this season of sorrow, reminding me that I am not alone.

"In His suffering, we find a source of strength that understands our pain."

ANGELS WATCHING OVER

"In all their affliction he was afflicted, and the angel of his presence saved them; in his love and in his pity he redeemed them; he lifted them up and carried them all the days of old."
Isaiah 63:9

DEVOTIONAL

There was once a woman named Sarah who, after losing her beloved husband, found herself wandering through the empty halls of her home. Each room echoed with memories, yet they also felt like whispers of loneliness. One particularly quiet evening, as she sat staring at the photo of them together, she felt a warmth envelop her. It was as if an unseen hand brushed across her cheek, and a soft voice whispered, "You are not alone." In that moment, she realized that the love they had shared continues to surround her, and she could feel the presence of angels watching over her heart, reminding her that she would be okay.

Remember, dear one, that the angels are near, watching over you, guiding you through each moment of your grief until you can walk into the light once more.

DAILY REFLECTION

What comforting signs have you noticed in your life lately that might be reminders of the love and care surrounding you, even in this time of loss? Sure, they may seem small, but how could they be messages from angels watching over you?

PRAYER

Dear God, as I navigate this new chapter of my life, please send your angels to surround me with peace and comfort. Help me to feel their presence and recognize the signs that remind me I am not alone.

"Even in our darkest moments, love remains a guiding light, illuminating our path ahead."

LET THE PSALMS SPEAK FOR YOU

"The Lord is my rock, my fortress, and my deliverer; my God is my rock, in whom I take refuge, my shield and the horn of my salvation, my stronghold." **Psalm 18:2**

DEVOTIONAL

As I walked through the quiet house, echoes of laughter and memories filled the air – a reminder of the love I once knew so deeply. The days following my husband's passing felt overwhelmingly heavy, each moment a struggle against the wave of sorrow that threatened to pull me under. In that stillness, I discovered the psalms, words steeped in heartache and hope, that spoke to my broken spirit. Psalm 18 reminded me that I was not alone; there was a rock to cling to, a fortress to shelter me from despair. In that sacred space, I learned to voice my pain and invite the Lord into my aching heart.

In the midst of your grief, allow the Psalms to voice your deepest sorrows and to remind you of the strength that God provides, for you are never truly alone.

DAILY REFLECTION

What emotions are surfacing for you today, and how might the words of the Psalms help you express them?

PRAYER

Dear God, as I walk this path of grief and healing, help me to find comfort in Your Word. May the Psalms resonate in my heart and guide me through this journey.

"In the silence, He hears my cries."

WHEN WORSHIP IS A WHISPER

"In repentance and rest is your salvation, in quietness and trust is your strength."
Isaiah 30:15

DEVOTIONAL

Sometimes we find ourselves in a place where words escape us, where our prayers feel more like a whisper than a song of praise. After the loss of a beloved partner, it can be challenging to lift our voices in worship. But in moments of deep sorrow, even the softest utterances hold immense power. Just like a child who approaches a parent with a quiet request, you can whisper your heart's longing to God. He hears every breath, every sigh, and every tear. There was a time when I sat in church, surrounded by a choir of voices, yet I felt utterly alone. Despite the noise around me, my heart was a gentle murmur of sorrow, but in that whisper, I found solace in knowing God was listening.

Your quiet heart is still a heart of worship; in your whispers, the Lord cradles your pain and transforms it into strength.

DAILY REFLECTION

What does it feel like to offer your heart to God when words seem too heavy to bear?

PRAYER

Dear Lord, in this quiet moment, help me to sense Your presence even in my silence. Remind me that my whisper of worship is heard and cherished by You.

"Even the softest sounds can resonate in the depths of despair, becoming a melody of faith."

YOUR SOUL STILL SINGS

*"Sing for joy, O heavens! Rejoice, O earth! Burst into song, O mountains! For the Lord has comforted His people and will have compassion on them in their suffering." **Isaiah 49:13***

DEVOTIONAL

Once, a widow named Sarah sat alone in her home, feeling overwhelmed by the silence that filled the rooms once vibrant with laughter. As she sorted through pictures, she stumbled upon a video of her husband serenading her on their anniversary. As she watched, tears flowed freely, transforming her sorrow into a bittersweet smile. In that moment, she realized that although he was gone, the love they shared was a melody that could not be silenced. It echoed within her, reminding her to sing her own song of hope and remembrance.

Your soul still sings, even in the silence of loss; let it be heard through your memories and your willingness to embrace the beauty of life anew.

DAILY REFLECTION

What are the melodies of joy and peace that your heart still yearns to embrace, even amidst the silence of loss?

PRAYER

Dear Lord, help me to feel Your presence in my sorrow and remind me that my soul still has the capacity to sing. Surround me with Your love as I navigate this new chapter of my life.

"Even in the silent spaces of grief, your soul can find a melody worth singing."

THE PRESENCE OF GOD IN GRIEF

*"Where can I go from your Spirit? Where can I flee from your presence? If I go up to the heavens, you are there; if I make my bed in the depths, you are there. If I rise on the wings of the dawn, if I settle on the far side of the sea, even there your hand will guide me, your right hand will hold me fast." **Psalm 139:7-10***

DEVOTIONAL

After losing her beloved partner, Carla found herself wandering through each day in a fog of sorrow, clutching onto their memories like lifelines. One particularly tough evening, as the shadows of loneliness wrapped around her, she decided to take a walk in the park where they used to spend their Sunday afternoons. As she sat on their favorite bench, tears streaming down her face, she noticed the sun beginning to set in vibrant hues, illuminating the fading day. In that moment, she felt an inexplicable warmth envelop her — it was like God's gentle embrace, reminding her that even in her deepest pain, she was not alone. The stillness of the park enveloped her, and she realized that God's presence was there in her grief, lovingly guiding her through the shadows.

In your deepest grief, remember that you are forever held in the comforting presence of God, who walks alongside you every step of this difficult journey.

DAILY REFLECTION

What aspects of your grief feel most overwhelming right now, and how might you invite God's comforting presence into those moments?

PRAYER

Dear God, as I navigate the waves of grief, help me to feel Your comforting presence. Show me signs of Your love and peace, reminding me that I am never truly alone.

"In the depths of sorrow, God's presence can transform our tears into strength and hope."

Halfway Through Our Journey

You are now halfway through this devotional journey.

Many women discover this book through the thoughtful reviews shared by readers like you.

If these pages have supported your faith and daily reflection, would you consider sharing a short review on Amazon?

Your voice may help someone else find encouragement today.

devo.anchoredgraces.com/grief

ASKING GOD FOR HEALING

"He heals the brokenhearted and binds up their wounds."
Psalm 147:3

DEVOTIONAL

There was a woman named Clara, who had recently lost her husband. Each morning felt heavier than the last, with memories flooding in like waves. One day, she found a quiet spot in her garden, a place they had cherished together. Sitting there, she closed her eyes and whispered her pain to God—each tear a release. As the sun warmed her face, she felt a gentle whisper in her heart: "You are loved, and I am with you." It was a moment of connection that shifted her heaviness into hope, reminding her that healing was a journey, not a destination.

In the midst of your grief, take time to be present with God; healing begins when we acknowledge our pain and invite Him into our brokenness.

DAILY REFLECTION

What parts of your heart feel broken or wounded right now, and how might you invite God into those spaces for healing?

PRAYER

Dear God, in this time of loss, I ask for Your gentle healing touch. Help me to know that I am not alone and give me strength as I navigate the path ahead.

Healing begins with acknowledging the wounds we carry.

FINDING LIGHT IN SCRIPTURE

"The unfolding of your words gives light; it imparts understanding to the simple."
Psalm 119:130

DEVOTIONAL

In a quiet little town, there lived a woman named Clara. Recently widowed, she felt the weight of solitude each day, the silence of her home echoing with memories. One evening, searching for comfort, she picked up her Bible, remembering her husband's love for reading. As she flipped through the pages, her eyes landed on a verse that spoke of hope and renewal. That night, Clara felt a flicker of light in her heart, realizing that though her husband was gone, the love and faith they shared would forever guide her through the shadows.

Life may feel overwhelming in the wake of loss, but God's Word is a steady light that offers clarity, hope, and understanding amid the confusion.

DAILY REFLECTION

What passages in Scripture bring you comfort, and how can you seek them out in the days ahead as you navigate this new season of life?

PRAYER

Dear God, wrap your arms around this precious woman as she journeys through her loss. Illuminate her path with your Word and help her to find solace and strength in your promises.

"Even in the shadows, His light shines through the cracks of our brokenness."

LETTING GOD HOLD YOU

"God is our refuge and strength, an ever-present help in trouble."
Psalm 46:1

DEVOTIONAL

After losing her husband, Clara felt as though she was drifting in an ocean of sorrow. Each day blended into the next, and the weight of loneliness often felt unbearable. One afternoon, as she sat quietly in her garden, she noticed a gentle breeze rustling the leaves. In that moment, she felt a warmth wrap around her, as if God was embracing her right there in her sorrow. It was a tender reminder that even in her darkest moments, she was held securely in the loving arms of her Savior, a truth that began to ease her heartache.

In the midst of your grief, allow God to hold you and fill your heart with His peace; you are precious to Him, and He is your constant companion.

DAILY REFLECTION

What feelings or fears come up when you think about surrendering your pain to God? How might your life look if you allowed Him to hold you through this season of grief?

PRAYER

Dearest Lord, in this moment of sorrow, I invite you to wrap your arms around me. Please comfort my heart and guide me through this difficult time, reminding me that I am never alone in my loneliness.

"Letting God hold you does not mean your pain will disappear,
but it allows His love to transform your heart, making space for new hope."

GRACE FOR THE NEXT STEP

"Let us then approach God's throne of grace with confidence, so that we may receive mercy and find grace to help us in our time of need." **Hebrews 4:16**

DEVOTIONAL

After losing her husband, Laura felt unmoored in a world that seemed to keep spinning without her. Every day brought waves of grief that sometimes washed over her, leaving her exhausted and disoriented. Yet, as she began to wake each morning, she found small moments of grace emerging: the warmth of the sun filtering through the window, a familiar song on the radio, or a friend's encouraging message. These reminders led her to realize that while the journey of grief was her own, each step was also met with divine grace that provided the strength to carry on.

In your journey of loss, remember that grace is not a distant concept but rather a guiding companion, inviting you to lean into each new step with trust and hope.

DAILY REFLECTION

What is one small step you can take today that honors both your feelings and your path forward? Consider how this step can lead you closer to healing.

PRAYER

Dear God, please walk beside me in this moment of change. Grant me the strength to embrace each new day with hope and your boundless grace.

"Every step taken in grace is a step towards healing."

ONE SMALL STEP AT A TIME

"Do not let your hearts be troubled. Trust in God; trust also in me. In my Father's house are many rooms; if it were not so, I would have told you. I am going there to prepare a place for you." ***John 14:1-2***

DEVOTIONAL

After losing her husband, Mary felt as if the world had plunged into darkness. She often found herself seated at the kitchen table, staring blankly at the untouched cup of coffee in front of her. One morning, she noticed a single flower poking through the cracks of the pavement outside her window. It reminded her that beauty can emerge from difficult places, and life continues to bloom even amid sorrow. From that day on, she committed to taking one small step every day—whether it was watering that flower, reaching out to a friend, or simply taking a walk. Each step brought light back into her life, revealing the strength she never knew she possessed.

One small step at a time can lead you toward unexpected renewal and hope, reminding you that healing is a journey, not a race.

DAILY REFLECTION

What small step can you take today that honors both your journey and the memory of your loved one?

PRAYER

Dear Lord, grant her comfort in this time of transition. May she find strength in her sorrows and hope in her tomorrows. Guide her as she learns to navigate this new path one gentle step at a time.

"Every small step taken with love is a tribute to the memories we cherish."

HOPE IS STILL HERE

"But God will never forget the needy; the hope of the afflicted will never perish." ***Psalm 9:18***

DEVOTIONAL

After a long battle with illness, Ellen found herself in a quiet home, the echoes of laughter and shared memories replaced by silence. Each room harbored fragments of her life with her beloved husband, the joyful moments tinged with heartache. One evening, as she sat on the porch wrapped in a shawl, she noticed a vibrant rose pushing through the cracks of the pavement. It stood tall, defying its harsh surroundings. That single bloom reminded Ellen that even in the most unexpected places, beauty and hope can flourish, reawakening the longing in her heart for brighter days and new beginnings.

Even in the depths of grief, allow yourself to believe that hope can blossom anew, revealing pathways you never thought possible.

DAILY REFLECTION

What does hope look like for you in this moment of your life? Can you take a moment to reflect on the small things that bring you comfort and joy, even in the midst of your sorrow?

PRAYER

Dear God, please wrap your arms around this heart that grieves. Help her to see the flickers of hope in her life and grant her peace as she navigates this challenging journey.

"Hope blossoms in unexpected places, even from the ashes of loss."

EMBRACING NEW ROUTINES

*"For I know the plans I have for you," declares the Lord, "plans to prosper you and not to harm you, plans to give you hope and a future." **Jeremiah 29:11***

DEVOTIONAL

After losing her beloved husband, Angela found herself in a void that felt insurmountable. The routines they had built together alongside their shared memories seemed disorienting. Each morning, as the sun peeked through the curtains, she would stare at the empty chair at the breakfast table and feel the weight of her loneliness. One day, with a lingering sense of determination, she decided to shift her habit of mourning into one of honoring him. She began to set new morning rituals: a cup of coffee enjoyed on the porch while savoring the beauty of nature, journaling her feelings, and dedicating time to planning her day with intention. Slowly, these small acts transformed her grief into gratitude, weaving new threads of purpose into her life.

Life is both a tapestry and a journey; allow yourself to embrace new routines that honor your past while embracing your future.

DAILY REFLECTION

What new routines could bring joy and peace to your days as you navigate this fresh chapter of life?

PRAYER

Dear God, guide my heart as I embrace these new routines. Help me find comfort in the small moments and strength in the adjustments I make. Thank you for your love and support in this journey.

"Each day is a new beginning, an opportunity to weave new threads into the fabric of our lives."

HEALING DOESN'T MEAN FORGETTING

*"Therefore, since we are surrounded by such a huge crowd of witnesses to the life of faith, let us strip off every weight that slows us down, especially the sin that so easily hinders our progress. And let us run with endurance the race God has set before us, keeping our eyes on Jesus, the champion who initiates and perfects our faith." **Hebrews 12:1-2***

DEVOTIONAL

In her quiet moments, Evelyn often found herself drifting back to memories of her late husband, the sound of his laughter, their shared dreams, and the simple joy of everyday life together. Initially, she fought these memories, believing that letting them linger somehow prevented her from moving forward. Yet, in a tender moment of reflection, she understood that healing doesn't mean forgetting; rather, it means cherishing those memories while learning to create a new life without him. Every smile she remembered became a gentle reminder of love, not loss, as she honored their journey while stepping into the next chapter of her own.

Healing is a testament to love, not a denial of it.

DAILY REFLECTION

What memories of your loved one bring you both joy and sadness? How can you hold these memories in a way that honors their life while also nurturing your own healing journey?

PRAYER

Dear God, as I navigate this path of healing, help me to remember my loved one with warmth and gratitude. Grant me the strength to embrace both the good and the painful, knowing that You are with me every step of the way.

"Healing may not mean forgetting;
it means carrying the love and memories forward as a cherished part of who we are."

WHEN YOU BEGIN TO SMILE AGAIN

*"Do not fear; you will not be ashamed. Do not be afraid; you will not be disgraced. For you will forget the shame of your youth and remember no more the reproach of your widowhood." **Isaiah 54:4***

DEVOTIONAL

In the stillness of her new reality, Sarah found herself clutching her husband's old sweater, a bittersweet reminder of days filled with laughter and shared dreams. The mornings were particularly heavy, layered with the weight of loss and solitude. Yet, one afternoon while tidying up, she discovered a long-neglected photo album filled with joyous memories. As she flipped through its pages, laughter unexpectedly bubbled up from deep within her, surprising her with its warmth. It was the first smile she had worn in months, a gentle reminder that joy can linger alongside grief, waiting patiently to be rediscovered.
Even in the hardest moments of loss, remember that joy can intertwine with grief, allowing your heart to smile again.

DAILY REFLECTION

When was the last time you felt a moment of joy, even amidst the heaviness of your grief? What small thing made you smile today?

PRAYER

Dear God, as I navigate this difficult journey, help me to find the seeds of joy hidden in my heart. May Your love surround me and guide me toward moments of light and laughter once again.

"Smiles are the whispers of the heart, speaking hope in the silence of sorrow."

THE DAY HE DIED

*"Brothers and sisters, we do not want you to be uninformed about those who sleep in death, so that you do not grieve like the rest of mankind, who have no hope. For we believe that Jesus died and rose again." **1 Thessalonians 4:13-14***

DEVOTIONAL

After losing her beloved husband, Clara found herself lost in a sea of memories. Each room echoed the laughter they once shared, and every corner held a reminder of their life together. One quiet morning, while sipping her coffee, she caught a glimpse of his favorite chair, and instead of sadness washing over her, a smile crept onto her face. She remembered his warmth, his encouraging words, and how they faced challenges together. In that moment, she realized that though he was gone, their love remained, endlessly entwined in her heart.
In times of deep grief, cherish the love that remains, for it is a steadfast anchor in the stormy seas of loss.

DAILY REFLECTION

What emotions have you felt most strongly since that day, and how can you allow yourself to process each one gently?

PRAYER

Dear Lord, wrap this woman in Your loving embrace as she navigates this painful season. Fill her heart with Your peace and remind her that she is never alone.

In the midst of loss, may we find moments of grace and strength to carry us forward.

SURPRISING BLESSINGS IN GRIEF

"Give thanks in all circumstances; for this is God's will for you in Christ Jesus."
1 Thessalonians 5:18

DEVOTIONAL

After losing her husband, Marge often found herself weeping alone in the quiet evenings, the silence of their home echoing her loss. One afternoon, she decided to sort through a box of memorabilia, and as she stumbled upon a collection of love letters they had exchanged during their courtship, she felt a comforting warmth envelop her heart. Those words, filled with passion and laughter, reminded her not just of the love they shared but also of the friendships they built together and the joy that had filled their lives. Through her grief, she began reaching out to those friends, sharing memories, and feeling a rebirth of connections that offered her solace and strength. Each new story and shared laugh became a surprising blessing amid her heartache.

In grief, unexpected blessings often await us, revealing the power of love and connection that surpasses our deepest sadness.

DAILY REFLECTION

What unexpected moments of beauty or connection have you discovered in the midst of your grief? How can you honor those moments as part of your healing journey?

PRAYER

Dear God, in this time of sorrow, help me to see the glimmers of hope and blessings that surround me. Give me the strength to embrace my memories while opening my heart to new experiences.

"Grief may cloud your vision, but God's light can still shine through the cracks."

A HEART OF GRATITUDE THROUGH SORROW

"Rejoice always, pray continually, give thanks in all circumstances; for this is God's will for you in Christ Jesus." **1 Thessalonians 5:16-18**

DEVOTIONAL

Just last week, I attended a small gathering where stories of love and loss were shared. One woman spoke of her late husband's favorite cup, which she now uses daily for her morning tea. Each sip became a tribute to the love they shared, reminding her of the simple joys that intertwined their lives. As she expressed her gratitude for those brief moments together despite her profound sorrow, I realized that remembering the good can illuminate even the darkest days.

Though the pain of loss is heavy, seek out small joys and allow your heart to embrace gratitude, for these moments honor the love you still hold.

DAILY REFLECTION

What in your life brings you moments of joy or gratitude, even amidst the sorrow you feel? Can you recall a memory that sparks a smile, or a simple blessing that reminds you of love and connection?

PRAYER

Dear Lord, in this time of aching loss, help me find the flickers of gratitude in my heart. May I cherish the memories and the love that once filled my life, holding them close as I walk through this season of sorrow.

"Gratitude can be a gentle guide, leading us through the darkest valleys toward the light of hope."

FINDING LIGHT AFTER DARKNESS

"For we walk by faith, not by sight."
2 Corinthians 5:7

DEVOTIONAL

After losing her husband of nearly thirty years, Linda wandered through her home feeling like a shadow of her former self. The vibrant colors of their shared memories seemed to fade into black and white, leaving her grappling with overwhelming silence. One evening, after a particularly hard day, she sat on the porch, wrapped in a blanket and a deep sense of loneliness. As she gazed at the stars emerging one by one, she felt the warmth of hope start to rekindle within her heart. In that moment, she realized that while darkness had been her companion, the light of memories and love would always twinkle in the night. It was a reminder that even in her grief, beauty and joy still lingered, waiting for her to embrace them again.

No matter how deep the darkness feels, remember that glimmers of light and joy can still shine through, guiding you back to life.

DAILY REFLECTION

What moments in your life have brought you the most light, even amidst the shadows? How can you invite those memories into this new chapter?

PRAYER

Dear God, please surround this woman with your comfort, guiding her through the shadows toward the light of hope and healing. May she feel your presence with her in every step of this journey.

"In the midst of darkness, let your heart seek the dawn."

THE FIRSTS WITHOUT HIM

"No temptation has overtaken you except what is common to mankind. And God is faithful; He will not let you be tempted beyond what you can bear." **1 Corinthians 10:13**

DEVOTIONAL

As I sat at the dining table, staring at the empty chair across from me, I felt a profound wave of loneliness wash over me. The first meal prepared without my husband felt like a monumental task, as if the very essence of our shared dinners had vanished. I poured the soup, and the warmth filled the bowl just as my love once filled our home. In that moment, I remembered how he would often say, "Let's make the best of what we have." So, I whispered a quiet gratitude for the memories, allowing the pain to mingle with the love that still remained.

Remember, it's okay to grieve the firsts without him; each small step forward is also a step toward healing.

DAILY REFLECTION

What emotions arise in you when you think about experiencing the first significant moments without him? How can you acknowledge those feelings while envisioning a path forward?

PRAYER

Dear God, grant her comfort in the moments of loneliness and strength in the challenges ahead. May she feel Your presence as she navigates through this time of loss and rediscovery.

"In the midst of sorrow, new beginnings can take root."

REVISITING SHARED PLACES

*"Every good and perfect gift is from above, coming down
from the Father of the heavenly lights." **James 1:17***

DEVOTIONAL

As I stood in front of the little café where we used to spend Saturday mornings, the memories flooded my mind—the laughter shared over coffee, the sunshine streaming through the window while we planned our week. It felt both comforting and painful to be in a place so full of life yet now filled with silence. I took a deep breath, closed my eyes, and whispered a prayer, asking for strength to embrace the remnants of our love in these shared spaces. Slowly, I began to notice the beauty that still lingered there, as each moment became a reminder of a life beautifully lived rather than a life lost.

It's okay to revisit places that hold memories; they can bring healing and strength as we honor the love we shared.

DAILY REFLECTION

What memories stir in your heart when you revisit the places you once shared with your spouse? How do these feelings shape your journey forward?

PRAYER

Dear God, comfort me in my moments of solitude as I walk through the cherished spaces that hold our memories. Help me to embrace both the joy and the sorrow they evoke, guiding me toward healing and hope.

'Revisiting sacred spaces can be a gentle reminder of love's enduring presence within us.'

SIFTING THROUGH HIS BELONGINGS

*"Set your minds on things that are above, not on things that are on earth."
Colossians 3:2*

DEVOTIONAL

As I sat on the floor surrounded by boxes filled with my late husband's belongings, I was enveloped by a whirlwind of memories. Each item stirred emotions; an old jacket, a favorite book, and photographs that captured laughter and love. It felt surreal to sift through his things, exposing the tangible remnants of a shared life. With each piece, I remembered the moments we built together—the places we traveled, the dreams we chased. It was both painful and cathartic, a bittersweet reminder of our love that would forever remain despite his absence.

The process of sorting through your loved one's belongings can be a profound journey of love and healing, reminding you that while he is physically gone, the essence of your shared life still lingers in your heart.

DAILY REFLECTION

What memories do you find most comforting as you sift through your loved one's belongings? How do they help you in this moment of reflection and grief?

PRAYER

Dear Lord, grant her the peace to navigate through these belongings with love and grace, reminding her of the beautiful moments shared. May she find solace in each memory, knowing she is held in Your gentle embrace.

'Every item holds a story, a moment of love now captured in memory.'

UNPACKING THE LAST CONVERSATION

*"Peace I leave with you; my peace I give you. I do not give to you as the world gives. Do not let your hearts be troubled and do not be afraid." **John 14:27***

DEVOTIONAL

Just last week, Clara found herself sitting alone in her kitchen, surrounded by memories that seemed to echo with every quiet tick of the clock. She could still hear the gentle hum of her husband's voice as they shared their last conversation about their dreams for the future, a hopeful exchange that now felt like a bittersweet farewell. As she reflected on those words, she realized that while he was no longer with her physically, the essence of their love remained—woven into every piece of laughter and tear shed together. Each time she replayed that conversation in her mind, it brought her both sadness and comfort, revealing the depth of a bond that transcended even this final goodbye. It was in unpacking those words that Clara began to understand the importance of holding onto the love while also allowing herself space to grieve.

Cherish the memories of your loved one, for within them lies the beauty of the love you shared and the strength you carry forward.

DAILY REFLECTION

What was the last thing your loved one said to you, and how does that moment resonate with your heart today?

PRAYER

Dear Lord, as I navigate this season of loss, help me to hold on to the tender memories of our conversations. May I find comfort and peace in the love we shared.

In every word spoken, there lies a treasure of connection and a legacy of love.

EMBRACING SELF-COMPASSION

*"See what great love the Father has lavished on us, that we should be called children of God! And that is what we are!" **1 John 3:1***

DEVOTIONAL

After years of selfless devotion to her family, Martha found herself navigating a world that felt painfully empty after losing her husband. The mornings were particularly hard as she faced the silence that filled the house, the echoes of laughter now replaced by solitude. One day, as she was sorting through old photographs, she stumbled upon a picture of them together, radiating joy. In that moment, she felt a rush of warmth, realizing that, although her heart ached, she needed to cherish those memories instead of losing herself in grief. Martha gave herself permission to cry, to remember, and to embrace the love they shared—allowing herself moments of compassion during this challenging season.

It's okay to grieve the love you once shared while also extending kindness and compassion towards yourself as you navigate this new path.

DAILY REFLECTION

What does it mean for you to be gentle with your heart during this time of loss, and how can you practice self-compassion in your daily life?

PRAYER

Dear God, hold this precious woman close to Your heart. Help her to remember that it's okay to grieve, and remind her to show herself the same kindness she would extend to a dear friend.

"Self-compassion is the gentle embrace needed to heal your wounded heart."

SAYING GOODBYE AGAIN AND AGAIN

*"Your husband will die and leave you; then you will be free to marry whoever you wish, but only if he believes in the Lord. The widow who is truly alone has placed her hope in God and continues to plead with Him day and night for her." **1 Corinthians 7:39***

DEVOTIONAL

After losing her husband, Ellen felt as though a part of her soul had been taken away. Each day brought reminders of him—his favorite chair still remained empty, and the scent of his cologne lingered in the bathroom. She often found herself having conversations with him in her mind, longing for the comfort of his presence. It was during one of these reflective moments that she realized that while she was saying goodbye to him, she was also saying hello to the memories and love they had shared. Each goodbye added depth to her heart, transforming her grief into a testament of their life together.

In the journey of grief, we continually say goodbye, but with each farewell comes the opportunity to cherish memories that shape who we are becoming.

DAILY REFLECTION

What emotions arise within you when you think about saying goodbye to your beloved? How do you honor those feelings while moving forward in your journey?

PRAYER

Dear God, hold her heart gently as she navigates through the waves of loss. Grant her peace in the moments of remembering and strength for the path ahead.

"Each goodbye is not just an end, but a space for love to continue growing in our hearts."

WHEN TEARS COME UNEXPECTEDLY

*"Our God is the Father of all comfort, who comforts us in all our troubles so that we can comfort those in any trouble. In moments of unexpected sorrow, He gently holds us, reminding us that we are never truly alone." **2 Corinthians 1:3-4***

DEVOTIONAL

After the loss of her husband, Jane often found herself caught off guard by sudden waves of grief. One afternoon, while sorting through a box of photographs, she stumbled upon a picture from their first vacation together. Without warning, tears began to flow, and her heart ached with the weight of cherished memories. In that moment, she felt an overwhelming sense of loss, but also a reminder of the love they shared, which even death could not diminish. As she cried, she whispered a prayer, feeling her husband's spirit wrap around her, reassuring her that it was okay to grieve deeply and love profoundly.

Your tears are a testament to the love you shared, and each unexpected moment of sorrow can lead you to deeper healing and connection with the one you've lost.

DAILY REFLECTION

What memories or thoughts tend to surface for you when tears catch you off guard? How can you embrace those moments as part of your healing journey?

PRAYER

Dear God, in moments when tears flow unexpectedly, help me to feel your loving presence. Wrap me in your comfort and remind me that vulnerability is a part of my healing.

Tears are not a sign of weakness; they are the language of a heart that once loved deeply.

HONORING THE LOVE THAT REMAINS

*"So we can say with confidence, 'The Lord is my helper; I will not be afraid. What can mere mortals do to me?'" **Hebrews 13:6***

DEVOTIONAL

After losing her beloved partner, Mary found herself at a crossroads. The house felt too quiet, the routines too empty, and each day lingered like a long shadow. Yet, as she sorted through their shared memories, she stumbled upon a box of letters he had written to her over the years. Each note echoed with love, laughter, and a promise of companionship that transcended even death itself. Instead of allowing sorrow to overwhelm her, Mary began to honor his memory by creating her own 'love letter' box—a reminder of the warmth they shared and a way to celebrate the enduring bond that still filled her heart.

Love does not diminish with loss; it transforms into a legacy that you carry forward with grace and gratitude.

DAILY REFLECTION

What memories bring you comfort when you think of your love? How can you honor those moments in your daily life?

PRAYER

Dear God, thank you for the love that remains in our hearts. Help us to cherish these memories and draw strength from them as we navigate this new chapter of our lives.

"Love transcends time and space, remaining a gentle whisper
in our hearts even when our beloved is gone."

HONORING HIS LEGACY IN EVERYDAY MOMENTS

"Where, O death, is your victory? Where, O death, is your sting?"
1 Corinthians 15:55

DEVOTIONAL

Last year, on what would have been his birthday, Jennifer stood in the kitchen making his favorite cake, her heart heavy with the ache of his absence. Each ingredient felt like a reminder of the many celebrations they had shared, the laughter echoing in the corners of their home. With tears streaming down her cheeks, she recalled how he would insist on blowing out the candles first, making silly wishes that always made her laugh. In that quiet moment of remembrance, she decided to set a slice of cake at his favorite chair, a small tribute to the love they had shared, and a way to keep his spirit alive in her heart.

Even as you navigate this painful milestone, remember that love endures beyond loss; it's okay to honor those memories and invite both joy and sorrow into your heart as you celebrate life in new ways.

DAILY REFLECTION

What memories come to mind when you think of celebrating birthdays together? How can you honor those moments while creating space for your own grief and healing today?

PRAYER

Dear God, as I navigate this difficult time, help me find comfort in Your presence. Embrace me with love and guidance as I remember and cherish the moments shared, even as I feel the void of absence.

"In our sorrow, we can still find the threads of joy woven into our memories."

THE ANNIVERSARY THAT HURTS

"And the peace of God, which transcends all understanding, will guard your hearts and your minds in Christ Jesus." **Philippians 4:7**

DEVOTIONAL

On what would have been their 35th anniversary, Mary sat alone at the dining table, the once vibrant space feeling achingly empty. She gazed at the two places set for dinner—flowers in the center, just as he had always done. Tears flowed as she recalled how they spent their years building a life together, creating memories in every corner of their home. But even amidst the ache, a soft whisper stirred within her spirit, reminding her that while his physical presence was absent, the love they shared was still a living thing, woven into the very fabric of her days. In that stillness, she felt a flicker of hope, a promise that even in grief, she could carry his legacy forward with grace and courage.

This anniversary may be a heart-wrenching reminder of loss, but it also opens the door for reflection on the love that remains with you, nurturing your spirit even in the absence.

DAILY REFLECTION

What memories surface for you when you think of this special day? How can you honor those feelings while also allowing space for healing and hope?

PRAYER

Heavenly Father, please be with me in this moment of remembrance. Help me to feel Your presence as I navigate the pain, and guide me toward the light of Your love and comfort.

"In the midst of grief, let us find a new way to celebrate love."

WHEN FRIENDS DON'T UNDERSTAND

"If any of you lacks wisdom, you should ask God, who gives generously to all without finding fault, and it will be given to you." **James 1:5**

DEVOTIONAL

After losing her husband, Marie felt a deep chasm between her and her friends. She sat in a circle of familiar faces, longing for solace, yet felt an invisible wall as they joked about the mundane worries of life. They meant well, but their laughter felt like a distant shore, unreachable in her stormy sea of grief. Each attempt to explain her heartache felt futile, leaving her feeling more isolated. One evening, she found herself writing in her journal about her experience, her pen flowing with her raw emotions. That night, she whispered her pain to God, finding solace in the understanding that He alone knew the depths of her sorrow.

Sometimes, the greatest understanding comes not from those around us, but from the heart of God, who is always willing to listen and embrace our pain.

DAILY REFLECTION

What are some feelings you've experienced that your friends might not fully grasp, and how can you express those emotions to them?

PRAYER

Dear Lord, please wrap your arms around this precious woman during her time of grief. Help her to find comfort in Your presence and guide her as she navigates relationships that may feel distant or misunderstood.

"Even in solitude, you are never truly alone; your heart knows the truth of your journey."

COUNTING BLESSINGS IN GRIEF

*"Do not be anxious about anything, but in every situation, by prayer and petition, with thanksgiving, present your requests to God. And the peace of God, which transcends all understanding, will guard your hearts and your minds in Christ Jesus." **Philippians 4:6-7***

DEVOTIONAL

In the midst of her heartache, Laura would often sit by the window, watching the seasons change outside. One quiet afternoon, as the sunlight spilled into the room, she noticed a little bird making a nest on the branch of the tree right outside. Intrigued, she began to observe the bird's tenacity—each twig carefully placed, the small bits of grass skillfully woven together. It struck her then, amidst the grieving, that life was still happening around her. Each tiny moment, like the bird's efforts, became a gentle reminder of the blessings around her: the warmth of the sun, the laughter of her grandchildren, and the love and support of caring friends.

In our grief, may we find the courage to count our blessings, no matter how small, for they often bring unexpected comfort.

DAILY REFLECTION

What small blessings can you identify today in the midst of your grief, and how might they help you move forward?

PRAYER

Dear God, as I navigate this difficult journey of loss, please help me to see the blessings that still surround me. Comfort my heart and open my eyes to the love and support that remains in my life.

"In the shadow of grief, blessings often whisper softly, waiting for us to listen."

LOSS IN THE QUIET MOMENTS

*"I will never leave you nor forsake you. So we can confidently say, 'The Lord is my helper; I will not fear; what can man do to me?'" **Hebrews 13:5-6***

DEVOTIONAL

After her husband's passing, Clara often found herself sitting alone in their sunlit living room, the silence echoing the absence of laughter and gentle conversations. In those quiet moments, she would feel the weight of loss creep in like a soft shadow, reminding her of the life they had shared. Yet, there were also moments when the stillness brought a newfound connection to God. One afternoon, with tears flowing freely, Clara realized that it was in those intimate, hushed hours that she could pour out her heart to the Lord, finding solace in His presence and the memories of love shared.

In the stillness of your darkest hours, seek the gentle presence of God, for it is there that you may find comfort and healing.

DAILY REFLECTION

What memories come to mind when you pause in the quiet moments of your day? How can you honor those memories while also moving forward in your journey?

PRAYER

Dear God, in this time of sorrow and healing, help me to find Your presence in the stillness. Comfort my heart and guide me through each quiet moment with Your unwavering love.

"In the stillness, we often find the depth of our loss, as well as the whispers of hope waiting to emerge."

WHEN MEMORIES TRIGGER PAIN

"May the God of hope fill you with all joy and peace as you trust in him, so that you may overflow with hope by the power of the Holy Spirit." **Romans 15:13**

DEVOTIONAL

There was a woman who found herself sitting alone in their favorite park bench, a spot they had cherished for years. As the sun set, casting a warm glow over the familiar paths, every rustling leaf, and gentle breeze flooded her heart with memories of laughter and companionship. But with each cherished memory came a wave of longing and an ache that felt insurmountable. In the midst of her sorrow, she closed her eyes and whispered a prayer, asking for the strength to embrace the beauty of those memories without the weight of pain. Gradually, she felt a soft whisper in her spirit reminding her that love, even in loss, could still be a source of strength and not just sorrow.

Embracing the memories can transform pain into a bittersweet reminder of love and resilience.

DAILY REFLECTION

What memories of your beloved rise to the surface, and how do they make you feel? Can you identify the pain that comes with those moments, and how you might find comfort in them?

PRAYER

Dear God, as I navigate the waves of memories that bring both joy and pain, hold me close. Help me to find healing in the love we shared and the strength to move forward with grace.

"Memories are a testament to love; while they can bring sorrow,
they also remind us of the beauty that once was."

CARRYING THE GRIEF WITH GRACE

"Blessed are those who mourn, for they will be comforted."
Matthew 5:4

DEVOTIONAL

After losing her husband, Helen found herself surrounded by photographs and memories that both comforted and haunted her. Each morning, she would awake to a quiet house, where laughter once filled the rooms. One day, while sorting through his belongings, she stumbled upon a letter he had written her years ago, filled with dreams and hopes for their future. In that moment, instead of allowing the grief to consume her, she chose to honor his memory by smiling at the joy they had shared, letting the tears flow as a testament to her love. It was a delicate balance, carrying the weight of her sorrow while also celebrating the life they had built together.

As you navigate this profound grief, remember that allowing yourself to feel the pain can coexist with moments of beauty and celebration for the love you experienced.

DAILY REFLECTION

What does carrying your grief look like for you today, and how can you honor your feelings while also seeking moments of peace?

PRAYER

Dear Lord, wrap your arms around the heart of this grieving woman. May she find comfort in Your presence as she navigates her sorrow, and help her to carry her memories with grace.

"Grief is not a burden to bear alone but a journey to walk with love and compassion."

KNOWN AND LOVED BY GOD

"Lord, you have examined my heart and know everything about me. You know when I sit down or stand up. You understand my thoughts even when I'm far away. You see me when I travel and when I rest at home. You know everything I do. You know what I am going to say even before I say it, Lord." **Psalm 139:1-4**

DEVOTIONAL

After losing her husband, Claire often found herself lost in the silence of her home. One evening, as she rummaged through old photo albums, she stumbled upon a picture of their wedding day. The image brought a wave of nostalgia but also a reminder of the tangible love they shared. With tears streaming down her face, she sensed God gently whispering to her heart, reassuring her that the love she experienced was a reflection of His deep love for her. In that moment, she realized that while her earthly companion was gone, she was never alone in her sorrow.

You are seen, understood, and unconditionally loved by God, even in your deepest grief.

DAILY REFLECTION

What are some ways you have felt God's love and presence in your life, especially during this challenging time? How can you lean into that love today?

PRAYER

Dear Lord, wrap your arms around her as she navigates this new chapter of life. Let her find comfort in Your unwavering love and support, reminding her that she is never alone.

"Even in the midst of sorrow, God whispers His love and understanding."

NURTURING FAITH IN UNCERTAINTY

"Do not consider his appearance or his height, for I have rejected him. The Lord does not look at the things people look at. People look at the outward appearance, but the Lord looks at the heart." **1 Samuel 16:7**

DEVOTIONAL

In the midst of her sorrow, Maria often found herself visiting the old oak tree in her backyard —the tree her husband had planted when they first moved in together. It stood tall and sturdy, a symbol of their life together. One blustery afternoon, as she watched the leaves dance to the ground, Maria noticed that even the strongest branches were swaying with the wind. Just like the tree, she realized that she too would sway in the storm of her grief but still remain rooted in faith. In that moment, Maria made the decision to nurture her relationship with God, for she knew He had always been her strength.

Even when life seems unpredictable and overwhelming, nurturing your faith can help you find peace and strength amid uncertainty.

DAILY REFLECTION

What does your heart long for in this season of uncertainty, and how can you invite faith to fill those spaces?

PRAYER

Dear God, in this tender time of loss, let Your love wrap around me like a warm blanket. Help me to find strength in Your presence and hope in my heart.

"Faith is the light that guides us through the shadows of uncertainty."

FINDING GOD IN THE SHADOWS

"The Lord himself goes before you and will be with you; he will never leave you nor forsake you. Do not be afraid; do not be discouraged."
Deuteronomy 31:8

DEVOTIONAL

After losing her husband, Sarah found herself wandering through the empty rooms of their home, feeling as if shadows had swallowed her joy. One quiet evening, she sat in their favorite spot, a chair by the window, the fading light casting long shadows on the walls. As she absorbed her surroundings, a thought came to her: even in the shadows, light still exists. With each passing day, she began to see little glimmers of God's love—through the calls from friends, a neighbor's gesture, and even in the gentle reminders of sweet memories shared. It was then she realized that darkness wasn't merely an ending; it could be a transition to a new chapter where God's presence could guide her through her grief.

Even in the darkest moments of loss, God walks with you, illuminating paths of hope and comfort amidst the shadows.

DAILY REFLECTION

What shadows in your life are you struggling to see beyond, and how might God be inviting you to find His presence within them?

PRAYER

Dear God, in this season of heartache, help me to sense your gentle presence. Comfort me in my grief and guide me through the shadows I face each day.

"Even in the darkest moments, God's light can seep through the cracks."

SCRIPTURE AS A HEALING BALM

"Weeping may endure for a night, but joy comes in the morning."
Psalm 30:5

DEVOTIONAL

In the midst of her grief, a woman named Martha found solace in the quiet rhythm of her small garden. Each morning, she would rise early, kneel in the soil, and tend to the flowers that brightly surrounded her. It was during those moments that she sensed God's presence most profoundly, whispering promises of new beginnings through the budding petals. Though her nights were often filled with tears, the morning light brought her a glimmer of hope, reminding her that healing could bloom even in the shadow of loss.

Even in our darkest nights, God's promises of renewal are waiting to greet us with the dawn.

DAILY REFLECTION

What verses bring you comfort in your time of grief? How might you lean into those scriptures to find healing in your heart?

PRAYER

Dear God, wrap your loving arms around her today. May she feel your gentle presence and find solace in Your Word as it nurtures her wounded spirit.

"Even in the depths of sorrow, Scripture can be the light that guides us back to hope."

GOD'S POWER IN MY WEAKNESS

"But he said to me, 'My grace is sufficient for you, for my power is made perfect in weakness.' Therefore I will boast all the more gladly about my weaknesses, so that Christ's power may rest on me." **2 Corinthians 12:9**

DEVOTIONAL

After losing her husband, Mary found herself engulfed in a fog of grief. Though the house felt empty and quiet, she began to notice small signs of life around her—a burst of spring flowers blooming in the garden he had tended, the laughter of children playing nearby, and a distant melody from a neighbor's porch. With each small moment, Mary discovered that even in her heavy sorrow, God's presence seemed to seep through her cracks, bringing hope and warmth. It was in her vulnerability that she began to experience a deeper connection to her faith, revealing a strength she never knew she possessed.
Sometimes, it is when we feel the most broken that we are best able to experience the transformative power of God's love and grace.

DAILY REFLECTION

What weakness are you currently facing that you can surrender to God today? How might His power transform that vulnerability into strength?

PRAYER

Dear Lord, in this challenging season of loss, remind me that even in my weakness, your power shines through. Help me to lean on you as I navigate this new path, trusting that you are with me every step of the way.

"In my frailty, I discover the depth of His strength."

A SMILE YOU DIDN'T EXPECT

"A joyful heart makes a cheerful face, but by sorrow of heart the spirit is crushed."
Proverbs 15:13

DEVOTIONAL

After the passing of her husband, Elaine felt as if the light had gone out of her world. Days turned into weeks where joy felt like a distant memory. One afternoon, while sorting through old photos, she stumbled upon a candid shot of their wedding day, both of them beaming with laughter. The memory struck her and, for the first time in a long while, a smile broke through her tears. In that moment, Elaine realized that even in her grief, the love they shared could still bring joy.

In the depths of sorrow, sometimes the unexpected reflections of joy can light the way ahead.

DAILY REFLECTION

What unexpected moments have brought you joy or a smile lately, even in the midst of your sorrow? How can you embrace these small blessings in your heart?

PRAYER

Dear Lord, as I navigate this new chapter of my life, help me to find the smiles hidden in every day. May your love shine through my grief and remind me of the beauty still surrounding me.

"Even in the depths of sorrow, joy can find a way to touch our hearts unexpectedly."

LETTING GO OF NEEDING ANSWERS

"For my thoughts are not your thoughts, neither are your ways my ways," declares the Lord. **Isaiah 55:8-9**

DEVOTIONAL

After losing her husband, Clara found herself drowning in questions. She spent hours poring over old photos and messages, trying to piece together the why's and how's of her new reality. One afternoon, while sorting through belongings, she stumbled upon a love letter he had written her years ago. In that moment, she realized that the memories they created together were far more important than the unanswered questions, allowing her heart to focus on love rather than sorrow.

In the midst of your loss, let go of the need for answers and embrace the love that remains.

DAILY REFLECTION

What are the questions you find yourself asking today, and how might you learn to let go of the need for those answers?

PRAYER

Dear God, grant me the peace to embrace uncertainty and the strength to trust in your plan, even when I don't understand it. Fill my heart with your love and comfort as I navigate this journey of healing.

"Sometimes, it is in the quiet spaces of uncertainty that we find the deepest strength and grace."

TOUCHED BY THE HOPE OF HEAVEN

*"Praise be to the God and Father of our Lord Jesus Christ! In his great mercy he has given us new birth into a living hope through the resurrection of Jesus Christ from the dead and into an inheritance that can never perish, spoil or fade." **1 Peter 1:3-4***

DEVOTIONAL

In the silence of a newly empty home, she found herself drawn to a worn Bible that had been a source of comfort for years. As she flipped through the pages, her fingers landed on old notes and highlights, memories of whispered prayers and quiet reflections. One particular evening, as the sun set boldly outside her window, she paused on the verses about hope and life everlasting. It struck her that beyond her present grief, there was a promise of reunion and joy that awaited her; each tear was indeed watering a seed of hope for what lay ahead. With each reading, she felt a gentle reminder that though her earthly companion had moved on, love endures and heaven beckons with open arms.

Even in the depth of your sorrow, remember that your loved one is safe in the arms of eternity, and hope is a promise that lights the way forward.

DAILY REFLECTION

What does the thought of heaven mean to you in this season of your life, and how can it bring you comfort in your loss?

PRAYER

Dear God, please wrap your loving arms around my heart today. Help me to feel your presence and the hope of what's to come, as I navigate this new path without my beloved.

"Hope is the light that guides us through the shadows of loss."

LETTING TEARS BECOME PRAYERS

*"You keep track of all my sorrows. You have collected all my tears in your bottle. You have recorded each one in your book." **Psalm 56:8***

DEVOTIONAL

In the quiet hours of the night, as Eileen sat on her bed clutching her husband's favorite shirt, tears freely flowed down her cheeks. Those tears spoke of love, loss, and countless memories that felt both beautiful and unbearable. She remembered a day spent at the beach, laughter echoing between them, and how her heart felt full. With each tear that fell, she silently transformed her sorrow into a heartfelt prayer, asking God to embrace her in her grief and provide comfort in the emptiness left behind. Before she knew it, those tears became a conversation with her Creator, turning her pain into a poignant declaration of faith and hope.

In the midst of your grief, let your tears flow freely, for they are not just signs of sorrow but channels through which your prayers can rise to God.

DAILY REFLECTION

What emotions are you holding onto right now, and how might you invite God into those feelings through your tears?

PRAYER

Dear Lord, as I navigate this season of loss, help me to transform my tears into prayers, trusting that you hear every cry of my heart. Surround me with your peace and comfort.

"Tears are not a sign of weakness; they are a bridge to deeper connection with the Divine."

CLINGING TO HOPE IN HIS WORD

"Be strong and take heart, all you who hope in the Lord."
Psalm 31:24

DEVOTIONAL

As I walked through her empty house, each room echoed with memories that only she could hear. Marie often found herself pausing at the kitchen table, where laughter once danced with the aroma of cinnamon and coffee. It was there she felt the weight of her loneliness and the silence that now filled her days. Yet, one morning, while flipping through her Bible, she stumbled upon a promise that God would be her refuge. It was a simple truth, but it began to unfurl hope in her heart that would guide her through the dark.

Hold on to the hope God provides, for even in your sadness, His promises illuminate the path forward.

DAILY REFLECTION

What passages in the Bible resonate deeply with your heart, and how do they guide you through your feelings of loss and loneliness?

PRAYER

Dear Lord, please wrap your loving arms around me as I navigate this difficult journey. Help me to find comfort and strength in Your Word, and let Your promises illuminate my path.

"Hope is the anchor for our souls, steadying us in the storms of life."

FINDING COMFORT IN CHRIST'S SUFFERING

"After we have suffered a little while, the God of all grace, who has called us to His eternal glory in Christ, will restore, confirm, strengthen, and establish us." **1 Peter 5:10**

DEVOTIONAL

A few months after losing her husband, Jane found herself wandering through the local park, the echoes of laughter and joy ringing hollow in her ears. The sun was shining, flowers blooming, and yet all she felt was an emptiness that seemingly had no end. One day, she stumbled upon a small group of women gathering for a picnic, their joy palpable. Hesitant, she approached and was welcomed with open arms and warm smiles. In sharing their stories of grief and loss, Jane slowly began to understand that there was a common thread in all their journeys—a thread woven with pain, resilience, and unexpected moments of grace. Through their laughter and tears, she felt a glimpse of hope beginning to bloom within her heart.

In the shared stories of loss and hope, we can find the gentle reminder that even in our suffering, there is a community and a Savior who walks alongside us, offering solace and understanding.

DAILY REFLECTION

What moments of Christ's suffering resonate with you as you navigate your own pain and loss? How can these reflections bring you comfort today?

PRAYER

Dear Lord, as I walk through this season of grief, help me to remember that You understand my pain. Embrace me with Your love and bring me peace amidst the sorrow.

"In my brokenness, I can lean into the depths of Christ's compassion, finding solace in His shared suffering."

SHELTERED IN DIVINE PRESENCE

"Lord, you have been our dwelling place throughout all generations."
Psalm 90:1

DEVOTIONAL

After a long and beautiful marriage, a woman named Mary found herself grappling with solitude after the loss of her husband. Each corner of her house echoed with memories; the laughter shared during dinner, the quiet moments watching the sunset together. One evening, she lit a candle and sat by the window, allowing herself to reflect on the warmth of their love. As the flickering flame danced, she felt an undeniable presence surrounding her, a gentle reminder that she was not alone. In that sacred moment, she chose to see her home not just as a place of memories but as a shelter filled with divine comfort and love, guiding her as she stepped into a new chapter.

In the arms of your memories, let the divine presence reassure you that you are never truly alone.

DAILY REFLECTION

What does it feel like to seek refuge in God's presence during this challenging season of your life?

PRAYER

Dear Lord, as I navigate the landscape of my grief, help me to find comfort and strength in Your divine presence. Surround me with Your love and peace as I learn to lean on You each day.

"In the stillness of sorrow, God's presence becomes my shelter and strength."

LETTING SCRIPTURE EXPRESS YOUR HEART

"Cast all your anxiety on him because he cares for you."
1 Peter 5:7

DEVOTIONAL

After losing her husband, Mary found herself surrounded by memories that stirred both love and heartache. Some days felt almost unbearable, as waves of grief washed over her at unexpected moments. One afternoon, feeling particularly lost, she stumbled upon a familiar passage that reminded her of the strength she could find in surrendering her burdens to God. In her quiet moments, she began to write her feelings in a journal, often turning her raw emotions into prayers. Each entry became not just a release of sorrow, but also a scriptural affirmation of God's relentless love and grace in her life.

Life is a journey marked by love and loss, and it's in our vulnerable moments that Scripture can give voice to our hearts' deepest yearnings.

DAILY REFLECTION

What verses have provided you comfort in your own quiet moments of loss, and how can you allow those words to express the deepest parts of your heart?

PRAYER

Dear Lord, in this tender season of grief, remind me that Your Word is alive and speaks to my soul. Help me to find solace and strength in the scriptures as I navigate this challenging journey.

"Even in sorrow, God's promises are still a light that guides our way."

WHEN WORSHIP IS A WHISPER

"Rejoice in the Lord always; again I will say, rejoice. Let your gentleness be known to everyone. The Lord is near. " **Philippians 4:4-5**

DEVOTIONAL

In the quiet moments of grief, a woman found herself sitting alone on a park bench, the weight of her loss hanging heavy in the air. As she watched the leaves gently fall from the trees, she felt a whisper of worship rise within her. It wasn't loud or boisterous; it was a soft, heartfelt acknowledgment of her love for her husband and the life they shared. With each breath, she released her sorrow, allowing the beauty of nature to remind her of God's presence. In those hushed moments, her heart began to heal, one whisper of gratitude at a time.

Even in your deep sorrow, the softest worship can bring comfort and connection to your heart and the Divine.

DAILY REFLECTION

What does it feel like for you to express your heart to God in moments of silence, when words seem too heavy to speak?

PRAYER

Dear Lord, in this season of grief, help me find comfort in the whispers of my heart. May I feel your presence in my quiet moments and know that you hear every unspoken word.

"Sometimes, the deepest worship comes not in our loudest shouts, but in our softest whispers."

YOUR SOUL STILL SINGS

"Oh sing to the Lord a new song, for he has done marvelous things; his right hand and his holy arm have worked salvation for him." **Psalm 98:1**

DEVOTIONAL

In the quiet of a Wednesday afternoon, Sarah sat alone in her living room, the silence heavy and pressing. It had been just three months since she had lost her beloved husband, and the memories seemed both vibrant and distant, like echoes in an empty hall. As she dusted off her old guitar, she recalled the nights they spent singing together, filling their home with laughter and melody. With hesitant fingers, she strummed a few notes, and suddenly, tears flowed freely. In that moment of vulnerability, she felt a flicker of joy emerge amidst the sorrow—her soul was still alive and capable of song, even in the depths of her grief.

Even when the world feels dark and heavy, remember that within you lies the ability to find joy and sing again.

DAILY REFLECTION

What melodies does your heart still hold, waiting to break free and be sung anew?

PRAYER

Dear God, in this moment of quiet sorrow, may your comforting presence fill the spaces in her heart. Help her to remember the joy and beauty that still resides within her soul, guiding her to moments of peace and grace.

"Even in grief, your spirit can still dance and your soul can still sing."

THE PRESENCE OF GOD IN GRIEF

"This is my comfort in my affliction, that Your promise gives me life."
Psalm 119:50

DEVOTIONAL

In the quiet stillness of my home, I often find myself surrounded by reminders of my husband—his favorite chair, the scent of his cologne lingering in the air, and the laughter we shared. On one particularly hard night, I wrapped myself in his beloved blanket, seeking warmth and comfort. As I closed my eyes, I sensed a gentle presence, a whisper that reassured me I was not alone. In my grief, I felt God enfolding me, reminding me that even in the sorrow, His promise of love and healing is ever-present.

In the depths of your grief, remember that God walks beside you, holding your heart with tenderness during your most vulnerable moments.

DAILY REFLECTION

What does it feel like to sense God's presence in your quiet moments of sorrow? Can you invite Him into your grief and share with Him the depth of your heartache?

PRAYER

Dear God, as I navigate through this season of loss, I seek your comfort and companionship. Wrap me in your presence, reminding me that I am never alone even in my darkest moments.

"In the depths of my sorrow, I discover the heights of Your love."

THE SHOCK OF GOODBYE

"Be still, and know that I am God."
Psalm 46:10

DEVOTIONAL

When Ruth's husband passed unexpectedly, she felt as though a black fog had enveloped her heart. The shock of goodbye was sudden, leaving her with a silence that filled the spaces where laughter and companionship once thrived. Each corner of her home held memories that now felt bittersweet, a reminder of the love they shared and the gaping void his absence had created. In the midst of her grief, she discovered an old journal, filled with their dreams and aspirations. As she read through the pages, she found comfort in the love they built together, realizing that though he was gone, the love they shared was an enduring gift that could never be fully lost.

Even in the depths of your grief, remember that the love you shared will always be a part of you, illuminating your path forward.

DAILY REFLECTION

What emotions rise within you as you confront the sudden absence of your beloved? How can you allow yourself to feel those emotions while still drawing strength from your cherished memories together?

PRAYER

Dear Lord, in this time of loss, wrap your arms around her, offering comfort amidst the pain. Give her the strength to embrace the memories, and the wisdom to find hope even in the shadows of grief.

"Though the pain of goodbye is profound, the love shared endures forever in our hearts."

WHEN SILENCE FEELS LOUD

*"Be still before the Lord and wait patiently for him;
do not fret when people succeed in their ways."* **Psalm 37:7**

DEVOTIONAL

After losing her husband, Mary often found herself sitting in the quiet of their home, where the silence echoed the absence of his laughter and love. Each creak of the floor or rustle of the leaves outside felt magnified, reminding her of the love that once filled her days. She would sometimes wonder if her heart would ever heal, feeling that the silence was both a privilege and a burden. One evening, she decided to make a cup of tea and, instead of filling the quiet with distractions, sat simply in her garden. As she listened to the whispers of the wind and the chirps of the evening birds, Mary realized that in this silence, God was drawing near, providing comfort in ways she couldn't yet understand.
In the stillness of silence, know that you are not alone; God is present, embracing you in your grief.

DAILY REFLECTION

What emotions do you feel when you sit in silence, and how can you honor those feelings as part of your healing journey?

PRAYER

Dear God, as I navigate this quiet season, help me to feel your presence in the stillness. Wrap me in your love and guide me through my grief.

In the silence, I can find the whispers of my heart's longing and the gentle embrace of hope.

LEARNING TO BREATHE AGAIN

"To everything, there is a season and a time for every matter under heaven."
Ecclesiastes 3:1

DEVOTIONAL

When Linda first lost her husband, she felt as though she was drowning in a sea of sorrow, each breath a labor and every day an endless march through grief. Friends would reach out, but their well-meaning words felt distant, like echoes in a vast canyon. One rainy afternoon, as she walked through the park, she was surprised to find herself laughing at a toddler chasing after raindrops. It was a simple moment, yet it reminded her that joy could co-exist with her pain, and that life, despite its grief, still had moments worth cherishing. Slowly, Linda began practicing gratitude, allowing herself to cherish both her memories and her new beginnings, learning that breathing again could be a beautiful act of courage and resilience.
Life can bring unexpected seasons of sorrow, but even amidst the pain, we can learn to find breath and beauty once more.

DAILY REFLECTION

What memories of your loved one bring a smile to your heart? How can you create space for both joy and sorrow as you take your next steps forward?

PRAYER

Dear God, as I navigate this new chapter without my beloved, help me find comfort in Your presence. May each breath I take be filled with peace and hope for the future.

"With each breath, I learn to embrace both my sorrow and my strength."

LEARNING TO ASK FOR HELP

"I lift up my eyes to the hills—where does my help come from? My help comes from the Lord, the Maker of heaven and earth." **Psalm 121:1-2**

DEVOTIONAL

In the weeks following her husband's passing, Linda felt overwhelmed by the sheer weight of her daily responsibilities. One afternoon, as she was struggling with a particularly challenging task, her neighbor stopped by to check on her. Hesitant, Linda shared her feelings of helplessness. To her surprise, her neighbor not only offered a listening ear but also volunteered to help with her yard work. Linda found comfort in allowing someone in, realizing that asking for help did not make her weak; it brought support and connection in her time of need.

It's okay to lean on others for support; asking for help opens the door to healing and community.

DAILY REFLECTION

What does it feel like for you to ask for help, and what fears or thoughts come to mind when you consider reaching out to others in this new chapter of your life?

PRAYER

Dear Lord, as I navigate this journey of grief and healing, help me to remember that it's okay to lean on those around me. Grant me the courage to ask for support and the wisdom to embrace the love offered to me in this time of need.

"Vulnerability is not a weakness; it is an invitation for connection and community."

MISSING HIS VOICE

"So do not fear, for I am with you; do not be dismayed, for I am your God. I will strengthen you and help you; I will uphold you with my righteous right hand." **Isaiah 41:10**

DEVOTIONAL

When Ruth lost her husband, she often found herself sitting in silence, longing for his familiar voice and the comfort it brought. The echoes of laughter and shared conversations filled her home, but now there was only stillness—a stark contrast to the life they lived together. On a difficult evening, she walked into their garden, a place where they had spent countless hours talking and dreaming. In that sacred space, she felt the soft whisper of the wind, reminiscent of his gentle words, reminding her that though he was gone, love transcended physical presence. It was in the quiet moments that she started to hear her own heart's voice—filled with love, memories, and the courage to move forward, one step at a time.

In times of deep loss, your heart may ache for the familiar sounds of your loved one, but within that silence, you may find his love guiding you toward healing and renewal.

DAILY REFLECTION

What is it about his voice that you miss the most, and how does it make you feel when you hear memories of it echo in your heart?

PRAYER

Dear Lord, please wrap her in your love as she navigates this painful time. Comfort her with your presence and remind her that she is never truly alone, for Your voice can fill the silence that feels so heavy right now.

In the quiet moments, His voice is still a whisper in the winds of your memories.

ACCEPTING IMPERFECTION IN GRIEF

*"We know that in all things God works for the good of those who love him, who have been called according to his purpose." **Romans 8:28***

DEVOTIONAL

Maggie sat by the window, her tea growing cold beside her as the clouds mirrored her mood. Since losing her husband, every corner of their home felt heavy with memories—some beautiful, some painful. She often found herself comparing how she thought she should feel to how she actually felt. One day, as she struggled with tattered family photos that held laughter and love, she caught a glimpse of a cracked picture frame. Instead of tossing it away, she decided to keep it, realizing that it was in those imperfections that the depth of love was most vividly displayed. It became a reminder that her own journey through grief didn't have to be perfect; it simply had to be real.

Embrace the fact that your grief is uniquely yours, allowing space for imperfection and healing in its own time.

DAILY REFLECTION

What does it feel like to embrace your grief without the need for perfection? How can you allow yourself the space to feel all your emotions, even the messy ones?

PRAYER

Dear Lord, grant her the strength to navigate this journey of grief. Wrap her in your loving embrace as she learns to accept her emotions, both the light and the heavy, knowing you are with her every step of the way.

"Grief is not a straight path; it is a winding road where every twist and turn leads to deeper understanding."

LIGHTNESS IN A HEAVY HEART

The Lord is a refuge for the oppressed, a stronghold in times of trouble. Those who know your name trust in you, for you, Lord, have never forsaken those who seek you."
Psalm 9:9-10
DEVOTIONAL

Just a few months after losing her husband, Martha found herself sitting on a park bench, surrounded by memories that felt both heavy and beautiful. As she watched families enjoying the sunshine, laughter and joy seemed to dance around her, making her heart ache a little more. Yet, in that stillness, she felt a gentle breeze brush past, whispering reminders of the love she once shared. With every breath, she began to acknowledge that while her heart felt heavy with loss, joy could coexist alongside sorrow. Slowly, she started to recall the small moments of light that her husband brought into her life, cherishing them like precious treasures, allowing her heart to expand in unexpected ways.

In the midst of your grief, allow the flickers of joy and memories of love to bring lightness to your heart, acknowledging that both sorrow and joy can walk hand in hand.

DAILY REFLECTION

What are some small moments of joy or comfort you can embrace today, even in the midst of your sorrow?

PRAYER

Dear Lord, help me to find light in my heart during this heavy time. Guide me to embrace moments of peace and comfort in the warmth of your presence.

Even in sorrow, joy can be a gentle whisper, reminding us that we are not alone.

FINDING JOY IN SMALL MOMENTS

"The Lord has done great things for us, and we are filled with joy."
Psalm 126:3

DEVOTIONAL

As I sipped my morning tea, watching the sun rise over the horizon, I felt a flicker of warmth spread within me. The world outside was awakening, vibrant and alive, and it reminded me of the evenings my husband and I would share laughter on the porch, the laughter echoing into the twilight. Though he was no longer by my side, those small memories engulfed me with a sense of comfort. I closed my eyes, allowing the aroma of the tea to linger, and I realized that joy could still blossom in these quiet moments if only I dared to pause and notice them, much like the sun's rays breaking through the clouds.

Joy often resides in the little things around us; embrace those small moments that speak nourishment to your soul and remind you that life still holds beauty.

DAILY REFLECTION

What small moments in your day bring you a flicker of joy? Can you pause and feel gratitude for these little gifts, even amidst your grief?

PRAYER

Dear God, help me to open my heart to the small, beautiful moments that exist in my daily life. Remind me that joy can still flicker in the shadows, bringing warmth and light to my journey ahead.

"Joy is often found in the stillness of a simple moment."

GRACE FOR YOUR REGRETS

"Come to me, all you who are weary and burdened, and I will give you rest."
Luke 11:28

DEVOTIONAL

After losing her husband, Sarah often found herself tangled in thoughts of what she could have done differently. She replayed moments over and over in her mind, wishing she had spoken more lovingly during disagreements or planned more adventures together. One quiet evening, as she sat with an old scrapbook, a particular photo caught her eye—a silly snapshot from a picnic they once had, where laughter was abundant and love was evident. In those cherished memories, Sarah remembered that they were not defined by their regrets, but rather by the grace of shared moments, the joy they created, and the support they gave each other. This realization became a balm for her heart, reminding her that love outshines regret.

You are not defined by your regrets; instead, allow the grace of your memories to guide you toward healing and newfound hope.

DAILY REFLECTION

What regrets are you carrying in your heart today, and how might you offer them to God for His grace and healing?

PRAYER

Dear God, I come before You with my regrets, trusting that Your grace covers all my shortcomings and fears. Help me to release these burdens and embrace the peace of Your love.

"Grace transforms our regrets into stepping stones for deeper faith."

BECOMING THROUGH BROKENNESS

"He will provide for those who grieve in Zion, to bestow on them a crown of beauty instead of ashes, the oil of joy instead of mourning, and a garment of praise instead of a spirit of despair." Isaiah 61:3

DEVOTIONAL

After losing her husband, Linda found herself wandering through the remnants of their life together, her home echoing with memories that were once filled with laughter and love. On a particularly heavy day, while cleaning out a closet, she stumbled upon a box of letters they had exchanged over the years. As she read each note, she was flooded not only with sorrow but also with the beauty of their shared journey—each letter a testament to the triumphs and tribulations they had faced together. In that moment, she realized that her broken heart was also a treasure chest holding the depth of their love, showing her that within her pain lay the seeds of new possibilities. Slowly, with each breath, she began to envision a future where her brokenness could lead to new beginnings.

Embrace your brokenness as an opportunity to discover deeper layers of strength and resilience that lie within you.

DAILY REFLECTION

What does the idea of becoming through your brokenness mean to you in this moment of your life? How can you begin to see your grief as a space for growth and transformation?

PRAYER

Dear God, please wrap your loving arms around her as she navigates this journey of loss. Grant her strength to embrace her brokenness and wisdom to see the beauty that can emerge from it.

"In the depths of sorrow, seeds of strength are sown, waiting patiently for the sun to shine again."

FORGIVING YOURSELF, GENTLY

"You are precious in my eyes, and honored, and I love you."
Isaiah 43:4

DEVOTIONAL

After the passing of her beloved husband, Karen found herself submerged in waves of guilt. She often replayed their last moments together, wondering if she had done enough to make him feel loved and cherished. It was during a quiet evening, surrounded by familiar shadows and memories, that she began to understand the importance of forgiving herself for those moments she deemed imperfect. She gently reminded herself that love is not measured in flawlessness, but in the vast, deep moments shared. In forgiving herself, Karen found a path toward healing, realizing that her love, while not without its shortcomings, was profound and true.

Forgiveness of oneself is often the hardest to give, yet it opens the door to peace and healing.

DAILY REFLECTION

What are the moments from your past that linger in your heart, and how can you begin to embrace forgiveness for yourself in those memories?

PRAYER

Dear God, wrap your loving arms around my heart as I learn to forgive myself. Help me to remember that I am worthy of grace and healing during this difficult time.

"Forgiveness is not forgetting; it's the gentle act of embracing our humanity."

DELIGHT IN THE MIDST OF LOSS

"Take delight in the Lord, and he will give you the desires of your heart."
Psalm 37:4

DEVOTIONAL

After losing her husband, Martha felt an emptiness that wrapped around her like a heavy blanket. As days turned into weeks, she noticed that her garden, once vibrant and alive, mirrored her heart - much of it needed tending. One quiet morning, she ventured outside, and as she pulled weeds and trimmed the overgrown branches, she stumbled upon a patch of blooming daisies, their cheerful faces shining bright against the green. In that moment, Martha realized that even in her sorrow, there was still beauty around her waiting to be discovered. She decided to nurture her garden anew, allowing it to be a source of joy as she reopened her heart to the world.

Sometimes, embracing the beauty in unexpected places can lighten the heaviness of our loss.

DAILY REFLECTION

What moments of joy have you discovered in your daily routine since your loss? How can you nurture them in this season of change?

PRAYER

Dear God, in the quiet spaces of grief, help me find the gentle delights you place along my path. Allow me to embrace the small joys that remind me of your love and presence.

"In sorrow, new beginnings can bloom."

PEACE IN THE UNKNOWN

"Cast your cares on the Lord and he will sustain you;
he will never let the righteous be shaken." **Psalm 55:22**

DEVOTIONAL

After her husband's passing, Carol often felt lost in the quiet of her home. The future seemed like a vast, uncharted sea, and she wondered how she would ever find her way. One afternoon, while sorting through old photographs, she remembered how her husband used to reassure her during storms, saying, "We'll get through this together." Now, she sensed God whispering those same words to her heart, reminding her that she was not alone, even in the unknown.

When life feels uncertain and overwhelming, you can find peace by letting God carry your worries and trusting that He will sustain you through each new day.

DAILY REFLECTION

What is one area of your life that feels uncertain right now, and how might you invite God's peace into that space?

PRAYER

God, in the quiet moments when I feel lost and unsure, please fill my heart with Your calming presence. Help me trust that You are guiding me, even when I cannot see the way ahead.

Even in the unknown, God's peace can gently hold your heart.

HOPE IS A HOLY THING

"Blessed is the one who perseveres under trial because, having stood the test, that person will receive the crown of life that the Lord has promised to those who love him." James 1:12

DEVOTIONAL

In the quiet of her home, Clara often found herself wrapped in the memories of her late husband, filling the silence with laughter that echoed from years gone by. One evening, while sorting through old photo albums, she stumbled upon a picture of the two of them during a joyful summer picnic, both bursting with laughter and surrounded by the beauty of nature. Suddenly, a wave of sorrow washed over her, shadowing the warmth of that memory. But as she gazed at the photograph, Clara felt a flicker of hope ignite within her; that love remained, a sacred thread connecting her past and her future. It struck her that while grief is heavy, it is hope that can guide her into her new chapter, shining like a light in the dark.

Hope is a holy thing that keeps the heart alive and whispers of the beauty yet to come.

DAILY REFLECTION

What hopes and dreams have you found stirring within you since your loss, and how might they guide you toward healing?

PRAYER

Dear God, as I navigate this difficult season, help me to find glimmers of hope in my journey. May Your presence be a comfort and a guiding light as I embrace the path before me.

"Hope is a gentle whisper that reminds us of love's enduring power."

LOOKING FOR THE LIGHT

"Now to him who is able to do immeasurably more than all we ask or imagine, according to his power that is at work within us." Ephesians 3:20

DEVOTIONAL

When Sarah lost her husband, the days felt long and heavy, each minute a reminder of her new reality. One evening, while sitting alone in her garden, she noticed a small flower pushing through the cracked earth. It was a reminder that even in difficult times, beauty could emerge from hardship. As the sun began to set, the sky transformed with hues of orange and pink, illuminating her surroundings and offering a glimpse of hope. That moment reminded Sarah that light could break through the darkness, signifying that life, though changed, could still be filled with grace and wonder.

Even in your darkest moments, remember that light can find a way to shine through the cracks in your heart.

DAILY REFLECTION

What brings you comfort in your moments of solitude, and how can you seek the light even within the shadows of your grief?

PRAYER

Dear Lord, as I navigate this journey of loss and longing, help me to find Your light even in the darkest moments. Surround me with Your warmth and guide my heart toward hope.

"In the midst of darkness, the smallest light can make a world of difference."

YOUR FUTURE IS NOT OVER

"For nothing will be impossible with God."
Luke 1:37

DEVOTIONAL

After losing her husband, Mary found herself walking through an empty house filled with memories. Each room was a reminder of laughter and love, now shadowed with silence. One day, while sifting through old photos, she stumbled upon a picture of a trip they had dreams of taking together. A thought ignited within her; perhaps she could still pursue that dream. With a mix of grief and newfound courage, she began planning for the journey—one that would honor his memory while opening up new possibilities for her own future.

Even in the depths of sorrow, your heart can find the courage to dream anew.

DAILY REFLECTION

What dreams or hopes have you put aside that you feel are waiting for you to rediscover?

PRAYER

Dear God, please hold me in your love as I navigate this new chapter. Remind me that I am not alone and that my future is still filled with possibilities.

"Your story is not finished; it is just beginning a new chapter."

JOY WILL RETURN

"I will turn their mourning into joy and will comfort them, and make them rejoice after their sorrow." **Jeremiah 31:13**

DEVOTIONAL

After her husband passed, Doris often found herself staring out the window, lost in memories of laughter and love that seemed distant now. One day, while walking through a local park, she noticed a group of children playing, their laughter echoing in the air. It struck her that joy, much like the blooming flowers around her, can re-emerge even after the coldest winters. Inspired, Doris took a deep breath, allowing a small smile to break through her sorrow as she remembered the love that would always be a part of her life, even in absence.

Your heart can heal and embrace joy again; it just takes time and the willingness to let it grow within you.

DAILY REFLECTION

What brings you moments of joy, even in the midst of your sorrow? Can you recall a time when laughter found its way into your heart despite the heaviness?

PRAYER

Dear God, you understand the depth of my grief and the longing for joy. Please cradle my heart in your love and help me find glimmers of hope each day.

"Joy is not the absence of sorrow, but the presence of hope."

TOMORROW CAN BE BEAUTIFUL

*"Forget the former things; do not dwell on the past. See, I am doing a new thing! Now it springs up; do you not perceive it? I am making a way in the wilderness and streams in the wasteland." **Isaiah 43:18-19***

DEVOTIONAL

After losing her husband, Mary found herself grappling with the emptiness that filled her home and heart. Each room echoed memories of laughter and love, but soon she realized that while the past was a cherished chapter, it was not the whole story. One day, as she sorted through old photographs, a picture of the two of them hiking in the mountains caught her eye. Inspired by that memory and the joy they shared, she decided to take a morning walk in nature. As she breathed in the fresh air, surrounded by the vibrant colors of spring, she felt a renewed sense of hope. Slowly, she began to discover new joys, like painting and volunteering, realizing that her life could still hold beauty.

Tomorrow can bring unexpected blessings, even amidst the pain of today.

DAILY REFLECTION

What small steps can you take today to embrace the promise of a brighter tomorrow?

PRAYER

Dear God, wrap your loving arms around her heart as she navigates this difficult time. Help her to find peace in the memories and hope in the dreams still to come.

"Though today may feel heavy, remember that each dawn brings the gift of a fresh start."

NEW CHAPTERS, NEW GRACE

"But be strong and courageous; do not be frightened or dismayed, for the LORD your God is with you wherever you go." Joshua 1:9

DEVOTIONAL

When Linda lost her husband of thirty years, she spent weeks in a fog, grappling with the silence of an empty home. Each day felt heavy with memories, and familiar routines became a haunting reminder of her loss. One afternoon, while sorting through their belongings, she stumbled upon their wedding album. As she flipped through the pages, the joy radiating from her past began to fill her heart once more. That moment sparked a realization: though her life had taken an unexpected turn, each cherished memory could become a stepping stone toward new beginnings. Inspired, Linda took a deep breath, committed to approaching life with an open heart, ready to embrace whatever new chapter God had in store for her. *It's in embracing the new chapters of our lives that we often discover the depths of God's grace and love.*

DAILY REFLECTION

What new chapter do you feel nudging at your heart, inviting you to embrace a different path or perspective in this season of life?

PRAYER

Dear God, as I stand at the threshold of this new chapter, grant me the grace to embrace change and the courage to step forward into the unknown with hope and faith.

"Each ending is a gentle reminder that life is a tapestry, rich with both loss and renewed beginnings."

THE NEXT SEASON

"In all this you greatly rejoice, though now for a little while you may have had to suffer grief in all kinds of trials. These have come so that the proven genuineness of your faith—of greater worth than gold, which perishes even though refined by fire—may result in praise, glory and honor when Jesus Christ is revealed." 1 Peter 1:6-7

DEVOTIONAL

As I sat alone in my kitchen, sipping my tea while watching the sun rise, memories flooded back of mornings shared with my beloved. I felt an ache in my heart, not only for his absence but also for the joy of what was. Yet, as the rays of light painted the walls, I remembered the beauty of new beginnings. Each day is a canvas waiting to be filled with colors yet unseen. Though my journey felt marred by loss, it also held the promise of a new season—a time to explore who I am now and what lies ahead in God's plan for me. *This next season of life may be filled with uncertainty, but it is also an opportunity to step forward in faith, embracing the unknown with hope and courage.*

DAILY REFLECTION

What does the next season of your life look like, and how can you embrace this new chapter with hope and purpose?

PRAYER

Dear God, as I navigate this new season, fill my heart with Your peace and guide me in discovering joy once again. Help me to see the beauty of each day and the possibilities that lie ahead.

"Each season brings its own beauty,
and this new chapter is filled with the potential for growth and renewal."

THE BEAUTY OF AUTUMN CHANGE

*"Consider the lilies of the field, how they grow: they neither toil nor spin, yet I tell you, even Solomon in all his glory was not arrayed like one of these." **Matthew 6:28-29***

DEVOTIONAL

As autumn approaches, the leaves begin to change, transforming the landscape into a breathtaking display of oranges, yellows, and reds. I remember a vivid autumn day after my own loss, walking through a park and feeling the crisp air brush against my skin. The beauty of the vibrant leaves resonated with me, reminding me that all things, even in their end, carry a beauty of change. Just like the trees let go of their leaves, I too was called to shed the weight of my sorrow, allowing new growth to emerge. It was in that moment, amidst the falling leaves, that I finally understood - change could bring both beauty and hope.

Embrace the changes, for in each ending lies the potential for a beautiful new beginning.

DAILY REFLECTION

What changes do you find most difficult to embrace in this season of your life? How might seeing these changes as moments of beauty help you heal?

PRAYER

Dear Heavenly Father, as the leaves transition and the days grow shorter, help me to find peace in the changes around me. Grant me strength and comfort in this season of transformation. Amen.

'Just as the leaves surrender to the wind, so too can we release
what no longer serves us and embrace the beauty of new beginnings.'

HARVESTING NEW BEGINNINGS

*"Those who sow with tears will reap with songs of joy; those who go out weeping, carrying seeds to sow, will return with songs of joy, carrying sheaves with them." **Psalm 126:5-6***

DEVOTIONAL

After losing her beloved husband, Sarah found herself surrounded by memories that filled her home with both comfort and heartache. One rainy afternoon, she stumbled upon a half-finished garden project they had planned together. Initially, she felt overwhelmed looking at the unkempt beds filled with weeds, but as she gingerly began to clear away the debris, she discovered life beneath—tender sprouts of flowers waiting for nurturing. Inspired, she decided not only to revive the garden but also to create new spaces for fresh blooms, symbolizing her hope for a future filled with color and brightness. Each plant she nurtured became a testament to her resilience and a reminder that even in loss, there is the potential for beauty and new growth.

Embrace each day as an opportunity to plant seeds of hope, knowing that joy can blossom from the depths of sorrow.

DAILY REFLECTION

What new opportunities for growth and renewal are you being called to in this season of your life? How can you embrace these changes with hope and courage?

PRAYER

Dear God, as I navigate this season of loss, help me to see the beauty in new beginnings. Grant me the strength to embrace the future with an open heart, trusting in Your guidance every step of the way.

'Each ending carries the promise of a new beginning, waiting to bloom in the light of hope.'

WHEN THE FOG BEGINS TO LIFT

"Even though I walk through the darkest valley, I will fear no evil, for you are with me; your rod and your staff, they comfort me." **Psalm 23:4**

DEVOTIONAL

As the fog enveloped the days following her husband's passing, Sarah felt lost in a world that no longer made sense. Each morning began with a heaviness that seemed to cling to her, making every simple task feel like an insurmountable challenge. She often found herself staring out the window, awaiting the sunlight that seemed to elude her. Yet, one crisp morning, as the sun began to break through the mist, she suddenly felt a subtle shift within her—the fog was starting to lift. The warmth of the light reminded her of her husband's embrace, letting her know he was still with her in spirit, and she felt a flicker of hope. Sarah realized that while the journey through grief was daunting, there would be brighter moments ahead.

Hope can flicker back to life when we allow ourselves the space to feel our grief and remember the love that remains.

DAILY REFLECTION

What small signs of hope or joy have you noticed recently, even amid your sadness?

PRAYER

Dear God, as the fog of grief starts to lift, help me see the rays of your light shining through. Fill my heart with your comfort and guide me in this new season of life.

"Hope is often found in the gentle moments of everyday life."

ANTICIPATING NEW JOY

"Yet the Lord longs to be gracious to you; therefore he will rise up to show you compassion." **Isaiah 30:18**

DEVOTIONAL

After losing her husband, Clara found herself in a quiet house that felt overwhelmingly empty. Each room echoed memories that brought both warmth and fresh waves of sorrow. One afternoon, as she dusted off the shelves, Clara stumbled upon a box of letters they had written to each other during their early years. Reading through their shared dreams and laughter rekindled a sense of connection. As tears turned to smiles, she felt a whisper of hope, realizing that even though her journey had changed, the love they shared would forever illuminate her path.

Every new day uncovers opportunities for healing and renewed joy, no matter how insurmountable today may feel.

DAILY REFLECTION

What activities or dreams have you set aside that you can begin to explore again as you step into this new chapter of your life?

PRAYER

Dear God, as I navigate this season of change, help me to embrace the possibilities ahead. May I find comfort in Your presence and joy in the new experiences that await me.

"In every ending, there is a whisper of a new beginning."

HOPE IN THE MORNING

"The Lord your God is with you, the Mighty Warrior who saves. He will take great delight in you; in his love, he will no longer rebuke you, but will rejoice over you with singing."
Zephaniah 3:17

DEVOTIONAL

As the sun began to rise one early morning, Mary sat on her porch wrapped in a shawl that her husband had gifted her. The dawn light filtered through the trees, casting delicate patterns across the yard, reminding her of the joyful mornings they had shared. Though his absence filled her heart with an ache that felt insurmountable, she took a deep breath and watched as the world awakened around her. It was in that stillness, amidst the chirping of birds and the gentle rustle of leaves, that she felt the tender embrace of hope wrapping around her like a warm blanket. Each morning now became a reminder that life continues to unfold, and in that unfolding, there was the promise of new beginnings.
In each dawn, find your heart awakened to the whispered promise of new hope waiting just outside your door.

DAILY REFLECTION

What new beginnings can you envision for yourself as you move into this next chapter of your life? How can you invite hope into your days, even amidst your sorrow?

PRAYER

Dear Lord, as dawn breaks and a new day begins, fill my heart with hope and remind me of your steadfast love. Help me to lean into the promise of tomorrow, trusting that brighter days are ahead.

"Morning is God's gentle reminder that every day holds the possibility of renewal."

ROOM FOR SOMETHING NEW

"Those who hope in the Lord will renew their strength."
Isaiah 40:31

DEVOTIONAL

After losing her husband, Marissa found herself wandering through familiar spaces that suddenly felt foreign. Days turned into weeks filled with emptiness and memories echoing in the silence of her home. One evening, as she sorted through old photographs, she stumbled upon a small journal he'd encouraged her to keep. With each entry, she rediscovered her dreams and passions—all the things they had talked about long ago. Inspired, she decided to step out and try a painting class she had always mentioned but never dared to pursue. Each brushstroke brought her joy and a sense of connection to herself, reminding her that it's never too late to embrace new beginnings.
In this time of transition, take heart that opening yourself to something new can be a gateway to healing and joy.

DAILY REFLECTION

What dreams and passions have been tucked away that you can now gently bring forward as you navigate this new chapter of your life?

PRAYER

Dear God, as I stand at this crossroads of grief and hope, help me to embrace the possibility of new beginnings. Fill my heart with courage to seek and explore the beauty that lies ahead.

"Even in the depths of loss, there is room for something beautiful to blossom."

TRUSTING GOD WITH THE UNKNOWN

"Trust in the Lord with all your heart and lean not on your own understanding; in all your ways acknowledge Him, and He will make your paths straight." **Proverbs 3:5-6**

DEVOTIONAL

After losing her beloved husband, Martha found herself standing at the threshold of a newly uncertain life. One evening, as she stared blankly at pictures that seemed to whisper memories, she felt a gentle nudge to step outside. The sun was setting, painting the sky with hues of orange and pink, and in that moment of beauty, she sensed God's presence reminding her that though she could not see the path ahead, He was with her. As she took a deep breath and allowed her heart to grieve, she also felt an unexpected flutter of hope bubbling within her. Perhaps the unknown wasn't a void, but a canvas for new beginnings.

Trusting God means embracing the unknown as an opportunity for growth and healing, knowing that He walks this journey with you.

DAILY REFLECTION

What uncertainties linger in your heart as you step into this new chapter of your life? How can you invite God into those unknowns today?

PRAYER

Dear God, in this season of loss and uncertainty, I ask for your comfort and guidance. Help me to trust in your plan, even when I cannot see the path ahead.

"Even in the shadows of grief, His light can guide us through the unknown."

PLANTING HOPE DAILY

"Wait for the Lord; be strong, and let your heart take courage; wait for the Lord."
Psalm 27:14

DEVOTIONAL

After losing her husband, Clara often found herself staring out the window, her eyes searching the garden they had once tended together. It was a tangled mess of thorns and weeds, much like the chaos in her heart. One afternoon, she decided to venture into that garden, pulling out the weeds and uncovering the dormant flowers beneath. With every little bloom she uncovered, Clara felt a flicker of hope ignite within her—a reminder that, although her life had changed drastically, there was still beauty to be found with patience and care.

In every season of grief, there is an opportunity for renewal and growth.

DAILY REFLECTION

What small step can you take today to nurture a seed of hope in your heart?

PRAYER

Dear Lord, as I navigate this new season of life, grant me the strength to plant seeds of hope each day. Help me to find joy in the little moments and to trust in your guidance with each passing day.

"Even in the darkest nights, stars can be found if you look up."

BUILDING A NEW IDENTITY

*"I praise you because I am fearfully and wonderfully made; your works are wonderful, I know that full well." **Psalm 139:14***

DEVOTIONAL

After losing her husband of 30 years, Mary found herself standing in an empty room that once echoed with laughter and shared dreams. She spent endless hours sifting through memories, overwhelmed by the silence that had taken his place. One day, she discovered a box of love letters they had written to each other, filled with hopes and adventures. Reading those words reminded her of not only the love they shared but also of the vibrant woman she was even before they met. She slowly began to explore new hobbies and reconnect with friends, realizing that while grief was a part of her story, it didn't have to define her future.

You are not just a widow; you are a beautiful tapestry of experiences, dreams, and strength that is waiting to be woven into your new identity.

DAILY REFLECTION

What steps can you take today to embrace your new identity and celebrate the strength you have gained through your journey?

PRAYER

Dear Lord, as I navigate this season of change, help me to discover the beauty in my new identity. Guide me with your love and wisdom as I build a life that honors both my past and my future. Amen.

"From heartache blooms new beginnings."

HEALING IN NATURE

*"The Lord will guide you always; he will satisfy your needs in a sun-scorched land and will strengthen your frame. You will be like a well-watered garden, like a spring whose waters never fail." **Isaiah 58:11***

DEVOTIONAL

There was once a woman named Clara who lost her husband unexpectedly. Feeling lost in her grief, she decided to take daily walks in a nearby park. During one of her outings, she came across a blooming garden alive with color and fragrance. As she sat on a bench, breathing in the beauty around her, the memories of her husband began to fall away. Instead, she felt a deep sense of peace and connection to the world around her. The gentle rustling of leaves and the soft warmth of the sun reminded her that life was still present and vibrant. Over time, these moments in nature became a sanctuary for her heart, allowing her to heal and discover hope once more.

Finding solace and strength in nature can be a gentle reminder of the beauty and continuity of life, even in our hardest moments.

DAILY REFLECTION

What does the beauty of nature whisper to your heart during this time of healing? How can you find solace in the sights and sounds around you?

PRAYER

Loving God, please surround her with your comforting presence as she walks through this season of loss. May the gentle breeze and blooming flowers remind her of the love that remains.

"In every petal and leaf, there is the promise of renewal,
a gentle reminder that life continues to unfold in beautiful ways."

PLANTING SEEDS OF JOY

*"Though you have not seen Him, you love Him; and even though you do not see Him now, you believe in Him and are filled with an inexpressible and glorious joy, for you are receiving the end result of your faith, the salvation of your souls." **1 Peter 1:8-9***

DEVOTIONAL

After losing her husband, Elaine found herself wandering through her days, often trapped in memories that brought both joy and sorrow. One day, while tending to her garden, she noticed a tiny sprout pushing its way through the soil. It reminded her that even in the midst of loss and sorrow, new life can emerge. Inspired, she began to plant more seeds—flowers that bloomed a vibrant hue, herbs that added flavor to her meals, and vegetables that nourished her body. Each time she tended to her garden, she felt a renewed sense of hope and purpose, as if the act of planting mirrored her journey of healing.

In the face of grief, allow yourself to nurture new beginnings, knowing that joy can sprout even from the most tender of places.

DAILY REFLECTION

What small moments have brought you joy today, even amidst your grief? Can you identify the seeds of happiness that are waiting to bloom in your heart?

PRAYER

Dear God, as I navigate this season of sorrow, help me to recognize and nurture the seeds of joy you've planted in my life. May I find comfort in small blessings and cherish each moment of peace.

"Joy can be a gentle whisper in the midst of life's loudest storms."

LETTING LOVE IN AGAIN

"Now abide faith, hope, love, these three; but the greatest of these is love."
1 Corinthians 13:13

DEVOTIONAL

After losing her husband, Marjorie felt as if the world around her had dulled. Memories of their laughter echoed in her heart, yet the silence in her home felt overwhelming. One day, while sifting through a box of old letters, she stumbled upon a note he had written, professing his love and encouraging her to always embrace new beginnings. Inspired, she decided to try something new, joining a local book club where she met warm-hearted women who shared their stories and laughter. Over time, Marjorie found herself slowly letting love in again, recognizing the beauty of friendship that could blossom from shared grief.

Opening your heart to new connections honors the love you've experienced while allowing fresh joy to enter your life.

DAILY REFLECTION

What does "letting love in again" look like for you in this new season of life? How can you open your heart to the possibility of joy and connection while honoring the love you have known?

PRAYER

Dear God, as I navigate this new chapter, help me to gently open my heart again to love. Please surround me with Your warmth and guide me in embracing both the memories and the possibilities that lie ahead.

"Love is a garden; even after the frost, it can bloom again."

THE LIFE YOU BUILT TOGETHER

*"I have loved you with an everlasting love;
therefore I have continued my faithfulness to you."* **Jeremiah 31:3**

DEVOTIONAL

When Sarah lost her husband after nearly four decades of shared experiences, she felt as if the foundation of her life had crumbled. Their home, once filled with laughter, conversations, and dreams, now echoed with silence. As she sorted through old letters and photographs, she stumbled upon a note he had written on their wedding day. "I promise to build a life filled with love and adventure," it read. In that moment, Sarah realized that although he was no longer physically present, the life they created together remained alive in her heart, teaching her the importance of cherishing memories while also finding the strength to forge ahead.

In the bittersweet journey of mourning, remember that the love you built together remains a lasting treasure that can inspire you to embrace your next chapter.

DAILY REFLECTION

What are the most cherished memories you built together, and how do they shape your heart today?

PRAYER

Dear God, embrace this precious soul with Your love as she navigates her grief. May the memories she holds close continue to bring her comfort and remind her of the joy they shared together.

"Even in the quiet spaces of loss, love remains, woven into the very fabric of our memories."

WHAT HE TAUGHT YOU

"Your word is a lamp for my feet, a light on my path."
Psalm 119:105

DEVOTIONAL

As I sat in the quiet of my kitchen one evening, reflecting on the life I shared with my late husband, I found myself remembering the small lessons he had taught me over the years. He had a way of turning mundane moments into treasured memories—like the time he showed me how to cook his favorite meal. Each ingredient was a reminder of our shared life, but more importantly, it was his patience during the process that touched me deeply. Even as I face the uncertainty of my new life, I realize that those lessons still illuminate my path, guiding me in ways I never anticipated.

Cherish the lessons learned in love, for they will light your way through the darkness.

DAILY REFLECTION

What has your journey with your partner taught you about love and resilience? Reflect on specific moments that have shaped your understanding of relationships and yourself.

PRAYER

Dear God, as I navigate this new chapter of my life, help me cherish the lessons learned and find peace in the memories. May each day remind me of the love that built my strength.

'Every love story leaves footprints on our hearts;
cherish them as reminders of the journey you walked together.'

CARRYING ON HIS KINDNESS

"Blessed are the merciful, for they will be shown mercy."
Matthew 5:7

DEVOTIONAL

After the passing of my husband, I felt a tidal wave of loneliness wash over me. One chilly evening, feeling particularly lost, I stepped out for a walk and that's when I noticed my neighbor struggling with her groceries. I hesitated but remembered how much I appreciated the small acts of kindness during my own dark days. As I helped her carry the bags, we started talking, and I learned she had also faced loss. In that moment, amidst shared stories and tears, I realized that kindness was my lifeline, connecting me back to the world and to others who understand my pain.

In moments of grief, remember that showing kindness not only helps others but also nurtures your heart.

DAILY REFLECTION

What does carrying on kindness look like in your daily interactions, especially now as you navigate life without your beloved partner?

PRAYER

Lord, as I find my way through this new season of life, open my heart to the simple acts of kindness that can uplift both me and others. May Your love shine through me in unexpected ways.

"Kindness is a thread that weaves connections, reminding us that even in loss, we can create moments of grace."

HIS FAVORITE SAYINGS

"But he said to me, 'My grace is sufficient for you, for my power is made perfect in weakness.' Therefore I will boast all the more gladly about my weaknesses, so that Christ's power may rest on me." **2 Corinthians 12:9**

DEVOTIONAL

The other day, I stumbled upon an old photo of my husband and me at a picnic, laughing under a sun-drenched sky. In that moment, it hit me how life can take such unexpected turns. I remember our favorite saying, "We can weather any storm together." As the days pass without him, that sentiment feels both comforting and heavy. I often find myself wanting to hear his voice, to share my daily musings. Yet, I've come to realize that even in this season of loss, the essence of those words continues to resonate within me. The storms I once navigated beside him now lead me to discover a deeper faith and resilience within.

Sometimes, the absence we feel opens a new avenue for strength we never knew we had.

DAILY REFLECTION

What are some of the comforting words or memories of your loved one that you hold dear in your heart? How can you carry those sayings forward as a source of strength and comfort in this new season of life?

PRAYER

Heavenly Father, embrace her heart as she navigates this journey of grief. May Your presence be a gentle reminder of hope and love, guiding her through each day.

"May the words of those we love continue to echo in our hearts, bringing us comfort and strength."

COOKING HIS FAVORITE MEAL

"And my God will meet all your needs according to the riches of his glory in Christ Jesus."
Philippians 4:19

DEVOTIONAL

When Laura entered her kitchen, the familiar scents of garlic and rosemary flooded her senses, stirring memories of evenings spent cooking with her late husband. His favorite meal, a hearty lasagna, had always been her way of showing love. As she chopped the vegetables, tears streamed down her cheeks, mingling with the laughter echoed in the pots and pans. In that moment, she realized that cooking his favorite meal wasn't just about recreating a dish; it was a way to honor their love and keep his spirit alive in her heart.

In moments of sorrow, the simplest acts of love can draw us close to cherished memories and remind us of the beauty that once filled our lives.

DAILY REFLECTION

What are some of the favorite sayings or verses that your late husband would often share with you, and how do they resonate with you in this season of your life?

PRAYER

Dear Lord, wrap your comforting arms around her today. May she find solace and strength in the cherished words and memories that remind her of Your everlasting love.

"Memories are the treasures of the heart."

A LEGACY OF LAUGHTER

"Our mouths were filled with laughter, our tongues with songs of joy."
Psalm 126:2

DEVOTIONAL

As Clara flipped through old photo albums, she stumbled upon a picture from their first vacation together. They were both laughing so hard, the joy in their eyes radiated through the pages. It reminded her of his playful spirit and how they would often find humor even in the mundane moments of life. Those memories of laughter wrapped around her like a warm embrace, allowing her to feel his presence, reminding her that joy could still exist even amidst the heaviness of grief. Clara realized that while he was gone, his spirit of laughter could continue to thrive in her heart and home.

Embrace the gift of laughter, for it is a legacy that can light your path forward.

DAILY REFLECTION

What memories make you smile when you think of your loved one? How can you carry that joy into your everyday life now?

PRAYER

Dear God, help me find joy in the little things and cherish the laughter that once filled my home. May I carry this legacy of joy in my heart each day.

"Laughter is the sunshine that breaks through the clouds, reminding us of the love that once was."

HIS STRENGTH IN YOU

"He gives strength to the weary and increases the power of the weak."
Isaiah 40:29

DEVOTIONAL

As Martha stared out the window, watching the world bustling by, she felt a profound emptiness that seemed to echo in every corner of her home. After losing her beloved husband, the days felt heavy and long, marked by the absence of their shared laughter. Yet, as she began to declutter their memories—sorting through old photos and letters—she found herself enveloped in warmth. Each memory told a story of resilience and joy, igniting a flicker of strength she thought had dimmed within her. It was in that moment of reflection that she realized, though he was gone, the love they shared continued to empower her.

You are not alone; His strength is within you, guiding you as you navigate this new chapter.

DAILY REFLECTION

What does it mean for you to lean into God's strength during this challenging season in your life? How can you invite Him into your daily moments of struggle and uncertainty?

PRAYER

Dear Lord, in this time of sorrow and transition, I seek Your strength to guide me through each day. Wrap your gentle arms around me, and help me feel Your presence in every moment of loneliness and doubt.

"In the cracks of despair, His strength becomes the light that guides your way."

WHAT HE'D WANT FOR YOU NOW

"I thank my God every time I remember you. In all my prayers for all of you, I always pray with joy because of your partnership in the gospel from the first day until now."
Philippians 1:3-5

DEVOTIONAL

As you navigate this new chapter without him, remember that you are not alone. Your love story, though it may feel paused for now, still carries forward in the hearts of those who knew him. Think of the memories shared, the laughter that echoed in your home, and the many moments that shaped your lives together. These memories are treasures that can sustain you and bring healing. It's in the quiet moments when grief seems overwhelming that you can pause and reflect on the love you both nurtured, recognizing that he would want you to keep living fully, embracing the joys and challenges that lie ahead.

Your journey of healing is not just about moving forward but also about celebrating the love and life you shared together.

DAILY REFLECTION

What dreams or joys do you believe your partner would want you to pursue now that they are gone?

PRAYER

Heavenly Father, comfort this dear woman in her loss, and guide her as she seeks to honor her late partner's memory. Fill her heart with hope and inspire her to embrace the new chapters of her life.

"Embracing the future doesn't mean leaving the past behind;
it's cherishing the memories while stepping forward with grace."

TELLING HIS STORY

"Your eyes saw my unformed body; all the days ordained for me were written in your book before one of them came to be." **Psalm 139:16**

DEVOTIONAL

Sitting in the quiet of her living room, Sarah found herself surrounded by memories. The photographs on the walls whispered tales of laughter, love, and shared dreams. It was here, amid the echoes of her husband's voice, that she began to craft her own narrative. With each memory that surfaced, she realized that their story together was not just a chapter in her life but a legacy that could inspire others. By sharing their journey—both the beautiful and the challenging—Sarah discovered a renewed purpose; one that could help heal her heart while telling of the love that had shaped her.

Every story carries the weight of love; in sharing her husband's legacy, she begins to weave her path forward.

DAILY REFLECTION

What story about your loved one do you cherish the most? How can sharing that memory create a sense of connection with those around you?

PRAYER

Heavenly Father, grant her comfort in her memories and strength to share the love that was woven into her life. May your peace fill her heart as she reflects on the gift of their time together.

"Every love story is a testament to the beauty of connection and the power of shared moments."

LIVING WITH HIS LOVE STILL

"This is how God showed his love among us: He sent his one and only Son into the world that we might live through him. This is love: not that we loved God, but that he loved us."
1 John 4:9-10

DEVOTIONAL

After losing her husband, Maria felt as if she were adrift in a sea of sorrow. Each day passed with a heaviness that seemed insurmountable, and she often asked herself how she would go on without his presence. One evening, as she sorted through old photos, she stumbled upon a snapshot of them dancing under the stars, their laughter echoing through the years. In that moment, she felt an overwhelming rush of love that transcended even death. A warmth enveloped her, reminding her that love is not confined to the physical presence of her beloved, but remains alive in her heart and spirit, an eternal connection.

Even in the face of profound loss, the love you shared can be a source of comfort and strength as you navigate your new path.

DAILY REFLECTION

What does it mean to you to experience God's love in a new way as you navigate this chapter of your life?

PRAYER

Dear Lord, thank you for the love that remains, even through heartache. Fill me with a sense of Your presence, guiding me as I walk this new path with Your comfort and grace.

"His love remains a steady harbor amidst the waves of change."

CHERISHING THE WEDDING VOWS

"There is no fear in love. But perfect love drives out fear."
1 John 4:18

DEVOTIONAL

When Sarah first navigated her days without John, she found herself surrounded by memories that brought joy and sorrow in equal measure. Every room whispered tales of laughter, challenges, and shared glances that spoke volumes. Instead of feeling overwhelmed, she began to take out their wedding album, slowly flipping through the pages of their blessed moments together. Each vow they had spoken echoed through her mind, reminding her of the promises that transcended life's circumstances, bringing her comfort in the knowledge that their love was real, tangible, and forever imprinted upon her soul.

Cherish the vows spoken in love, for they are a lasting testament of connection that can guide and uplift you in times of loneliness.

DAILY REFLECTION

What do your wedding vows mean to you now, and how can they continue to inspire your life moving forward?

PRAYER

Dear God, wrap your loving arms around this heart that is learning to navigate life without its beloved partner. Help her to find peace in the cherished memories and strength in the vows that still hold significance.

"Love is not diminished by absence; it is deepened and cherished in memories."

WHAT HE LOVED ABOUT YOU

"Know that the Lord is God. It is he who made us, and we are his; we are his people, the sheep of his pasture." **Psalm 100:3**

DEVOTIONAL

After decades spent with her beloved husband, Sarah found herself looking at their wedding album one quiet afternoon. Each photo told a story, each smile a memory, and as she turned the pages, she couldn't help but notice how her husband had always looked at her with a love that seemed to soften even the hardest moments. Through shared laughter and quiet evenings, he had loved her for her kindness, her strength, and her carefree spirit. Though she felt lost without him, she realized she was still the same woman he adored, capable of moving forward and embracing life again.

You are cherished, not just in memory but in the essence of who you are; your worth remains profound, even in his absence.

DAILY REFLECTION

What are the qualities or moments that you now cherish most about your relationship, and how do they reflect the beauty of who you are?

PRAYER

Dear Lord, wrap your arms around this woman as she navigates her grief. Help her to see the love that surrounded her and to embrace the precious memories that reveal her worth. May she feel your comfort and find strength in the love that remains.

"You were loved deeply, and that love still lives within you."

LESSONS FROM A LIFE TOGETHER

"Many are the plans in a person's heart, but it is the Lord's purpose that prevails."
Proverbs 19:21

DEVOTIONAL

As I hold onto the memories of our life together, I reflect on the simple moments that wove our years into a tapestry of love. I remember how we used to sit on the porch, sipping our coffee and sharing dreams. Those quiet mornings offered a comfort that now feels like a cherished echo. The plans we laid out together often changed with unexpected twists, yet each moment brought us closer and grounded us in shared purpose. I have come to realize that though he is gone, the love we built still guides me through this journey of healing, reminding me that each unfolding day carries a whisper of our shared dreams.

Every ending is a new beginning, and the love you shared continues to shape your path forward.

DAILY REFLECTION

What memories from your life together bring you comfort today, and how can those memories guide you in moving forward?

PRAYER

Dear God, thank you for the love that once filled my life and for the lessons learned through it. Please grant me strength to cherish those memories while embracing the path ahead.

"Love leaves a lasting imprint on our hearts,
guiding us through the shadows of grief into the light of hope."

A MEMORY THAT WARMS YOU

"My flesh and my heart may fail, but God is the strength of my heart and my portion forever." **Psalm 73:26**

DEVOTIONAL

As she sorted through the old photographs that afternoon, Jane's fingers brushed against a picture of her and Tom at their favorite seaside resort. His arm was draped around her shoulder, and both of them were laughing freely—joy radiating from their smiles. In that moment, she felt the warmth of those memories wrap around her like a cozy blanket, reminding her that love, once shared, can never truly be taken away. The ache of loss was palpable, but so was the profound gratitude for the moments they had together, a reminder that joy can coexist with sorrow.

You are not alone in your grief; cherish the memories that evoke warmth and comfort, for they are the treasures that hold your love close.

DAILY REFLECTION

What is a cherished memory of your loved one that brings a smile to your heart, even in moments of sadness?

PRAYER

Dear Lord, thank You for the beautiful memories we've made. Please help us to hold onto those moments, finding comfort and warmth in them as we navigate this new chapter in life.

"Memories are the threads that weave love into the fabric of our lives."

SHARING HIS MEMORY WITH OTHERS

"Precious in the sight of the Lord is the death of His saints."
Psalm 116:15

DEVOTIONAL

After losing her beloved husband, Sarah found herself lost in the weight of her grief. As she rummaged through old photo albums, she stumbled upon a picture of their wedding day. The smiles they wore filled her heart with warmth, prompting a sudden desire to share those memories. She decided to host a small gathering with close friends and family, inviting them to share their own memories of her husband. That evening turned into a profound celebration of love and laughter, allowing her to feel his presence in a fresh and comforting way.

In grief, sharing memories transforms sorrow into a tapestry of connection and love that honors those we have lost.

DAILY REFLECTION

What memory of your late partner brings a smile to your face, reminding you of the warmth of your shared moments? How can you carry that memory into today, finding comfort in it?

PRAYER

Dear God, as I navigate this season of loss, help me to cherish the memories that warm my heart. May I find peace in remembering the love we shared and the joy he brought into my life.

"Memories are the hugs that keep our loved ones close."

PASSING DOWN HIS VALUES

"Let your light shine before others, that they may see your good deeds and glorify your Father in heaven." **Matthew 5:16**

DEVOTIONAL

As Sarah navigated the quiet days after losing her husband, she often found herself reflecting on the values he cherished. Their home was a tapestry woven with kindness, laughter, and a deep faith that shaped their lives together. One evening, while sorting through old photographs, she stumbled upon a picture of him helping a neighbor fix her fence. It sparked a realization: those small acts of love and service were not just memories but seeds he had sown in her heart. Inspired, Sarah began to reach out to others in her community, embodying his spirit of generosity and teaching her children the importance of helping those around them. In sharing his values, she found healing and hope, creating a legacy that would last beyond her own days.

The essence of love and service you carry within you can illuminate the path for others, creating a legacy that honors those you've lost.

DAILY REFLECTION

What values do you hold dear that you wish to pass down to those you love, and how can you embody them in your daily life?

PRAYER

Dear God, in this journey of loss and transition, help me to carry your values in my heart. May I find solace and strength in sharing your love and wisdom with those around me.

"Your legacy is not just what you leave behind, but how you live each moment today."

A Moment of Gratitude

If this devotional has brought moments of peace, strength, or reflection into your life, a short review on Amazon can help others discover it too.

devo.anchoredgraces.com/grief

Even a few words about your experience can make a meaningful difference.

Thank you for continuing this journey.

A TRIBUTE IN EVERYDAY LIVING

*"Every good and perfect gift is from above, coming down from the Father of the heavenly lights, who does not change like shifting shadows." **James 1:17***

DEVOTIONAL

During a quiet moment in her kitchen, Sarah found herself making a simple cup of tea, a ritual shared with her late husband for years. As she stirred the honey into the warm liquid, memories flooded back—the laughter, the late-night conversations, and the comfort of companionship. Yet, today, they became bittersweet reminders. She took a deep breath and decided to make the most of her solitude. A thought blossomed: could she honor his memory through the everyday moments of her life? That day, Sarah chose to embrace her routine with gratitude, infusing each task with love, transforming simple acts into a tribute of remembrance for all they had shared.

In honoring those we've lost, we often find the strength to celebrate life's everyday moments.

DAILY REFLECTION

What small act of kindness could you incorporate into your daily routine that pays tribute to your loved one's memory?

PRAYER

Dear God, as I navigate this new chapter, guide me to find moments of love and remembrance in the everyday. Help me cherish the memories we created together while allowing my heart to heal.

"Each day can be an expression of love, a living tribute to those we've lost."

HIS FAVORITE HYMN

*"May the God of hope fill you with all joy and peace as you trust in Him, so that you may overflow with hope by the power of the Holy Spirit." **Romans 15:13***

DEVOTIONAL

After losing her beloved husband, Margaret found solace in the familiar melodies of hymns they used to sing together. One particular hymn, "Great is Thy Faithfulness," became her refuge. Each day, she would sit by the window, humming its verses, feeling the presence of her husband beside her as she praised God for His unwavering faithfulness. The simple act of singing reminded her that even in grief, God's love remained a steadfast anchor, comforting her soul and igniting her hope.

In your journey of healing, let the hymns you cherish be a connection to both your past and the promise of God's continued faithfulness in your life.

DAILY REFLECTION

What hymn has carried you through your darkest days, reminding you of hope and love even in the midst of grief? How does it speak to your heart now, as you navigate this new and challenging chapter of your life?

PRAYER

Dear Lord, envelop this heart in your gentle embrace, guiding each step through sorrow with the light of your love. May the melodies of your presence soothe and uplift, granting strength and peace in moments of reflection.

"In every note of sorrow, there is a promise of healing."

A LETTER TO HIM IN HEAVEN

*He will wipe every tear from their eyes. There will be no more death or mourning or crying or pain, for the old order of things has passed away." **Revelation 21:4***

DEVOTIONAL

After losing my husband, I found myself wandering through our favorite park, the place where we shared countless moments of laughter and love. I could almost hear his laughter in the rustling of the leaves, and it brought both comfort and sadness. One afternoon, as I sat by the pond, I picked up a letter I had tucked away in my purse—a love note from him on an ordinary Tuesday. Reading his heartfelt words felt almost like a warm embrace, reminding me that while he may no longer be physically present, the essence of our love remains forever imprinted on my heart. I closed my eyes, whispered my gratitude for our memories, and sent my love up towards heaven, knowing it would reach him there.

Treasure the memories you shared, for they are the threads that will continue to weave your heart into his, even in his absence.

DAILY REFLECTION

What are the words you long to share with him today, and how can you honor that love in your heart?

PRAYER

Dear God, help me to find comfort in the memories we shared and strength in the love that endures. May I feel his presence in the gentle whispers of your creation and cherish the moments that still bind us together.

'Love transcends time and space; it remains a guiding light even in absence.'

YOU LOVED WELL

"We love because He first loved us."
1 John 4:19

DEVOTIONAL

When Anne lost her husband after decades of companionship, the silence in their home felt unbearable. Yet, as she went through their photo albums one evening, she began to relive the moments of joy, laughter, and love that filled their lives together. With each photograph, the bittersweet memories transformed her sorrow into gratitude. She realized that the love they shared lived on in her heart and encouraged her to embrace life more fully. Instead of merely mourning, she began to celebrate the love they had built, allowing its warmth to guide her forward.

Your love will always be a guiding light, illuminating the path through your grief and reminding you of the beautiful life you shared.

DAILY REFLECTION

What are some of the memories that bring a smile to your face when you think about the love you shared?

PRAYER

Dear God, wrap this beloved soul in Your peace today. Help her to remember the beauty of the love she shared and the joy it brought, even amidst the pain of loss.

"Love never truly leaves us; it becomes a part of who we are."

ACCEPTING HELP WITH GRACE

"Come to me, all you who are weary and burdened, and I will give you rest."
Matthew 11:28-30

DEVOTIONAL

After losing her husband, Sarah found herself submerged in a sea of loneliness and overwhelming tasks that felt insurmountable. She often turned down offers of help from friends and family, believing she should carry her burdens alone. One afternoon, a kind neighbor brought over a warm casserole, and for the first time, Sarah accepted assistance. As she shared a meal and stories, she found that this small act of kindness brought her comfort and a renewed sense of community. Realizing that accepting help didn't mean she was weak but rather human, she began to open her heart to those around her.

Embracing the support of others can be a source of strength and healing as you navigate this new chapter in your life.

DAILY REFLECTION

What does accepting help from others mean to you in this season of your life, and how can you embrace it as an opportunity for connection and healing?

PRAYER

Dear God, in this time of loss, help me to remember that it is a sign of strength to lean on others. May I find comfort in their presence and support, knowing that I am not alone.

"Accepting help is not a sign of weakness,
but a beautiful testament to the bonds that hold us through life's most challenging moments."

WHEN YOU NEED A FRIEND

"Two are better than one, because they have a good reward for their toil. For if they fall, one will lift up his fellow, but woe to him who is alone when he falls and has not another to lift him up." **Ecclesiastes 4:9-10**

DEVOTIONAL

After losing her husband, Sarah found herself in a world filled with silence and solitude. The evenings felt the longest as she sat in the living room, the empty chair next to her a constant reminder of her loss. One day, as she sorted through old photographs, she stumbled upon a picture of her and her best friend from decades ago. That prompted her to call her friend, and they ended up sharing stories and laughter for hours. In that moment, Sarah realized that though life had changed drastically, the love and support of friends could fill the void and bring warmth back into her life.

Sometimes, the companionship and understanding of a friend are the lifelines that help us navigate through our grief and solitude.

DAILY REFLECTION

What does friendship mean to you in this new season of your life? Who comes to mind when you think of reaching out or being reached out to for support?

PRAYER

Dear Lord, in this time of solitude, help her to recognize the friends You have placed in her life and to reach out for comfort and companionship. May she feel Your presence as a gentle reminder that she is never truly alone.

"A friend is always a bridge to the heart in times of need."

SUPPORT GROUPS AND SACRED CIRCLES

"Bear one another's burdens, and so fulfill the law of Christ."
Galatians 6:2

DEVOTIONAL

After losing her husband, Linda felt increasingly isolated, like a ship drifting without its anchor. One afternoon, she decided to attend a local support group for widows, unsure of what to expect. As she walked into the warm, inviting room filled with familiar mournful yet hopeful faces, she quickly realized that sharing her story among others who understood her pain created a powerful bond. They laughed and cried together, forming a sacred circle that felt like a safe haven, allowing her to heal through shared experiences. Linda discovered that by supporting one another, they found strength not only in their shared grief but also in the loving community they began to build together.

In the midst of grief, seeking community can transform isolation into connection and healing.

DAILY REFLECTION

What feelings emerge for you when you think about opening your heart to a support group or a sacred circle? How might sharing your story with others provide comfort or healing?

PRAYER

Dear God, as I navigate this new chapter of my life, help me find the strength to reach out and connect with others. May I feel Your presence in every circle I enter, comforting me and guiding my journey.

In shared vulnerability, we discover the power of grace and connection.

FINDING COMFORT IN OTHERS' STORIES

"Though the mountains be shaken and the hills be removed, yet my unfailing love for you will not be shaken, nor my covenant of peace be removed," says the Lord, who has compassion on you. **Isaiah 54:10**

DEVOTIONAL

In the days following her husband's passing, Sarah often found herself at a crossroads, torn between grief and the comfort she desperately sought. One afternoon, she attended a local support group for those who had lost partners. As the women shared their stories, Sarah was struck by the raw honesty of each experience. One woman spoke of finding solace in nature, another in art, and yet another in the laughter of her grandchildren. It was in listening to their journeys that Sarah began to recognize glimpses of her own potential path towards healing. Each story, a thread woven into a collective tapestry of resilience, offered Sarah hope that though the journey was difficult, she was not alone.

In the shared stories of others, we can find the strength and hope we need to navigate our own grief.

DAILY REFLECTION

What stories have you heard from others that resonate with your own experience? How have those stories brought you comfort or perspective in this season of your life?

PRAYER

Dear Lord, in this tender time of loss, may I find solace in the shared experiences of others. Help me to listen with an open heart, embracing the stories that give me strength.

"Every story shared is a thread in the tapestry of healing."

WHEN SOMEONE REALLY LISTENS

*"Whether you turn to the right or to the left, your ears will hear a voice behind you, saying, 'This is the way; walk in it.'" **Isaiah 30:21***

DEVOTIONAL

After losing her husband, Mary often found herself feeling invisible in social gatherings, her laughter now just a distant echo. One day, a close friend invited her over for tea and, with genuine concern, asked her how she was really doing. Instead of filling the silence with platitudes, she listened intently, allowing Mary to speak freely about her emotions, her memories, and her fears. In that conversation, Mary felt seen and understood; the weight on her heart began to lighten as her friend validated her feelings, reminding her she was not alone.

Sometimes, the most healing gift we can receive is the presence of someone who listens with an open heart.

DAILY REFLECTION

What stories of love, resilience, or healing have you encountered lately that resonate with your journey? How do these narratives lift your spirit and remind you of the shared experiences of others?

PRAYER

Dear God, surround me with your warmth and the comforting embrace of community as I navigate this new chapter in my life. Help me to find solace in the stories of others, and may their journeys inspire hope and healing in my own heart.

"In the tapestry of life, your thread weaves in and out of many stories, each one a vibrant reminder that while some chapters end, new ones are waiting to unfold."

COFFEE WITH A KIND SOUL

"She opens her mouth with wisdom, and the teaching of kindness is on her tongue."
Proverbs 31:26

DEVOTIONAL

After losing her beloved partner of many years, Sarah found solace in her morning routine. Each day, she brewed a strong cup of coffee, the aroma wrapping around her like a warm hug, calling her to sit quietly in the sunlight streaming through the window. One chilly morning, she noticed a neighbor, Mrs. Johnson, sitting on her porch, looking lonely. Sarah decided to take her cup of coffee outside and share it with Mrs. Johnson, initiating a conversation that began to heal them both. Through this small act of kindness, Sarah discovered that in giving, she also received the comfort of companionship.

In the midst of loss, sharing kindness can bridge the gap of loneliness and foster new connections.

DAILY REFLECTION

What does a kind soul look like to you in this season of your life, and how can you invite more moments of connection into your days?

PRAYER

Dear Lord, I thank You for the kindness that surrounds us, even in the midst of our grief. Help me to reach out and connect with those who bring warmth to my heart. May I find comfort in the kindness of others and be a source of comfort as well.

"In the heart of every sorrow, a spark of kindness can light the way to healing."

SHARING A TEAR AND A LAUGH

"A joyful heart is good medicine, but a crushed spirit dries up the bones."
Proverbs 17:22

DEVOTIONAL

After losing her husband, Mary found herself walking a delicate line between sorrow and joy. One afternoon, as she sorted through old photographs, she stumbled upon a picture of them dressed as clowns for a charity event. She chuckled out loud, remembering his silly antics and the way he'd cheekily painted a smile on her face, even on their hardest days. Tears flowed, but they were mixed with laughter as she reminisced about their shared moments of joy amid the struggles. It was in that quiet moment she realized that grief and joy could coexist, allowing her to honor her feelings while celebrating his memory.

Cherish the moments of laughter, for they hold the power to heal even the deepest of wounds.

DAILY REFLECTION

What are some moments when you've felt both the weight of your loss and the joy of a fond memory, and how did that duality make you feel?

PRAYER

Dear God, as I navigate this journey of grief, help me to embrace both my tears and my laughter. May I find your comfort in the moments that bring both sadness and joy, remembering the love that continues to surround me.

"Even in our sorrow, laughter can be a bridge to healing."

GRIEF SHARED IS GRIEF HALVED

"Surely he took up our pain and bore our suffering; yet we considered him punished by God, stricken by him, and afflicted." **Isaiah 53:4**

DEVOTIONAL

In the days following her husband's passing, Laura felt a heaviness settling upon her heart. Each morning she would awaken, the silence of the empty home echoing the absence of shared laughter and quiet moments. Seeking solace, she attended a grief support group where she met other women who understood her sorrow all too well. As they shared their stories, Laura found a peace she hadn't expected—talking about her husband brought back not just pain, but also warm memories that seemed almost buried. With tears mingling with laughter, she realized that sharing her grief with others lightened her load and reminded her of the joy he had given her during their years together.

Grief shared is grief halved, and opening your heart to others can heal wounds in ways you never imagined.

DAILY REFLECTION

What memories do you cherish most about your loved one, and how can sharing those moments lighten your heart today?

PRAYER

Dear God, as we gather in our grief, may we find comfort in Your presence and in the stories we share. Help us to hold one another up as we navigate this journey, finding strength in our memories and connection.

In sharing our sorrow, we allow love to grow amidst the pain.

ENCOURAGEMENT FROM UNEXPECTED PLACES

*"I waited patiently for the Lord; he inclined to me and heard my cry. He drew me up from the pit of destruction, out of the miry bog, and set my feet upon a rock, making my steps secure." **Psalm 40:1-2***

DEVOTIONAL

After losing her husband, Sarah felt adrift in a world that seemed to have lost its color. One rainy afternoon, while walking in her neighborhood, she noticed a vibrant flower blooming bravely through a crack in the concrete. Its beauty in such an unlikely place struck her deeply. She realized that, like that flower, she too could find strength and hope even amidst her sorrow. In that moment, she felt an unexpected wave of encouragement wash over her, reminding her that joy can emerge from the harshest conditions and that life still holds surprises and beauty, even in pain.

True encouragement can flourish in the most unexpected moments, inviting us to find strength and beauty in places we never thought to look.

DAILY REFLECTION

What unexpected places have you found comfort or encouragement in since your loss? Can you remember a moment, however small, where you felt a spark of hope or connection?

PRAYER

Dear God, in these moments of loneliness, may I find your presence in the most unexpected places. Help me to see the beauty and encouragement woven through my days, and guide me as I journey forward.

"Sometimes, the gentlest reminders of love come from the most surprising corners of our lives."

NEW FRIENDSHIPS IN NEW SEASONS

*"Do not be afraid, for I have redeemed you; I have summoned you by name; you are mine." **Isaiah 43:1***

DEVOTIONAL

After losing her husband, Margaret often found herself wandering through the local park, lost in her thoughts and memories. One day, she noticed a woman sitting alone on a bench, and something compelled her to sit down and strike up a conversation. This small act led to a friendship that blossomed over shared cups of coffee and long talks about life, loss, and hope. Through this connection, Margaret discovered new joys and laughter, uncovering that even in her grief, it was possible to build a new life with new friends.

Sometimes, embracing new friendships can light the path to healing and help us redefine our journey in this new season of life.

DAILY REFLECTION

What does the idea of forging new friendships mean to you in this season of your life? How might opening your heart to new connections bring you joy and healing?

PRAYER

Dear God, embrace this woman with your love as she navigates the path of new friendships. May she find comfort and encouragement in the company of others, reminding her that she is never truly alone.

"Every friendship is a new thread woven into the tapestry of our lives."

LETTING OTHERS IN AGAIN

"He heals the brokenhearted and binds up their wounds."
Psalm 147:3

DEVOTIONAL

After losing her husband, Claire felt more isolated than she had ever been. The quiet sometimes felt too loud, and the shadows of memories pressed heavily upon her heart. One day, a friend from her church reached out, inviting her for coffee. At first, Claire hesitated, doubting that she was ready to share her grief or let someone else step into her world. But finally, she accepted, and as they talked, she realized that sharing her pain not only eased her burden but also deepened her connection with someone who genuinely cared. In that moment, Claire learned that allowing others in doesn't diminish her love for her husband; it honors it and encourages her healing.

Opening your heart to others again can be a way to honor your past while embracing the potential for new connections in your life.

DAILY REFLECTION

What fears or feelings arise when you think about letting others back into your life? How might it feel to take small steps towards connection again?

PRAYER

Dear God, in this time of uncertainty and change, help me to open my heart to those around me. Guide me as I navigate this new chapter, embracing the possibility of friendship and support.

"Vulnerability can be a bridge to healing and new beginnings."

BUILDING SISTERHOOD IN SORROW

"Bear one another's burdens, and so fulfill the law of Christ."
Galatians 6:2

DEVOTIONAL

In the wake of her husband's passing, Sarah found herself in an unexpected solitude, wrestling with not only her grief but also the silence that permeated her days. One evening, she decided to reach out to an old friend from her church who had also experienced loss. As they sat together, sharing their stories, a sense of understanding washed over them both. They discovered that in their shared sorrow, there was a unique bond that emerged—a sisterhood formed not merely through joy, but through the deep valley of grief. They vowed to meet regularly, offering each other a listening ear and a comforting shoulder, reminding themselves that they didn't have to walk this path alone.

In sorrow, we find the strength to build connections that can lighten our burdens and bring us hope.

DAILY REFLECTION

What emotions do you find yourself wrestling with as you seek comfort in the company of other women who share your grief?

PRAYER

Heavenly Father, wrap your loving arms around those who mourn and bless the bonds of sisterhood that are forming in the midst of sorrow. May we find strength in each other as we navigate this new path together.

"In the depths of our sorrow, we discover the beauty of shared hearts."

OFFERING SUPPORT TO ANOTHER WIDOW

*"For I know the plans I have for you," declares the Lord, "plans to prosper you and not to harm you, plans to give you hope and a future." **Jeremiah 29:11***

DEVOTIONAL

After losing her husband, Mary felt an overwhelming sense of isolation. One Sunday, she noticed a new woman sitting alone in the back pew, tears streaming down her face. Remembering her own days of silent suffering in crowded rooms, Mary felt compelled to reach out. She introduced herself and sat down, sharing a few comforting words about loss, their shared journey, and the hope that still flickered in their hearts. That simple gesture forged a bond that soothed not only the new widow but also Mary, reminding her that even in grief, they could find strength in one another.

Supporting another widow is a beautiful way to heal; your willingness to share your journey can brighten someone else's path.

DAILY REFLECTION

What has your journey through widowhood taught you about reaching out to others who are also grieving? How might your experiences guide you in offering support to a fellow widow?

PRAYER

Dear God, grant me the compassion to understand the heartache of others and the courage to extend my hand in support. Help me to be a comforting presence to someone else on a similar path.

"In sharing our wounds, we find healing together."

PHONE CALLS THAT SOOTHE

*"Be still, and know that I am God; I will be exalted among the nations, I will be exalted in the earth." **Psalm 46:10***

DEVOTIONAL

In the weeks that followed my husband's passing, there were days when I felt lost in the silence of our home. One afternoon, I picked up the phone and, hesitantly, called a dear friend. As we shared stories, laughed at the memories of our time together, and even shed a few tears, I felt my heart begin to uncoil from the tightness of sorrow. That simple call turned into a weekly ritual, a moment of connection that soothed the ache of loneliness, reminding me that I was not alone in my grief.

In times of loss, reaching out to others can help ease the weight of our sorrow and remind us of the love and support that still surrounds us.

DAILY REFLECTION

What calls to mind the voices of love and comfort in your life? Who in your circle provides that soothing presence when you feel overwhelmed by your grief?

PRAYER

Dear Lord, we come to you seeking comfort in our solitude. Wrap your loving arms around her, reminding her that she is never truly alone, and guide her to those who uplift her spirit.

"Sometimes, the softest whispers carry the deepest love."

A HUG THAT HEALS

"For your Maker is your husband, the Lord Almighty is his name; the Holy One of Israel is your Redeemer; he is called the God of all the earth." **Isaiah 54:5**

DEVOTIONAL

In the quiet moments of evening, after the world fades to a whisper, I found myself wrestling with memories. I would sit in his favorite chair, clutching a faded sweater, trying to gather the remnants of our shared laughter and love. One evening, I noticed a single star shining brightly in the sky—it felt like a comforting presence, reassuring me that I was not alone in my struggles. That star became my beacon, reminding me that while my loving husband had departed, the love we shared was eternal, woven into the very fabric of who I am.

Even in the depths of sorrow, you are accompanied by a love that transcends earthly ties, bringing you comfort and strength for the journey ahead.

DAILY REFLECTION

What phone call have you received that lifted your spirits and reminded you of the love surrounding you? How can you open yourself to those connections now, even in your grief?

PRAYER

Dear Lord, surround her with Your soothing presence, offering comfort through each call she receives. May she feel Your love in the voices of her friends and family, reminding her she is never truly alone.

"Every call is a reminder that love transcends even the darkest of times."

THE MINISTRY OF PRESENCE

"Rejoice with those who rejoice, and weep with those who weep."
Romans 12:15

DEVOTIONAL

When Sarah lost her husband, moments felt unbearably heavy and silence loomed where laughter once thrived. One day, she sat at a local café, lost in her thoughts when a dear friend walked in. Instead of diving into small talk, her friend simply sat down, held her hand, and quietly offered her presence. In that moment of shared silence, Sarah felt understood and less alone, realizing that sometimes the most profound kindness is simply being there for one another in our pain.

The greatest gift we can offer a grieving heart is not words, but our presence.

DAILY REFLECTION

What does being present in the moment mean to you, especially as you navigate through this season of change and grief? How can embracing the ministry of your presence bring comfort to yourself and those around you?

PRAYER

Dear God, in this time of solitude and reflection, help me to find peace within my moments. May I feel Your presence guiding me and may I share that warmth with those who need it.

"Your presence is a gift, a gentle reminder that love can be felt even in silence."

SAYING "YES" TO INVITATIONS

*"Behold, I am doing a new thing; now it springs forth, do you not perceive it? I will make a way in the wilderness and rivers in the desert." **Isaiah 43:19***

DEVOTIONAL

After losing her beloved husband, Mary found herself spending most of her days alone, held captive by memories and a heart heavy with grief. One rainy afternoon, a letter arrived from a friend inviting her to a small book club. The thought of stepping out into the world filled her with dread, but she felt a gentle nudge in her spirit. That evening, with a mix of trepidation and hope, Mary decided to say "yes." To her surprise, the warmth of new friendships, laughter, and shared stories began to cultivate a garden of healing in her heart. Each meeting became a safe space where she could be seen and supported, reminding her that life could still be vibrant and full of possibility.

Saying "yes" to invitations can open the door to new connections and experiences that nurture your spirit and help you heal.

DAILY REFLECTION

What invitations might you say "yes" to this week that could lead to new connections or experiences?

PRAYER

Dear God, guide my heart as I navigate this new chapter. Help me embrace opportunities and friendships that bring light and joy. Amen.

"Every invitation can be a step toward healing and renewal."

REBUILDING COMMUNITY

*"Therefore if there is any consolation in Christ, if any comfort of love, if any fellowship of the Spirit, if any affection and mercy, fulfill my joy by being like-minded, having the same love, being of one accord, of one mind." **Philippians 2:1-2***

DEVOTIONAL

After losing her husband, Sarah felt as if she was walking through a fog, unsure of how to navigate her life alone. In moments when loneliness threatened to overwhelm her, she began attending a local support group for widows. There, she discovered a warm community that embraced her, shared their grief, and celebrated the small joys of life together. This new circle of friends reminded her of the importance of connection; they laughed, cried, and supported one another, allowing Sarah to slowly rebuild the tapestry of her life, one precious thread at a time.

Community, even in grief, can be a source of strength and hope, reminding you that you are never alone on this journey.

DAILY REFLECTION

What are some small steps you can take today to reconnect with those who care about you or to seek out new friendships that nourish your spirit?

PRAYER

Dear God, as I navigate this season of loss, help me to open my heart to those around me. Grant me the courage to reach out and embrace the community that supports and uplifts me.

"In the embrace of community, we find the strength to heal and the joy to rebuild."

FINDING YOUR PEOPLE AGAIN

"God sets the lonely in families."
Psalm 68:6

DEVOTIONAL

Mary found herself at a crossroads after losing her husband of thirty-five years. She spent months cocooned in her home, surrounded by memories of laughter and love. One day, a neighbor invited her to a small gathering of women who had also walked through loss. Tentatively, she attended. Sharing stories and tears with those who understood her pain helped her feel seen again. The warmth of companionship began to mend her heart as she realized that it was possible to find joy and connection once more.

You are worthy of connection, and opening your heart to others can lead to unexpected healing and friendships.

DAILY REFLECTION

What does "finding your people" mean to you in this season of your life, and how can you take the first step towards reconnecting with others around you?

PRAYER

Dear God, as I navigate this new chapter, remind me of the beauty of connection and the warmth of community. Help me to open my heart to new friendships and rekindle old ones.

"Connection can heal, and companionship can bring new joy."

SPEAKING YOUR STORY ALOUD

"He lifts the poor from the dust and the needy from the ash heap; He seats them with princes, with the princes of His people." **Psalm 113:7-8**

DEVOTIONAL

After losing her partner of many years, Linda felt invisible, as if her essence had vanished into the shadows of grief. One rainy afternoon, she discovered a notebook tucked away in a drawer, filled with stories they had written together about their dreams and adventures. As she read through their shared memories, she felt the stirrings of her own voice emerging from the depths of sorrow. Inspired by those moments, she began to narrate her journey of love and loss to a small support group, discovering that her experiences resonated deeply with others. Speaking her story aloud became not only a source of healing for herself but a way to connect with those who needed to hear it.

Your voice carries the power to heal not only your heart but also the hearts of those who need to hear your truth.

DAILY REFLECTION

What stories do you carry within you that deserve to be spoken aloud, not just for others to hear but for your own healing and understanding?

PRAYER

Dear God, as I navigate this journey of loss, grant me the courage to share my story and the comfort to know that I am heard. Help me find the words that reflect my heart and my experiences.

"Your voice holds the power to transform pain into purpose."

PERMISSION TO REST

*"He makes me lie down in green pastures. He leads me beside still waters. He restores my soul." **Psalm 23:2-3***

DEVOTIONAL

After losing her beloved husband, Sarah often felt overwhelmed by the pains of her new reality. Each day seemed to demand more than she had to give. One afternoon, she decided to sit in her garden, where she could hear the birds chirping and feel the warmth of the sun. In that peaceful moment, with flowers blooming around her, she realized that it was okay to take a step back and just breathe. Slowly, she learned to embrace these small pockets of rest, understanding that in giving herself permission to pause, she was allowing God to mend her heart.

Remember that in your journey of grief, it is perfectly acceptable to take moments for rest and reflection; your healing is a process that deserves gentle care.

DAILY REFLECTION

What does rest mean to you right now, amidst the whirlwind of emotions and changes in your life? Are you allowing yourself grace to pause and breathe, even for a moment?

PRAYER

Dear God, as I navigate this journey of loss, help me to embrace rest as a gift, allowing my heart and spirit to heal. May I find comfort in Your presence, knowing that I am not alone.

"Rest is not a sign of weakness; it is an act of courage in the face of grief."

TAKING CARE OF YOU

*"My soul is weary with sorrow; strengthen me according to your word." **Psalm 119:28***

DEVOTIONAL

This season of mourning can feel like an unending winter, where the warmth of your past seems just out of reach. Sarah often found herself reminiscing about the joy and laughter she shared with her husband, feeling lost in a house once filled with love. One day, she discovered a dusty cookbook on a shelf, filled with notes and memories of meals they had created together. As she flipped through the pages, she decided to revive a few recipes, inviting friends over to share and create new memories. In taking time to nourish herself and connect with others, she began to feel her spirit lifting in ways she hadn't thought possible.

Sometimes, taking care of yourself means allowing the warmth of community and cherished memories to gently guide you forward.

DAILY REFLECTION

What does taking care of yourself look like in this new chapter of your life? How can you honor your feelings and needs as you navigate this journey of grief and healing?

PRAYER

Dear God, in this time of loss and transition, guide her to find peace and strength within herself. May she embrace self-care as a way to honor both her heart and her healing journey.

"Nurturing yourself is not indulgent; it's a necessary step toward wholeness."

NOURISHING BODY AND SOUL

*"God comforts us in our troubles, so we can in turn be a comfort to others. In times of deep sorrow, this verse invites us to open our hearts to the divine source of healing and nourishment." **2 Corinthians 1:3-4***

DEVOTIONAL

After losing her husband, Mary often found herself wandering through familiar places, each reminding her of laughter and love now silenced. One evening, as she prepared a simple meal for herself, she felt an overwhelming wave of loss wash over her. Yet in that quiet moment, Mary began to nourish not just her body with the food before her, but her soul with memories of joy. She whispered thankfulness for the years they shared and allowed those memories to fill her spirit. This experience taught her that even in solitude, she could cultivate love, joy, and warmth within her heart.

Nourishing your body with healthy food can be a gentle reminder to also nourish your soul with gratitude and cherished memories.

DAILY REFLECTION

What ways can you nourish your body and soul today, even amidst the heaviness of your recent loss?

PRAYER

Dear Lord, as I navigate this challenging journey, help me to remember to care for my body and soul with your love guiding my steps. Fill me with your peace and strength as I seek to embrace each day.

"Nourishing your spirit in these moments is as vital as nourishing your body—
both are essential for healing."

WALKING FOR HEALING

"I will not leave you orphaned; I am coming to you."
John 14:18

DEVOTIONAL

In the quiet of the early mornings after her loss, Mary found herself walking through the nearby park with a heavy heart. Each step felt like a reminder of the days before when laughter filled the air and the gentle presence of her husband brought her comfort. As she walked, she began to notice the beauty around her—the delicate unfolding of new blooms and the sun peeking through the clouds, bringing warmth. It struck her that, just like those flowers, healing would take time but could still bring life and hope back into her world.

Healing begins with embracing small steps in the journey forward, allowing yourself to feel and grow in the light of love that remains.

DAILY REFLECTION

What does healing look like for you in this season, and how can you take your first step toward it today?

PRAYER

Dear Lord, as I navigate this journey of healing, help me to feel Your presence by my side. May each step I take be filled with Your love and comfort.

"Every step forward is a small victory on the path to wholeness."

A CUP OF TEA AND STILLNESS

"Weeping may stay for the night, but joy comes in the morning."
Psalm 30:5

DEVOTIONAL

In the quiet moments after her husband passed, Linda found solace in brewing a cup of tea each afternoon. As she sat by the window, she watched the world go by, allowing herself to feel the weight of her grief. Each sip was a gentle reminder of the warmth that once filled her home, yet also a beacon of hope. The fragrant steam rising from her cup symbolized the sweetness life could still offer, even in sorrow. Over time, these moments of stillness became a sacred ritual, a space where memory and healing could intertwine.

In stillness and reflection, we often discover hidden strength and the promise of tomorrow.

DAILY REFLECTION

What does your heart whisper to you during your quiet walks, and how might those whispers guide you toward healing?

PRAYER

Dear God, as I take this journey of healing, help me feel Your presence with each step I take. Grant me peace and comfort as I navigate through this new chapter, reminding me that I am never alone.

"Every step on this path is a step toward discovering new strength within you."

JOURNALING FOR RELIEF

"Cast your cares on the Lord and he will sustain you;
he will never let the righteous be shaken." **Psalm 55:22**

DEVOTIONAL

After losing her husband, Sarah found herself overwhelmed with a whirlwind of emotions. Each day felt heavy, and her heart ached with the memories they had shared. One evening, she committed to writing her thoughts down in a simple journal. What started as a way to cope transformed into a sacred space where she could pour out her heart, share her grief, and even celebrate the beautiful moments they had together. As her pen glided over the paper, she began to feel a lightness lifting her spirit—each word was a step towards healing. Journaling became a refuge, allowing her to trace the contours of her grief and gradually find light amidst the shadows.

Writing can be a powerful tool for healing, enabling you to process your feelings and discover comfort in your memories.

DAILY REFLECTION

What emotions have you been carrying with you since your loss, and how might writing them down help lighten your heart?

PRAYER

Dear God, wrap your loving arms around me as I navigate this journey of grief. Help me find solace in the words I write, and let them guide me towards healing and understanding.

"Journaling is a gentle way to pour out your heart and allow your soul to mend."

FINDING SOLACE IN CREATIVITY

"Create in me a clean heart, O God, and renew a right spirit within me."
Psalm 51:10

DEVOTIONAL

After losing her husband, JoAnn found herself overwhelmed by the silence of their once bustling home. One rainy afternoon, in an effort to mend her aching heart, she picked up a paintbrush and began to express her emotions on canvas. As colors swirled and blended under her fingertips, she felt a sense of release she hadn't known in months. Each stroke carried not just her sorrow, but also her memories and hopes for a new beginning. Over time, this creative outlet became her sanctuary, a place where her grief transformed into something beautiful and meaningful.

Empower your healing journey by embracing creativity, allowing it to weave joy and pain into a tapestry of renewal.

DAILY REFLECTION

What creative outlets have brought you peace and joy in the past, and how might you explore them again in this season of your life?

PRAYER

Dear God, in this time of loss, help me to find comfort in my creativity. May each brushstroke, word, or note bring healing to my heart and remind me of the beauty that still surrounds me.

"Creativity is a gentle whisper from the soul, inviting us to celebrate life even in the shadows of grief."

READING THAT RESTORES

"Surely God is my salvation; I will trust and not be afraid. The Lord, the Lord himself, is my strength and my defense; he has become my salvation." **Isaiah 12:2**

DEVOTIONAL

After losing her husband, Mary found herself drowning in loneliness and sadness. One evening, she stumbled upon a collection of love letters they had exchanged years ago. As she began to read, each word wrapped her in sweet memories, whispering tales of joy and laughter. Though her heart ached, the pages became a sanctuary where she could dwell on the warmth of their love. In pouring over those letters, Mary discovered not just sorrow, but also the resilience of cherished memories that could carry her through her darkest days.

In times of deep loss, embrace the words and stories that bring you comfort; they have the power to restore pieces of your heart.

DAILY REFLECTION

What book or passage has brought you comfort lately, and how has it impacted your journey of healing?

PRAYER

Dear God, as I navigate this difficult season, I ask for Your peace to envelop my heart. Help me find solace in the words I read, and lead me to stories that bring restoration and hope.

"Every page turned can be a step toward healing, inviting light into the darkness."

DECLUTTERING THE PAIN

"When the righteous cry for help, the Lord hears and delivers them out of all their troubles. The Lord is near to the brokenhearted and saves the crushed in spirit." **Psalm 34:17-18**

DEVOTIONAL

Once, a woman named Sarah found herself surrounded by memories after the passing of her beloved husband. Each item in their home told a story, but as she struggled with grief, she realized that some memories felt like burdens. One day, with great trepidation, she began to declutter. To her surprise, as she let go of things that no longer served her, she discovered joy hidden among the memories. She kept what truly mattered—the love and laughter they shared—and found space for new beginnings.

In the process of decluttering your life, remember that letting go of physical reminders can be a step toward healing your heart.

DAILY REFLECTION

What pain are you holding onto that might be time to release? How can letting go of this burden open space for healing in your heart?

PRAYER

Dear God, grant her the courage to face her pain and the strength to let it go. Surround her with Your love as she begins to declutter her heart and embrace the hope of new beginnings.

"Just as we tidy our homes, we can also choose to tidy our hearts, making room for what brings us peace."

MUSIC THAT SOOTHES THE HEART

*You will keep in perfect peace those whose minds are steadfast because they trust in you." **Isaiah 26:3***

DEVOTIONAL

One evening, as the sun dipped low, painting the sky with hues of orange and pink, Sarah sat on her porch, feeling the weight of silence since her husband's passing. Suddenly, a gentle breeze carried the sound of a distant piano playing a familiar melody. It was a song they used to dance to during their happiest moments, a tune that reminded her of love, laughter, and shared dreams. As the notes wafted through the air, she closed her eyes and allowed the music to wrap around her, soothing the ache in her heart. That night, she realized that while the absence felt heavy, music could bring her comfort, echoing the love that still resided within her.

In moments of grief, let the music of cherished memories and gentle melodies soothe your heart and remind you that love endures beyond loss.

DAILY REFLECTION

What song resonates with you the most in this season of your life? How does it bring you comfort and remind you of cherished moments?

PRAYER

Heavenly Father, as I navigate this journey of loss, I welcome Your soothing presence through music. May each note bring healing to my heart and remind me of the love that never fades.

"Music is the language of the soul; it speaks when words fail."

GRATITUDE AS MEDICINE

*"Rejoice always, pray continually, give thanks in all circumstances; for this is God's will for you in Christ Jesus." **1 Thessalonians 5:16-18***

DEVOTIONAL

After losing her husband, Sarah found herself in a fog of sorrow, consumed by memories and what-ifs. One chilly morning, she took a walk through her neighborhood, taking in the vibrant colors of the leaves and the soft glow of sunlight filtering through the trees. As she walked, she began to recall the small joys her husband had brought into her life—his laughter, the warmth of his embrace, and the love he had for their garden. Almost without realizing it, she started to whisper thanks for those moments, finding that each word lifted a layer of her heartache, allowing her to see past the immediate sorrow and into a place of remembrance that honored both her grief and her gratitude.

Gratitude can be a balm, reminding us of the love that still surrounds us, even in our lowest moments.

DAILY REFLECTION

What moments from your day, even the small ones, can you find gratitude for right now?

PRAYER

Dear Lord, as I navigate this season of my life, help me to see the blessings amidst the sorrow. May my heart be open to recognizing the beauty in the world around me.

"Gratitude transforms what we have into enough and more."

A DAY OF NO EXPECTATIONS

"Come to me, all you who are weary and burdened, and I will give you rest."
Luke 12:25-26

DEVOTIONAL

In the quiet moments after losing her husband, one woman found solace in the simple act of sitting outside with a cup of tea. Each day had seemed heavy with expectations—what to do, how to feel, who to talk to. But on one unexpected morning, she resolved to simply watch the world unfold without a single plan. She noticed the way the sun played among the leaves and how the birds chirped sweetly, savoring their own little moments. It was in this unstructured peace that she discovered comfort, reminding her that there is beauty and healing in embracing what is, rather than striving for what could be.

Even in your grief, allow yourself days where you let go of expectations and simply be.

DAILY REFLECTION

What would it look like to embrace today without any expectations, allowing yourself to simply be in the moment? How might this freedom change the way you experience your day?

PRAYER

Dear God, amidst the heaviness of loss, help me to find comfort in the simplicity of today. Grant me the grace to let go of what I'm holding onto and find peace in the stillness of your presence.

"Sometimes, the most profound moments of healing come
when we allow ourselves the grace to live without expectations."

THE POWER OF TOUCH (MASSAGE, SPA)

"My dear, as a mother comforts her child, so will I comfort you."
Isaiah 66:13

DEVOTIONAL

After losing her husband, Clara found herself moving through life in a fog, unsure of how to emerge from the shadows of her grief. One afternoon, a friend invited her to a local spa for a much-needed escape. Reluctantly, Clara agreed, and as the soothing hands of the massage therapist worked on her weary body, tears flowed freely. In that moment of gentle touch, she felt a warmth restoring her spirit, rekindling a sense of hope and healing that she thought had vanished. The power of human connection, even through the simple act of massage, reminded her that she was still worthy of care and comfort.

Healing is not only found in time's passage but also in the nurturing embrace of compassionate touch.

DAILY REFLECTION

What does touch mean to you in this season of your life? How might integrating moments of gentle, nurturing touch help you heal and connect with yourself in this journey?

PRAYER

Heavenly Father, as I navigate this new chapter, may I find comfort in the gentle embrace of self-care and healing. Help me to lovingly tend to my heart and spirit, finding peace in the power of touch and connection.

"In the stillness of your solitude, may you discover the strength in gentle caress and tender care."

BREATHING THROUGH ANXIETY

*"Do not be anxious about anything, but in every situation, by prayer and petition, with thanksgiving, present your requests to God. And the peace of God, which transcends all understanding, will guard your hearts and your minds in Christ Jesus." **Philippians 4:6-7***

DEVOTIONAL

After losing her husband, Julia found herself overwhelmed by the weight of her sorrow and the incessant waves of anxiety that lapped at her heart. While sorting through old family photos, she stumbled upon a picture of their wedding day, where they were bathed in sunlight, laughter, and hope. This moment became a turning point; rather than allowing her anxious thoughts to consume her, she took a deep breath, offering her pain and longing as a prayer. As she inhaled deeply, she envisioned that sunlight wrapping around her—a reminder that joy can coexist with grief, each breath becoming a tether to the enduring love they shared.

In the midst of your anxiety, remember to take deep breaths, allowing each exhale to carry your worries to God and each inhale to fill your heart with His peace.

DAILY REFLECTION

How does your heart respond to the waves of anxiety that sometimes crash upon you, and what small step can you take today to breathe through them? Think about a moment when you've felt God's presence bringing you peace.

PRAYER

Dear God, in this time of deep sorrow and uncertainty, please hold her close. Grant her the strength to breathe through each anxious moment and fill her heart with Your calming love.

"Each breath is a reminder that you are still here, still loved, and still moving forward, one step at a time."

SETTING BOUNDARIES WITH GRACE

"Above all, love each other deeply, because love covers over a multitude of sins."
1 Peter 4:8

DEVOTIONAL

After losing her beloved husband, Sarah found her world spun into a whirlpool of emotions. Friends and family rallied around her, showering her with love and support. Yet, their well-meaning advice often felt overwhelming, leaving her drained. One afternoon, as she sat at her kitchen table staring out the window, she realized that she needed to carve out sacred space just for herself. She began setting boundaries gently, letting others know when she needed quiet time to reflect or grieve. Slowly, she learned that saying "no" didn't mean rejecting others; rather, it meant saying "yes" to her own healing.

In the midst of grief, it is essential to honor your own needs and set boundaries that support your journey toward healing.

DAILY REFLECTION

What does it mean for you to set boundaries in your life right now, especially as you navigate new emotions and relationships? How can these boundaries reflect your needs while honoring the memory of your loved one?

PRAYER

Dear God, please grant her the wisdom to know her limits and the strength to express them with love and grace. Surround her with peace as she learns to care for herself in this new chapter of life.

"Boundaries are not walls; they are bridges to a healthier life."

CHOOSING JOY WITHOUT PRESSURE

"I have told you this so that my joy may be in you and that your joy may be complete."
John 15:11

DEVOTIONAL

After losing her beloved husband, Clara often found herself caught in a cycle of sadness, feeling as though she was expected to grieve a certain way for a set period of time. One sunny afternoon, she decided to visit the park where they used to have picnics. As she sat on their favorite bench, she closed her eyes and breathed in the fresh air, allowing the warmth of the sun to envelop her. In that moment of tranquility, she began to recall joyful memories and started to smile. It was then she realized that honoring her husband's memory didn't mean she had to linger in sorrow; it was instead an invitation to find joy in the beauty surrounding her, even in her pain.

Choosing joy is not about forgetting your loved one, but about allowing yourself to feel the beauty of life again, without any pressure to conform to how that joy should look.

DAILY REFLECTION

What boundaries do you need to set in your life right now to honor your feelings and personal space as you navigate this new chapter?

PRAYER

Dear God, grant me the strength to establish healthy boundaries filled with grace. Help me to find peace in saying no when I need to and yes to what truly nourishes my spirit.

"Setting boundaries is a beautiful act of self-respect and love, especially in times of transformation."

CRYING AS A CLEANSING RITUAL

"Jesus wept."
John 11:35

DEVOTIONAL

When my beloved husband passed, I was consumed by a storm of emotions. In those quiet moments alone, I found myself crying—sometimes softly and other times in deep, shaking sobs. Each tear felt like a release, a way to pour out the love and loss I carried within me. I learned that crying is not a sign of weakness, but rather a powerful and necessary part of healing. It was in those moments of vulnerability that I felt his spirit closest to me, reminding me that it's okay to grieve, to feel, and to allow those emotions to flow freely.

Crying can be a cleansing ritual, allowing the soul to express its pain and ultimately helping to pave the way for healing and peace.

DAILY REFLECTION

What emotions have you felt in your journey of grief that you need to allow yourself to fully express?

PRAYER

Dear God, in this time of healing, grant me the courage to embrace my tears as a sign of love and remembrance. Help me to find peace in the release that crying brings, and comfort in Your presence.

"Every tear shed is a testament to love and an invitation for healing."

WATER AS HEALING: BATH OR OCEAN

*"O God, you are my God; earnestly I seek you; my soul thirsts for you; my whole body longs for you, in a dry and weary land where there is no water." **Psalm 63:1***

DEVOTIONAL

After losing my husband, I found myself drawn to the ocean. The rhythmic sound of the waves seemed to echo the ebb and flow of my grief. One particular day, I waded into the water, feeling the coolness envelop my feet. As each wave lapped against my ankles, I imagined each one washing away a fragment of my pain. With each retreating wave, I felt lighter—a small reminder that healing is gradual and gentle, much like the waters of life.

Just as water can cleanse and heal, allow yourself to immerse in the love and mercy of God, letting Him wash over your heart and soothe your spirit during this time of transition.

DAILY REFLECTION

What images or memories does the presence of water evoke for you, and how can these moments serve as a source of healing during this challenging time in your life?

PRAYER

Dear God, as I stand at the edge of the water, I ask for your comfort and peace. Help me to embrace the healing that comes with each gentle wave and flowing stream, reminding me that I am not alone.

"Just as water refreshes and renews, it can wash away the pain, allowing space for hope and healing."

RELEASING THE NEED TO "BE STRONG"

*"Do not fear, you worm Jacob, little Israel, do not fear, for I myself will help you," declares the Lord, your Redeemer, the Holy One of Israel. **Isaiah 41:14***

DEVOTIONAL

Once, a woman named Helen found herself grappling with her widowhood after losing her husband of over thirty years. Everyone told her how strong she needed to be, but she felt anything but strong. One day, while sitting alone in her garden, she broke down in tears, allowing the pain to flow without reservation. In that vulnerable moment, she noticed a small flower pushing through the cracks in the concrete. It symbolized resilience, not because it was strong, but because it simply existed, accepting its reality and blooming in its own time. This revelation brought her peace; she didn't have to be strong—she just had to be.

It's in our moments of sorrow and weakness that we can truly lean on God's strength and find comfort in our vulnerability.

DAILY REFLECTION

What does "being strong" look like to you in this moment, and what might it feel like to release that expectation and allow yourself to simply be?

PRAYER

Dear God, as I navigate this season of loss, help me to let go of the need to be strong. Surround me with your gentle love, giving me the courage to embrace my vulnerability and lean on you for comfort.

"Strength isn't always about holding it together; sometimes it's about letting go."

A DAY TO DO NOTHING

"For God alone, my soul waits in silence; from him comes my salvation. He alone is my rock and my salvation, my fortress; I shall not be greatly shaken." **Psalm 62:5-6**

DEVOTIONAL

In the quiet hours of the day, after the whirlwind of emotions has settled somewhat, you might find yourself craving a moment to simply be—to do nothing. It's as if time slows down, allowing the memories and emotions to wash over you without the pressure to act. One recent widow, Sarah, shared how she spent an entire afternoon in her garden, just sitting among the flowers she had planted with her husband. She didn't worry about weeding or planting anything new; she just soaked in the peace of the moment, letting the beauty of nature soothe her weary heart. These moments, she realized, were sacred, allowing her to be still and connect with her soul as she navigated this new chapter of life. *Sometimes, embracing solitude in quiet moments allows your heart to heal and cultivate a deeper relationship with God.*

DAILY REFLECTION

What does a day of rest and stillness mean to you right now in this season of your life?

PRAYER

Dear God, in this moment of quietness, I invite your comfort and peace to fill my heart. Help me to embrace the stillness and find rest in Your presence.

"Even in our busyness, the soul craves moments of stillness to heal and reflect."

A DAY TO DO NOTHING

"For God alone, my soul waits in silence; from him comes my salvation. He alone is my rock and my salvation, my fortress; I shall not be greatly shaken." **Psalm 62:5-6**

DEVOTIONAL

In the quiet hours of the day, after the whirlwind of emotions has settled somewhat, you might find yourself craving a moment to simply be—to do nothing. It's as if time slows down, allowing the memories and emotions to wash over you without the pressure to act. One recent widow, Sarah, shared how she spent an entire afternoon in her garden, just sitting among the flowers she had planted with her husband. She didn't worry about weeding or planting anything new; she just soaked in the peace of the moment, letting the beauty of nature soothe her weary heart. These moments, she realized, were sacred, allowing her to be still and connect with her soul as she navigated this new chapter of life. *Sometimes, embracing solitude in quiet moments allows your heart to heal and cultivate a deeper relationship with God.*

DAILY REFLECTION

What does a day of rest and stillness mean to you right now in this season of your life?

PRAYER

Dear God, in this moment of quietness, I invite your comfort and peace to fill my heart. Help me to embrace the stillness and find rest in Your presence.

"Even in our busyness, the soul craves moments of stillness to heal and reflect."

WHAT I MISS MOST TODAY

*"Brothers and sisters, we do not want you to be uninformed about those who sleep in death, so that you do not grieve like the rest of mankind, who have no hope. For we believe that Jesus died and rose again, and so we believe that God will bring with Jesus those who have fallen asleep in him." **1 Thessalonians 4:13-14***

DEVOTIONAL

Lila sat on the porch as the sun began to set, the beauty of the glowing sky contrasting sharply with the emptiness beside her. It was in these quiet moments that she felt the void of her husband's absence most acutely. They used to share this space, exchanging stories and laughter about their day. Now, the silence was deafening, amplifying her heartache and longing for the small, cherished moments. Yet, as she breathed in the cool evening air, she felt a flicker of warmth; a reminder of the love they had shared and the hope that held her tight in the shadows of her grief.

Embrace your memories, for they are treasures that keep your loved one's spirit alive within you.

DAILY REFLECTION

What do you miss most about your beloved companion today, and how can those memories shape your joy moving forward?

PRAYER

Dear Lord, envelop her in your loving presence as she navigates her grief. May she find comfort in the cherished memories and the love that still surrounds her. Amen.

"Grief may alter our world, but love remains a guiding light through the darkest days."

WHAT WOULD I SAY TO HIM?

*"Even though I walk through the darkest valley, I will fear no evil, for you are with me; your rod and your staff, they comfort me." **Psalm 23:4***

DEVOTIONAL

As I sat alone in the quiet of the evening, I found myself reflecting on the countless conversations I had shared with my husband. There was a rhythm to our lives, a deep understanding that felt like a second skin. Now, in this vast silence, I often catch myself wishing I could tell him how much I miss him, how my heart feels heavy with memories and dreams unfulfilled. I wonder what I would say if he were here—if he could hear my whispers of love and longing, or my questions about how to navigate this new path without him by my side. Each moment feels like a dialogue with his spirit, as I learn to carry forward the beautiful lessons he taught me.

In this season of grief, remember that your heart carries the love and wisdom of those who have shaped you, and even in silence, you can still converse with their memory.

DAILY REFLECTION

What would you say to him if you could gather the memories of your heart and form them into words? What comfort or understanding would you seek to share with him about the life you cherished together?

PRAYER

Dear God, as I navigate the waves of grief, help me to feel your presence close to my heart. Allow me to cherish the memories I hold dear while trusting in your promise of peace. Amen.

In the quiet of your heart, those unsaid words can become a bridge to healing.

THREE THINGS I'M GRATEFUL FOR

"I will give thanks to you, Lord, with all my heart; I will tell of all your wonderful deeds."
Psalm 9:1

DEVOTIONAL

As I sat on my porch one quiet afternoon, sipping tea and watching the leaves dance in the gentle breeze, I found myself reflecting on the moments that made life beautiful, even in the midst of sorrow. My late husband had always cherished these moments, often pointing out the colors of a sunset or the laughter of our grandchildren. In that stillness, I realized that while he was gone, the memories we created together were still alive in my heart. I felt an overwhelming gratitude for those shared years, knowing I could hold onto them forever. Each sip of tea became a reminder of the warmth and love that had filled our home, and instead of sadness, I found a gentle peace within me.

In the face of loss, cultivating gratitude allows you to celebrate the beauty of the past while moving forward with hope.

DAILY REFLECTION

What is one moment from your day that brought you a sense of warmth or peace, and how can you nurture that feeling in yourself?

PRAYER

Dear God, in this moment of sorrow and remembrance, help me to see the blessings in my life. May I find comfort in Your presence while I search for joy in the little things.

"Even in the shadows of loss, gratitude can shine a light on the path ahead."

A PRAYER FROM MY HEART

"Call to me and I will answer you and tell you great and unsearchable things you do not know." **Jeremiah 33:3**

DEVOTIONAL

When Sarah lost her beloved husband, the world felt dimmer and colder. Each day, she woke up to the silence of an empty home, the echoes of laughter replaced by solitude. Yet, through her sorrow, she discovered an unexpected solace in journaling. Each night, she poured her heart onto the pages, praying for strength, for peace, and for a glimpse of hope amidst her sadness. Over time, these words became a sacred dialogue with God, a healing balm that slowly began to light her path forward.

Your heart's prayers are sacred, and in your grief, God waits to hear from you, offering unconditional love and guidance as you navigate this new chapter of your life.

DAILY REFLECTION

What does it feel like to bring your heart's deepest sorrow to God in prayer, and how can you invite His comfort into your life today?

PRAYER

Dear Lord, as I navigate this unfamiliar path of grief, I open my heart to You. Please wrap me in Your love and guide me through each moment with Your unwavering presence.

"In the quiet of your heart, God hears every unspoken word."

A SCRIPTURE THAT SPEAKS TODAY

"The Lord Himself goes before you and will be with you; He will never leave you nor forsake you. Do not be afraid; do not be discouraged." **Deuteronomy 31:8**

DEVOTIONAL

As you navigate through the complexities of your grief, remember that you are not alone. A close friend of mine faced the devastating loss of her husband after a long and happy marriage. In her darkest moments, she found comfort in her garden, where she had spent countless hours with him. It was there, amidst the blooming flowers and the gentle rustle of leaves, that she felt his presence wrapped around her like a soft embrace. Each day, as she tended to the garden they had nurtured together, she realized that while he was physically gone, their love continued to bloom in every petal and leaf.

Even in the depths of sorrow, trust that God's unchanging presence guides you into new beginnings.

DAILY REFLECTION

What feelings swell in your heart today as you think about your journey ahead without your beloved companion?

PRAYER

Dear God, in this moment of quiet, I come to You, seeking solace and connection. Wrap me in Your love, and grant me the strength to embrace each day with hope and purpose.

"Even in the depths of sorrow, Your light can guide my steps forward."

WHAT I'VE LEARNED THROUGH GRIEF

"For everything there is a season, and a time for every matter under heaven."
Ecclesiastes 3:1

DEVOTIONAL

When I first found myself alone after years of partnership, the silence was deafening. Morning coffee felt like a ritual stripped of its joy, and evenings became a reminder of what used to be. Yet, as I navigated through this valley of sorrow, I discovered small moments of grace. A friend's unexpected visit, the warmth of sunshine on my face, and the sound of laughter from children playing nearby gradually pieced my heart back together. Each day brought a new realization that while the love I once held dear was gone, the lessons and memories remained etched in my spirit.

Grief teaches us that love never truly leaves; it transforms, allowing us to carry cherished memories into a future filled with new beginnings.

DAILY REFLECTION

What emotions have surfaced in you since your loved one passed, and how can you honor their memory amid the pain?

PRAYER

Dear Lord, wrap your loving arms around me as I navigate this journey of grief. Please grant me strength and comfort as I learn to carry my loved one in my heart while moving forward in faith.

Grief is not just a passage through sorrow; it's a doorway to deeper love and understanding.

WHERE I FOUND COMFORT THIS WEEK

"The tongue has the power of life and death."
Proverbs 18:21

DEVOTIONAL

Each evening, as the sun dips below the horizon, I remember the evenings spent with my husband on the porch, sharing stories and laughter. The quiet stillness now feels overwhelming, and I often find myself wishing for just one more day with him—to hear his voice, to feel his warmth beside me. One particular day, I found solace in preparing his favorite meal, feeling the love we had shared infuse every ingredient. It prompted a flood of memories, reminding me that while he may no longer be by my side, the moments we cherished together continue to shape my heart and make me who I am today.

Treasure the memories of your loved one, for they are the beautiful threads woven into the fabric of your life.

DAILY REFLECTION

What would you say to your beloved if you could have just one more day together? What memories or words would you share that hold meaning for both of you?

PRAYER

Lord, in this moment of longing, surround her with your comfort and peace. Help her to cherish the love she experienced while embracing the hope of her future. Amen.

"Love's echoes remain in our hearts, even when we can no longer hold the ones we love."

IF I COULD HAVE ONE MORE DAY

"I am the resurrection and the life. Whoever believes in me, though he die, yet shall he live, and everyone who lives and believes in me shall never die." **John 11:25-26**

DEVOTIONAL

When I lost my husband, the days felt countless and the nights excruciatingly long. On what would have been our anniversary, I found myself reminiscing about our life together. I walked through our favorite park, clutching a bouquet of flowers, wishing I could share the moment with him one more time. There, I spotted a lone butterfly flitting among the blooms, reminding me of his joyful spirit. In that moment, I felt both the weight of my pain and the lightness of cherished memories. Sometimes, when longing fills our hearts, we can find solace in the beauty that surrounds us, as it reminds us of love that outlasts even our hardest days.

Love doesn't disappear with death; it transforms, reminding us to embrace every moment and seek joy even in our grief.

DAILY REFLECTION

What would you say or do if you could have just one more day with your loved one? How would you express the feelings that perhaps were left unsaid?

PRAYER

Dear God, as I navigate these days filled with longing, please bring comfort to my heart. Help me cherish the precious memories while finding the strength to move forward in love.

Every moment we shared is a thread woven into the fabric of my heart,
a testament to our love that endures even in separation.

WHAT I NEED TO RELEASE

"Brothers and sisters, I do not consider myself yet to have taken hold of it. But one thing I do: Forgetting what is behind and straining toward what is ahead, I press on toward the goal to win the prize for which God has called me heavenward in Christ Jesus."

Philippians 3:13-14

DEVOTIONAL

After losing her beloved husband, Margaret found herself in a fog of memories, clinging tightly to every moment they shared. She would often sit in silence, staring at the empty chair beside her, feeling the weight of what once was. One day, while sorting through old photographs, she had an epiphany; the love they shared would never fade, but holding onto the past was anchoring her to sorrow. With a deep breath, she decided to create a memory scrapbook, celebrating their journey together, but also leaving room for new experiences. In doing this, she began to notice small joys returning to her life, reminding her that love transcends time. *Letting go of what no longer serves you allows space for healing and new blessings to grow in your life.*

DAILY REFLECTION

What burdens and memories from your past might you be holding onto that could be released to make space for new joys and healing? What steps can you take to let go of them?

PRAYER

Dear God, in this time of sorrow and transition, guide me to let go of what no longer serves me. Grant me the strength to release my pain and embrace the hope that lies ahead.

"Releasing the past opens the door to a future filled with grace."

WHAT BRINGS ME PEACE

"Cast all your anxiety on him because he cares for you."

1 Peter 5:7

DEVOTIONAL

When Linda lost her husband after decades of companionship, the world around her felt unbearably heavy. Days turned into a blur as she walked through a fog of grief, finding it difficult to navigate the simplest of tasks. One evening, while sorting through some of their old photographs, she stumbled upon a picture of them dancing at their favorite restaurant. In that moment, she remembered that love has a way of imbuing memories with warmth. Even in her sorrow, Linda found comfort in knowing that the love they shared still lingered, wrapping her in a blanket of peace that brought a fleeting smile to her lips. With each tender memory, she recognized that their love story was not over; it simply transformed, becoming a source of strength on her path toward healing. *Peace can often be found in cherishing the memories we hold dear, allowing love to sustain us through our grief.*

DAILY REFLECTION

What brings you peace in this season of your life? Can you recall a moment, big or small, when you felt a gentle calm wash over you?

PRAYER

Dear God, in these quiet moments of longing and remembrance, envelop me in Your peace. Help me to find comfort in Your presence, knowing that I am never truly alone.

"Peace isn't the absence of chaos; it's the presence of a strength that holds you steady."

WHO HAS SHOWN ME KINDNESS?

*"Do not forget to show hospitality to strangers, for by so doing some people have shown hospitality to angels without knowing it." **Hebrews 13:2***

DEVOTIONAL

After the passing of her husband, Sarah felt loneliness set in like a shroud. One afternoon, as she sat in her garden, a neighbor she barely knew stopped by with a warm plate of cookies. They sat together, sharing stories about their lives, and in that moment, Sarah felt a flicker of connection. It was that simple, yet profound gesture that reminded her kindness still lingered around her, even when grief seemed all-consuming.

Even in the depths of our sorrow, we can find solace in the kindness of others, reminding us that we are never truly alone.

DAILY REFLECTION

Who has shown you kindness during this challenging time in your life? As you think about the people around you, can you remember a specific moment when someone reached out in love or support?

PRAYER

Dear God, I thank You for the kindness that surrounds me, even in my sorrow. Help me to recognize and cherish those who have shown me love during this difficult time. May I find comfort in their presence as I navigate this new chapter of my life.

"Kindness is a bridge that connects us, reminding us we are never truly alone."

MY HOPES FOR THE FUTURE

"Now faith is confidence in what we hope for and assurance about what we do not see."
Hebrews 11:1

DEVOTIONAL

After losing her beloved husband, Sarah often found herself wandering through their favorite park, each empty bench reflecting her loneliness. She would sit on one and remember their conversations, the laughter they shared, and the dreams they had planned together. One day, while lost in thought, a young couple sat next to her laughing and sharing stories, easily drawing her back to the present moment. Their joy reminded her that life continues, and perhaps it was time to allow new connections to form, to welcome the future with open arms, just as her husband would have wanted.

Hope is not the absence of pain; it is the recognition that beyond grief, a new chapter awaits, filled with possibilities yet to be realized.

DAILY REFLECTION

What are your dreams and hopes for the future that God has placed in your heart, and how can you take the first step towards pursuing them today?

PRAYER

Dear God, as I stand at the crossroads of my life, fill me with hope and clarity for the journey ahead. Help me to embrace each day with courage and anticipation for the beautiful plans you have for me.

"Hope lights the way when the path seems dark."

WHAT I'M AFRAID OF NOW

"Be strong, and let your heart take courage, all you who wait for the Lord."
Psalm 31:24

DEVOTIONAL

After the loss of her husband, Sarah found herself grappling with a mixture of emotions. Each day felt heavier, shadowed by a deep sense of uncertainty about the future. She worried about managing the household alone, navigating social situations without him by her side, and even facing the silence that now filled their once vibrant home. One evening, as she sorted through some old photographs, she stumbled upon a picture of them laughing together on a joyful day. In that moment, she realized that while her heart was aching, the love they shared would never fade, giving her hope to face the new challenges ahead.

In your moments of fear and uncertainty, remember the strength that has carried you through before; love endures beyond loss.

DAILY REFLECTION

What fears stir in your heart now? Take a moment to sit quietly and let them come to the surface. What do you find yourself most afraid of during this season of change?

PRAYER

Dear Lord, as I navigate this uncertain path, please grant me the courage to face my fears. Fill my heart with your peace and remind me that I am never alone in my struggles.

"Sometimes, the bravest thing we can do is feel our fear and allow ourselves to be vulnerable."

A LETTER TO GOD

"Not only so, but we also glory in our sufferings, because we know that suffering produces perseverance; perseverance, character; and character, hope." **Romans 5:3-4**

DEVOTIONAL

In the quiet moments of grief, a woman sat at her kitchen table, a letter in front of her, pen trembling in hand. With each stroke, she poured out her heart to God, sharing her loneliness, her pain, and her uncertainty about the future. As she wrote about the memories they created together, tears mixed with ink, yet as she reflected on their love, she felt a warmth in her heart—a reminder of the promise of joy that follows sorrow, even when it seems so far away. By the end of her letter, she realized that this act of writing wasn't just for God but also for herself; it was a path toward healing, a way to process her deep emotions and find hope amidst despair.

Healing begins when we openly share our hearts with God, allowing ourselves the space to feel both grief and hope.

DAILY REFLECTION

What thoughts and feelings fill your heart as you consider writing a letter to God? What would you choose to express in that moment of honesty and vulnerability?

PRAYER

Dear God, I come before You with a heart that feels both heavy and hopeful. Thank You for always listening, even when my words seem insufficient. Wrap me in Your love as I seek Your guidance and peace.

"Every tear you shed will one day turn into a message of hope."

WHAT STILL MAKES ME SMILE

"Delight yourself in the Lord, and he will give you the desires of your heart."
Psalm 37:4

DEVOTIONAL

After the loss of my husband, I found it hard to remember what brought me joy. Every day felt like a grey shadow of what life used to be. One afternoon, while sorting through old photographs, I stumbled upon a picture of us laughing during a picnic in the park. That moment of joy began to tug at my heart; it reminded me of the small, simple pleasures that still existed in my life. I took a walk to that same park, feeling the sun on my face and the gentle breeze in my hair. As I sat on our favorite bench, I began to smile, realizing that while grief will always be a part of my journey, there is still beauty to be found in the world around me.

In the midst of your grief, remember that moments of light still await you, beckoning you to experience joy once more.

DAILY REFLECTION

What simple moments throughout your day still bring a smile to your face, reminding you of the joys of life?

PRAYER

Dear God, thank You for the warmth of cherished memories and the beauty in small moments that still bring us joy. Help me to embrace each day with gratitude, finding sparks of happiness even in the midst of sorrow.

"In the midst of loss, joy can still be discovered in the smallest gifts of life."

MY SAFE PLACE

"For you have been my refuge, a strong tower against the enemy."
Psalm 61:3

DEVOTIONAL

In the quiet moments of the evening, when solitude settles in like a thick blanket, the reality of loss can feel overwhelming. I remember one particular night, staring out the window, watching the moonlight dance softly across the yard, and wishing for just a glimpse of the warmth I had lost. It was then I realized that in these moments of aching loneliness, I could turn my heart towards God, the one who has always been my refuge and my safe place. It was as if I could hear Him whispering, reminding me that even in my sadness, I had not been abandoned. Embracing this truth allowed me to start feeling safe again, surrounded by divine love.

Find solace in God's unwavering presence, for He is your safe place amidst the storms of grief.

DAILY REFLECTION

What does "safety" feel like to you in this moment? Where do you find comfort and peace amidst the waves of change in your life?

PRAYER

Dear Lord, embrace this dear woman with your loving presence. Wrap her in your comfort and help her to find her safe place in you, now and always.

"In your vulnerability, you may discover a deeper strength waiting to be embraced."

WHAT I WANT MY KIDS TO KNOW

"Train up a child in the way he should go; even when he is old he will not depart from it."
Proverbs 22:6

DEVOTIONAL

One chilly evening, after the day's bustle faded, I found myself sifting through old photographs. I stumbled upon a picture of my late husband and me with our little ones, each of us smiling broadly in that perfect snapshot of happiness. It was a bittersweet moment that sometimes feels like a second life. As I navigated through the pangs of missing him, I found solace in reflecting on the lessons I wanted to pass on to my children: that love is eternal, that it's okay to grieve, and that amidst sorrow, we can still find joy in each other. Those laughter-filled days, the heartaches, and the love woven through it all tell them that even amidst loss, life teaches us to cherish every moment.

Through every heartache, embrace the opportunity to show your children how to live fully, love deeply, and find strength even in sorrow.

DAILY REFLECTION

What lessons and values do you wish to pass on to your children that you have learned in your journey, especially in this new chapter of your life?

PRAYER

Dear Lord, grant me the strength to share the lessons of love and resilience with my children. Help me to guide them through the pain and show them the beauty of cherished memories. Amen.

"Love is a legacy that transcends time and loss; it is the gift we give even when we are apart."

HIS VOICE IN MY HEART

"What then shall we say to these things? If God is for us, who can be against us? He who did not spare his own Son but gave him up for us all, how will he not also with him graciously give us all things?" **Romans 8:31-32**

DEVOTIONAL

After losing her beloved husband, Sarah found her world abruptly changed. The emptiness echoed in every corner of her home, where laughter once thrived. One evening, while sorting through old photographs, she stumbled upon a note he had written during a time when life felt uncertain for both of them. In his beautiful penmanship, he had penned verses of hope and reassurance, reminding her of God's faithfulness. In that moment, Sarah felt the weight of his absence transform into a gentle reminder of their shared faith, a tether connecting her heart to a love that still transcended time and space.

You are not alone; in every whisper of your heart, God is speaking His love and care, guiding you through this journey one tender moment at a time.

DAILY REFLECTION

What has your heart been whispering to you since your loss, and how can you tune into His voice amidst the silence?

PRAYER

Dear Lord, in this tender moment of solitude, help me to hear Your voice more clearly. Comfort my heart as I navigate this journey of grief and remind me of Your unwavering presence.

"In the stillness of grief, His voice becomes the gentle companion we never knew we needed."

ONE STEP FORWARD

"Therefore, if anyone is in Christ, the new creation has come: The old has gone, the new is here!" **2 Corinthians 5:17**

DEVOTIONAL

In the months following my husband's death, I often found myself struggling to return to life as I once knew it. One dreary afternoon, I decided to take a short walk, a small step forward into the world outside my home. On that walk, I noticed vibrant flowers blooming along the pathway, their colors defying the grey clouds above. For the first time, I took a deep breath and felt a glimpse of hope. Each step I took felt heavier at first, but as I moved, I began to feel lighter. It was as if the act of stepping outside was a gentle reminder that life could still bring beauty, and that I was still part of it.

No step is too small; each moment is a chance to find a new beginning.

DAILY REFLECTION

What does taking just one step forward look like for you today, and how can you honor your journey as you navigate this new chapter of life?

PRAYER

Dear God, as I face this day filled with both challenges and possibilities, help me to take one small step forward. Grant me comfort in knowing that Your love surrounds me and guides my path.

"One step forward is still progress, no matter how small."

YOU ARE STRONGER THAN YOU KNOW

"Be strong and courageous; do not be frightened or dismayed, for the Lord your God is with you wherever you go." **Joshua 1:9**

DEVOTIONAL

After losing her husband, Clara felt as though the world around her had dimmed. Every morning she woke up dreading the empty space next to her, but she also felt a flicker of determination within her. One day, she decided to go for a walk in the park where they used to stroll together. As she walked, she noticed the beauty of the flowers blooming around her, a gentle reminder that life continues even in seasons of grief. With each step, she sensed a growing strength; though her heart felt heavy, she realized that the love they shared had cultivated resilience within her. Clara returned home with a renewed sense of purpose, knowing that while the journey ahead was uncertain, she possessed an inner strength she had yet to fully discover.

You are capable of more than you realize; your strength will guide you through the shadows of loss into the dawn of new beginnings.

DAILY REFLECTION

What hidden strengths within you do you discover in moments of quiet reflection, and how might you lean into them as you navigate this new chapter of your life?

PRAYER

Heavenly Father, as I walk through the valleys of grief, help me to uncover the resilience you have planted within me. Remind me that each day presents an opportunity to draw upon your love and strength.

In your vulnerability, you will find your power.

STRENGTH IN STILLNESS

"For God alone, my soul waits in silence; my hope is from him. He alone is my rock and my salvation, my fortress; I shall not be shaken." **Psalm 62:5-6**

DEVOTIONAL

After losing her husband, Clara found herself in a world filled with noise and chaos. Each day felt overwhelming, with voices clamoring for her attention and emotions battling for expression. One evening, seeking refuge, she stepped into her garden, where a gentle breeze whispered through the trees. In that still moment surrounded by nature, she closed her eyes and allowed herself to feel—a mix of sorrow and grace. It was there, in the embrace of silence, that she began to unravel her grief, realizing that in stillness, she could find strength and wisdom to navigate her new path.

In the quiet moments of your day, allow yourself to sit in stillness and listen for the whispers of God's comfort and strength.

DAILY REFLECTION

What does it mean for you to find strength in moments of stillness, especially when faced with your grief?

PRAYER

Dear Lord, in this time of deep sorrow, may I seek Your presence in the quiet moments. Bring comfort to my heart as I learn to embrace stillness and find strength in You.

"In the silence of sorrow, God whispers the loudest."

GOD IS YOUR REFUGE

"God is our refuge and strength, a very present help in trouble. Therefore we will not fear, though the earth gives way, though the mountains be moved into the heart of the sea."
Psalm 46:1-2

DEVOTIONAL

After losing her husband, Linda found herself standing in the quiet of their living room, surrounded by reminders of joy, laughter, and shared moments. The emotional heaviness felt insurmountable, and loneliness wrapped around her like a heavy blanket. One evening, as rain fell softly outside, she picked up her Bible, almost instinctively. As she read the words of Psalm 46, she felt a whisper in her heart—a gentle reminder that even when everything around her felt chaotic and uncertain, God was her safe haven. In that moment, she learned to lean into her grief while also opening her heart to the presence of divine comfort.

Though the storm of grief may feel overwhelming, trust that God is your shelter, offering peace and strength in your time of need.

DAILY REFLECTION

What does it mean for you to seek refuge in God during this time of loss? How can you consciously invite His presence into your daily life as you navigate this new chapter?

PRAYER

Dear God, wrap your comforting arms around me as I mourn my loss. Help me to see you as my shelter and guide, filling my heart with peace and strength in my grief.

"In the quiet of your heart, God whispers promises of hope and healing."

WHEN COURAGE LOOKS LIKE GETTING OUT OF BED

"I waited patiently for the Lord; he turned to me and heard my cry. He lifted me out of the slimy pit, out of the mud and mire; he set my feet on a rock and gave me a firm place to stand." Psalm 40:1-2

DEVOTIONAL

After losing her husband, Linda found herself trapped in a haze of grief, each morning feeling like a mountain to climb. The weight of her sorrow made even the simple act of rising from bed an overwhelming challenge. One day, she decided to take a small step— she reached for the framed picture of her husband on the nightstand and whispered a soft, "Thank you." That tiny act of gratitude brought a flicker of courage. She realized that every day she chose to rise was a day dedicated to honor his memory and embrace life, however heavy her heart felt.

Courage isn't always seen in grand gestures; sometimes, it's found in the simple act of getting out of bed and facing a new day.

DAILY REFLECTION

What does it mean for you, in this moment, to take that first step out of bed and face the day ahead?

PRAYER

Dear God, as I navigate this season of my life, grant me the strength to rise each morning and embrace the courage within me. Help me to find comfort in your presence and peace in each new day.

"Courage is not always about grand gestures;
sometimes, it's found in the simple act of getting out of bed."

BUILDING A NEW LIFE, BRICK BY BRICK

"Remember not the former things, nor consider the things of old. Behold, I am doing a new thing; now it springs forth, do you not perceive it?" Isaiah 43:18-19

DEVOTIONAL

After the loss of her partner, Elise found herself standing in the living room surrounded by memories—pictures on the walls, two cups on the counter, a familiar scent lingering in the air. Each corner of her home was a reminder of a life built together, yet she couldn't shake the feeling that she needed to rebuild. One day, amidst her grief, she decided to fill the empty spaces with new memories. She invited friends over for coffee, painted an accent wall a vibrant color, and started a new hobby. Slowly, the home that once echoed with sadness transformed into a place of warmth and new beginnings. With each step forward, she realized that building a new life didn't mean abandoning the old one; instead, it was about weaving in the beautiful threads of the past with the promise of tomorrow.

You have the strength to rebuild your life, honoring your past while embracing new opportunities for joy and connection.

DAILY REFLECTION

What small step can you take today that aligns with your vision for this new chapter in your life?

PRAYER

Dear God, as I navigate this journey of rebuilding, grant me strength and courage in the moments of doubt. Help me to see the beauty in every small step I take towards a new life.

"Every moment of rebuilding is an opportunity for growth and renewal."

GRIEF AND GRACE CAN COEXIST

"Rejoice with those who rejoice, and weep with those who weep."
Romans 12:15

DEVOTIONAL

In a small, quiet town, a woman named Sarah found herself alone after the passing of her beloved husband. The once vibrant home felt empty, and each day brought waves of sorrow that threatened to drown her. One chilly afternoon, while sorting through old photographs, she stumbled upon a picture of them dancing at their wedding, laughter frozen in time. In that moment, a soft smile broke through her tears, accompanied by a gentle warmth in her heart that reminded her of their love. Sarah realized that grief was not a barrier to grace; it was a pathway to cherish the beautiful memories they had created together. In acknowledging her sorrow, she also embraced the comfort of grace that surrounded her, reminding her that joy and grief could coexist.
You can find beauty in shared memories, even amidst the deepest sorrow.

DAILY REFLECTION

What does it feel like for you to hold both your grief and the grace you've received in this season of change? How can you allow each to teach you and coexist in your heart?

PRAYER

Dear God, I invite Your warmth into my heart as I navigate this journey of grief. Help me see the grace in small moments and the beauty in memories, trusting that I am never alone.

"Grace is the comfort that cradles me in the ache of loss."

YOU CAN DO HARD THINGS

"Be strong and courageous. Do not be afraid or terrified... for the Lord your God goes with you; He will never leave you nor forsake you." **Deuteronomy 31:6**

DEVOTIONAL

After losing her beloved husband, Maria felt as if the world had crumbled around her. Every morning was a reminder of the void left in her life, and simple tasks felt insurmountable. One day, she decided to plant flowers in the garden they once tended together. As she nurtured the soil and saw the flowers bloom, she realized that, while life could be painful, it could also be beautiful. Each flower stood as a testament to the love they shared, reminding her that even in loss, new beginnings could take root.
You have the strength within you to embrace each day, finding beauty and hope amid heartache.

DAILY REFLECTION

What hard things are you facing right now that you never expected to tackle alone?

PRAYER

Dear God, please guide my heart through this challenging time. Grant me strength and clarity as I navigate the difficult path ahead. Help me to see that I can rise up to face each day with courage.

In the midst of deep sorrow, strength can blossom in unexpected ways.

GOD IS STILL WRITING YOUR STORY

"He who began a good work in you will carry it on to completion until the day of Christ Jesus." **Philippians 1:6**

DEVOTIONAL

As you sit in the quiet moments of your day, memories of your loved one may often flood your heart, bringing both warmth and sorrow. These bittersweet recollections are threads woven into the fabric of your life, but remember, the story is not over yet. Just as an author crafts each chapter, God holds the pen to your narrative, carefully writing each line with purpose and grace. Each day may feel daunting, yet within those moments lies the promise that brighter pages are ahead, filled with hope, restoration, and new beginnings. Trust that in His divine orchestration, your story is still unfolding; it is rich with possibilities and love yet to be experienced.

Your journey is not defined by what you've lost but by the hope of what God is still creating within you.

DAILY REFLECTION

What dreams and desires do you still hold close to your heart, even amidst your grief? Can you envision how God might fulfill those dreams in unexpected ways?

PRAYER

Dear God, please remind her that Your story for her life is still unfolding. Give her peace as she navigates this new chapter and inspire her courage to embrace the future.

"Every ending is a beginning in disguise, woven by the gentle hands of God."

THE POWER OF ENDURANCE

"Therefore, since we are surrounded by such a great cloud of witnesses, let us throw off everything that hinders and the sin that so easily entangles. And let us run with perseverance the race marked out for us, fixing our eyes on Jesus, the pioneer and perfecter of faith." **Hebrews 12:1-2**

DEVOTIONAL

In the aftermath of grief, Sarah found comfort in tending to her garden. Each day, she would pull weeds and plant new seeds, a process that mirrored her own healing. At times, the garden would seem bare, reflecting the emptiness she felt inside. But as days turned into weeks, vibrant flowers began to emerge, reminding her that beauty could still flourish even in the wake of loss. It taught her that enduring through the hard times, pouring love into the soil of her life, allowed new beginnings to take root.

Your endurance during this season is a testament to the life and love you carry forward, illuminating paths of hope for others who may walk a similar journey.

DAILY REFLECTION

What does endurance mean to you in this season of your life, and how might it be a pathway to healing and strength?

PRAYER

Dear God, grant me the strength to endure through this painful journey. Help me to feel Your presence with each step I take and remind me that I am never alone.

"Endurance is the bridge that leads us from grief to hope."

WHEN YOU FEEL BRAVE AGAIN

"God is within her, she will not fall; God will help her at break of day."
Psalm 46:5

DEVOTIONAL

When Mary lost her beloved husband, the world felt impossibly heavy. Each morning became an exercise in courage as she faced days colored by profound loss. Yet, in her solitude, Mary discovered moments of unexpected bravery. The first time she ventured outside her home, feeling the sun on her face-like a gentle whisper reminding her of life, she realized that bravery doesn't always roar; sometimes, it simply takes the form of a quiet, steadfast heart that chooses to embrace the day. Slowly, with each passing moment, she weaved together a new tapestry of life, filled with fragments of joy amidst sorrow and laughter amidst tears.

Bravery isn't the absence of fear; it's the decision to take the next step anyway.

DAILY REFLECTION

What small step can you take today that would make you feel brave and empowered as you navigate this new chapter of your life? How can you honor your courage in moving forward?

PRAYER

Dear God, as I step into each new day, grant me the strength to embrace the unknown and the wisdom to recognize my own bravery. Help me to find peace in the journey ahead and the joy in the little victories.

"Courage is not the absence of fear, but the strength to rise again, one step at a time."

FINDING STABILITY IN CHANGE

"When you pass through the waters, I will be with you; and through the rivers, they shall not overwhelm you; when you walk through fire you shall not be burned, and the flame shall not consume you." **Isaiah 43:2**

DEVOTIONAL

In our lives, change can feel as daunting as navigating a stormy sea alone. After the loss of a partner, it's as if the very ground beneath you has shifted, creating a sense of uncertainty that can be overwhelming. Someone once shared with me how, after losing her husband, she found solace in her garden. Each day, she tended to her flowers, watching them bloom and fade with the seasons, drawing parallels to her own life. With every new blossom, she felt a sense of renewal, a reminder that even in times of grief, there is beauty and growth waiting to emerge.

Each day may bring new challenges, but remember, you have the strength to navigate these changes, and God walks with you through every wave.

DAILY REFLECTION

What aspects of your life feel most uncertain right now, and how can you find a sense of stability amidst these changes?

PRAYER

Dear Lord, as I navigate this season of change, grant me peace and clarity. Help me to feel Your presence in every moment, guiding my heart towards hope and healing.

"Even in the midst of a storm, I can find my anchor in faith."

A DAY WITHOUT PANIC

"When anxiety was great within me, your consolation brought me joy."
Psalm 94:19

DEVOTIONAL

After her husband passed away, Maria often found herself engulfed in moments of panic—sometimes over trivial things, like deciding what to make for dinner or managing household bills. It felt as though every choice was steeped in the magnitude of loss. One afternoon, while organizing his old tools in the garage, she discovered a hidden note he had written long ago, reminding her to "breathe and take one day at a time." Tears filled her eyes, but she felt the weight begin to lift. That day marked a change; she focused on gratitude and found joy in small tasks, letting go of what needed to be perfect.

Amidst grief, remember that it's okay to pause, breathe, and embrace each moment without panic.

DAILY REFLECTION

What would a day without panic look like for you? What small changes could you make to invite peace into your heart and mind today?

PRAYER

Dear Lord, I ask for Your comforting presence to fill my heart today. Help me find moments of stillness and serenity amidst the storm. Remind me that Your love surrounds me, providing strength and peace.

"Amidst the waves of grief, I choose to breathe calmly, letting each moment unfold with grace."

RESTING IN GOD'S PROTECTION

"Whoever dwells in the secret place of the Most High will rest in the shadow of the Almighty. I will say of the Lord, 'He is my refuge and my fortress, my God, in whom I trust.'"
Psalm 91:1-2

DEVOTIONAL

After a long day of sorting through memories and questions, Mary found solace by her bedroom window. The setting sun painted the sky in hues of orange and pink, reminding her of shared sunsets with her late husband. As she gazed out, she imagined she could feel his presence beside her, whispering words of comfort. In the quiet moments that followed, Mary felt the weight of her grief begin to lift just a little, replaced by a gentle assurance that there was a higher purpose in her sorrow. She silently prayed, seeking refuge in the understanding that God's protection enveloped her like a warm blanket, even in her loneliness.

Resting in God's protection allows us to feel safe and cherished, even in our moments of deepest pain.

DAILY REFLECTION

What do you need to release into God's care today, trusting in His protection for your heart and your future?

PRAYER

Dear Lord, surround me with Your love and peace as I navigate this difficult time. Help me to lean on You, finding comfort in Your presence and strength in Your promises. Amen.

"Rest in the refuge of His wings, for He is your shelter in every storm."

Near the End of Our Journey

You have spent many days reflecting through these devotionals.

If this book has supported your spiritual journey, sharing a short review on Amazon helps more women discover these pages of encouragement.

devo.anchoredgraces.com/grief

Your story may be the reason another woman finds hope.

RESILIENCE THROUGH FAITH

"The Lord is my shepherd; I shall not want. He makes me lie down in green pastures. He leads me beside still waters. He restores my soul." **Psalm 23:1-3**

DEVOTIONAL

After losing her husband, Marie felt lost, as if she were wandering through an endless fog. The days felt long and the nights, even longer. One morning, as she sipped her tea, she noticed the sunlight breaking through the clouds, illuminating her garden. A single bloom, resilient in the chill of the dawn, stood tall amidst the faded petals—a reminder of the beauty that can emerge from sorrow. In that moment, she realized that like the flower, she too was capable of growing and thriving, even in the wake of heartache.

True resilience comes from trusting in God's unfailing presence and love, recognizing that your journey through grief is a path toward renewal.

DAILY REFLECTION

What is one way you can lean into your faith today to find strength in this moment of loss?

PRAYER

Dear Lord, as I navigate this challenging time, help me to feel Your presence beside me. Grant me the strength to find solace in my faith and the courage to embrace each day ahead.

"Faith is the anchor that holds us steady in the storms of life."

HOLDING ON AND LETTING GO

"I can do all things through Christ who strengthens me."
Philippians 4:13

DEVOTIONAL

In the quiet moments of the evening, Mary often found herself holding onto the memories of her husband, clinging to every laugh, every shared glance, and every comfortable silence they had experienced together. Yet, as she sifted through the remnants of their life—a collection of old photographs, love letters, and the familiar scent of his favorite cologne—she discovered that holding on sometimes made the ache of loss more intense. One evening, as she sat down with a cup of tea, an idea took root. What if she began to let go of some items, not as an act of forgetting but as a way to honor their love? With each object she parted with, she felt a weight lift. It became a testament to their journey together, a bittersweet affirmation that love transcends even physical separation. With each release, she invited the healing power of remembrance through tears and laughter, knowing her husband would always hold a cherished place in her heart.

Letting go can be a pathway to healing, allowing the love you shared to transform into something that nurtures your spirit rather than weighs it down.

DAILY REFLECTION

What memories do you cherish the most from your time together, and how can those memories help you find peace in letting go?

PRAYER

Lord, as I navigate this journey of loss, fill my heart with comfort and guide me to embrace both the love I hold and the memories I need to release. Help me transition through this season with grace and strength.

In the dance of holding on and letting go, may your heart find the rhythm of healing.

THE WOMAN YOU'RE BECOMING

*"Dear brothers and sisters, when troubles of any kind come your way, consider it an opportunity for great joy. For you know that when your faith is tested, your endurance has a chance to grow." **James 1:2-3***

DEVOTIONAL

Sarah sat quietly at her kitchen table, her heart still heavy with the loss of her husband. Each day felt like a battle as she navigated a world that seemed to move on without her. One morning, as she sipped her coffee, she noticed a flower that had pushed through the cracks of the sidewalk outside her window. It stood tall and vibrant, a testament to resilience in the face of adversity. In that moment, Sarah realized that like the flower, she too was beginning a new journey of becoming—a journey that required patience and faith, and ultimately, the embrace of her own strength.

You are not defined by your loss, but by the woman you are becoming through it.

DAILY REFLECTION

What do you see when you think about the woman you are becoming in this new chapter of your life? How can you embrace this change as an opportunity for growth and renewal?

PRAYER

Dear God, as I navigate this new journey, help me to find strength in my vulnerability and joy in my transformation. Surround me with Your love and guidance as I discover the woman You intend for me to be.

"Your grief is a pathway to uncovering the strength and grace that already reside within you."

SMALL VICTORIES, BIG GROWTH

"But thanks be to God! He gives us the victory through our Lord Jesus Christ."
1 Corinthians 15:57

DEVOTIONAL

After losing her husband, Susan found herself overwhelmed by the heaviness of grief, struggling to complete even the simplest of tasks. One day, she decided to take a walk around her neighborhood, which felt monumental in its own way. As she stepped outside, she noticed the beauty of blooming flowers and the laughter of children playing. That small decision to step out of her home turned into a daily ritual, allowing her to find solace in nature and gradually reclaim her joy. Each step became a small victory that led to greater emotional healing, reminding her that life could bring new beginnings even after profound loss.

Every small victory you achieve can lead to monumental growth in your heart and spirit, revealing the strength you didn't know you had.

DAILY REFLECTION

What small victories have you experienced this week that brought you a sense of hope or peace? How did they contribute to your growth in this new season of life?

PRAYER

Dear Lord, grant her the strength to acknowledge each small victory, and help her see how these moments lead to personal growth. Surround her with Your love and comfort as she navigates this journey of healing.

"Even the smallest seed can grow into a beautiful tree with time and care."

THE VOICE OF STRENGTH WITHIN

"She is clothed with strength and dignity; she can laugh at the days to come."
Proverbs 31:25

DEVOTIONAL

When Sarah lost her husband, her home felt empty and silence hung heavily in the air. Each room held memories filled with laughter and love, now shadowed by the ache of loss. Yet, on one quiet evening, as she made her tea, she noticed a scrap of paper taped to the fridge. It was a note from him, simply saying, "You are stronger than you know." Those words began to resonate within her, awakening a newfound voice of strength. Through tears, Sarah started to pray and write down her thoughts, reclaiming her identity bit by bit, building a bridge from sorrow to hope, discovering that even in her pain, she could find power within.

Embrace the voice of strength within you; it is a gift that can guide you through even the darkest valleys.

DAILY REFLECTION

What strength can you discover within yourself as you navigate this new chapter of your life? How can you listen to the gentle whispers of resilience that call you forward?

PRAYER

Dear God, as I walk through this season of loss, help me to hear the voice of strength within me. Wrap me in Your comforting presence, guiding me step by step with hope and courage.

"Within every heart lies a reservoir of strength, waiting to be tapped into in even the hardest of times."

BLOOMING THROUGH BROKENNESS

"Consider how the wildflowers grow. They do not labor or spin. Yet I tell you, not even Solomon in all his splendor was dressed like one of these." **Luke 12:27**

DEVOTIONAL

In the winter of grief, it may feel as though the world has come to a standstill. A once vibrant flower now appears wilted and fragile, cradling the heartache of loss like a weight too heavy to bear. Yet, just as the wildflowers in spring find their way through the frost, so too can we. I remember standing by my window one chilly morning, gazing at the barren garden outside. I had not yet discovered that amidst the cold soil lay the promise of new life just waiting for warmth and light. Slowly but surely, I learned that it was okay to feel both broken and beautiful, as the petals of my spirit began to unfurl, nourished by love and hope.

In the depths of sorrow, allow yourself to grieve but also to seek the gentle sunlight of new beginnings, for it is through the cracks of our brokenness that we can bloom anew.

DAILY REFLECTION

What does blooming through your brokenness look like for you in this season of your life? How can you nurture the seeds of hope that are waiting to grow within you?

PRAYER

Dear Heavenly Father, please wrap your comforting arms around this precious woman as she navigates the pain of loss. Help her to see the beauty that can emerge from her brokenness and give her the strength to embrace each new day with grace and hope.

"From the ashes of sorrow, beauty can still rise."

December 23

BRAVE ENOUGH TO BEGIN AGAIN

"God places the lonely in families; He sets the prisoners free and gives them joy."
Psalm 68:6

DEVOTIONAL

After losing her husband, Sarah found herself overwhelmed by the silence of their once bustling home. The days stretched long, and the shadows of memories felt almost suffocating. Yet, one quiet afternoon, she stumbled upon an old box of photographs. As she flipped through each snapshot, joy mixed with sorrow, reminding her of cherished moments. Inspired, Sarah began to journal her feelings, capturing both the heartache and healing. Each entry slowly transformed into a narrative of her journey forward, encouraging her to embrace life anew, one brave step at a time.

This season of loss is a call to courageous rebirth; remember, every ending can bloom into a beautiful new beginning.

DAILY REFLECTION

What does it mean for you to embrace the possibility of starting anew? How can you take small steps toward finding joy and purpose in this next chapter of your life?

PRAYER

Dear God, in this moment of grief and transition, remind her that You hold her future in Your hands. Give her the courage to embrace the beauty of beginnings and the strength to step forward with hope.

"Every ending is a gentle invitation to a new beginning."

December 24

JOY THAT FINDS YOU IN SORROW

"You make known to me the path of life; in your presence there is fullness of joy; at your right hand are pleasures forevermore." **Psalm 16:11**

DEVOTIONAL

When Mary lost her husband of forty years, she felt as if the very ground beneath her had crumbled away. Days turned to weeks, and while she struggled to face each morning alone, she noticed the sweet, melodic sounds of birds singing outside her window. One day, she sat quietly and listened, realizing that their joyful notes had not ceased, even with her sorrow. As she contemplated their cheerful existence amidst the changing seasons of life, a soft warmth began to envelop her heart. In the simplest of moments, she found flickers of joy reminding her that while grief can feel isolating, the world still spins in beauty and grace.

Even in the midst of sorrow, joy is waiting to be uncovered in the smallest of moments.

DAILY REFLECTION

What memories of joy do you hold onto that still bring a smile to your heart, even amidst the pain of loss? How can you honor those moments today?

PRAYER

Dear God, as I navigate this season of sorrow, I ask for your gentle presence to guide me. Help me to find glimpses of joy that remind me of love, laughter, and hope in my life.

"Even in the dimmest moments, joy can flicker like a candle, guiding you toward warmth and light."

COPING WITH HOLIDAYS ALONE

"May your unfailing love be my comfort, according to your promise to your servant."
Psalm 119:76

DEVOTIONAL

There was a woman named Clara who faced her first holiday season after losing her beloved husband. Every twinkling light in the neighborhood seemed to mock her grief, and she felt even more alone as friends celebrated around her. One afternoon, as she gazed at a photo of them together, Clara felt an unexpected warmth wash over her. Instead of shutting herself in, she decided to attend a local service that welcomed everyone, especially those who might be alone. Surrounded by kind souls, she realized that while her heart was forever changed, she could still feel the comfort of community and the peace of shared stories. It was that night, amidst laughter and even some tears, that she learned it's okay to embrace both grief and joy simultaneously.

You are not defined by your loneliness; instead, let your heart open to the love and warmth that others can provide during this difficult time.

DAILY REFLECTION

What feelings arise within you as the holidays approach this year? How can you honor your loved one while embracing new traditions or memories that bring you comfort?

PRAYER

Dear God, in this time of solitude, help me to feel Your presence. Comfort my heart as I navigate these holidays, and remind me of the love that continues to surround me.

"Though I walk this path alone, I am never truly without love."

SEEING WITH NEW EYES

"The eye is the lamp of the body. If your eyes are healthy, your whole body will be full of light. But if your eyes are unhealthy, your whole body will be full of darkness."
Matthew 6:22-23

DEVOTIONAL

When Ellen's husband passed, she felt as though the world had lost its color. Days turned into a blur of gray, and the laughter they once shared echoed like a distant memory. One afternoon, as she sorted through their old photographs, a particular picture caught her eye—freezing a moment of joy at the beach. As she gazed at the smiles they wore, she felt a warmth stir within her. It reminded her that while the loss was profound, it did not erase the beautiful life they had shared and the love that would continue to carry her. With each remembrance, Ellen began to see her life anew—recognizing that love could coexist with grief, illuminating her path forward.

Your eyes can become a source of light, allowing you to see the love that remains and the future that awaits you.

DAILY REFLECTION

What new perspectives might you discover about yourself or your future as you navigate this journey? How can you honor your past while embracing the possibilities ahead?

PRAYER

Dear God, as I walk this new path, help me to see the beauty in the changes around me. Grant me courage to embrace each new day and find hope in unexpected places.

"Sometimes, it takes losing everything to gain a clearer vision of what truly matters."

LOVE AHEAD

"For I am convinced that neither death nor life, neither angels nor demons, neither the present nor the future, nor any powers, neither height nor depth, nor anything else in all creation, will be able to separate us from the love of God that is in Christ Jesus our Lord."
Romans 8:38-39

DEVOTIONAL

Her heart felt heavy as she stood in the kitchen, the place where countless meals had been shared, laughter echoed, and love blossomed. Every corner reminded her of the life they built together—a story now paused. Yet, in the silence, a whisper of hope began to rise within her. One quiet evening, she opened an old photo album, each snapshot serving as a love letter from the past. As memories flooded her mind, she realized that love wasn't confined to the past; it could transcend time and pain, offering a promise of connection that remains even in absence. It was a gentle reminder that while her beloved was gone, the essence of love still wrapped around her, encouraging her to embrace the future with open arms.
Love doesn't end with loss; it transforms and guides us into tomorrow.

DAILY REFLECTION

What does it mean to you to embrace the idea of 'Love Ahead' in this new chapter of your life? How can you open your heart to new relationships and joys, even in the midst of your loss?

PRAYER

Dear Lord, as I navigate this journey of grief, help me to see the promise of love that lies ahead. Comfort my heart and guide me to embrace each new day with hope and faith.

"Beyond the pain of loss, love invites us to look forward with courage and anticipation."

HOPE AND HEALING GO HAND IN HAND

We have this hope as an anchor for the soul, firm and secure."
Hebrews 6:19

DEVOTIONAL

Once, a woman named Sarah found herself lost in a world that felt unbearably dark after her husband's passing. Each morning she woke up feeling like a shell of her former self, until one day she spotted a small, vibrant flower growing in the crack of her driveway. It thrived against all odds, reminding Sarah that beauty can emerge from hardship, and that healing, like that flower, can take root even in the hardest of circumstances. Inspired, she began to nurture her own heart, planting small seeds of hope daily—allowing herself to mourn, but also to hope.
Healing comes visibly in steps, and those steps are often illuminated by the flicker of hope within us.

DAILY REFLECTION

What are some small joys or glimmers of hope you can cling to today, even in the midst of your sorrow? How can you invite healing into your heart as you navigate this journey?

PRAYER

Dear God, in this time of deep sorrow, help me feel Your comforting presence. May I find the strength to embrace hope and healing, knowing that both can dwell within my heart.

"Hope can light the way even in the darkest moments of grief."

YOUR ANNIVERSARY

"Weeping may stay for the night, but rejoicing comes in the morning."
Psalm 30:5

DEVOTIONAL

It was Sarah's first anniversary without her husband. The house felt emptier than ever, the memories echoing like soft whispers in the rooms they once shared. As she gathered her thoughts, she decided to honor their love by lighting a candle and reflecting on the beautiful moments they had shared. Tears flowed, but amidst the pain, she also felt a deep gratitude for their time together. It was a blend of grief and love, and she realized that while her heart was aching, it was also filled with cherished memories.

Every anniversary, whether alone or with loved ones, is a reminder to celebrate the love that shaped you, even in the midst of heartache.

DAILY REFLECTION

What emotions rise within you as you think of your wedding anniversary this year? How might you honor the love shared and the memories created on this special day, even in this new season of your life?

PRAYER

Dear God, as I navigate this bittersweet day, fill my heart with Your comforting presence. Help me to cherish the memories while finding peace in the journey ahead.

"Love lives on, not just in memories, but in the legacy we continue to create."

YOUR BIRTHDAY WITHOUT HIM

"For I know that my Redeemer lives, and at the last he will stand upon the earth."
Job 19:25

DEVOTIONAL

As you face another birthday without the warmth of his presence, remember that though he may no longer share in the celebration, your life still holds precious purpose. One woman described her first birthday alone, feeling an ache that resonated deeper than she had anticipated. Yet, as she collected thoughts, memories, and encouragement from family and friends, she discovered new ways to honor his memory. Instead of feeling alone, she embraced the stories shared, the laughter—and even the tears—that came from remembering all that he meant to her. Those moments not only filled her heart but also reminded her that love endures, even as life shifts.

Your birthday can still be a day of remembrance and hope, transforming sorrow into gratitude for the love you shared.

DAILY REFLECTION

What memories or feelings do you associate with celebrating your birthday together, and how can you honor those moments while also allowing space for new beginnings?

PRAYER

Dear Lord, as I approach this birthday without my loved one, grant me the comfort of Your presence. Help me to cherish the memories while also embracing the hope and new possibilities You have in store for me.

"Every birthday is a reminder of love that transcends time, shining brightly even in absence."

HOPE FOR TOMORROW

*"Therefore do not worry about tomorrow, for tomorrow will worry about itself. Each day has enough trouble of its own." **Matthew 6:34***

DEVOTIONAL

After losing her husband, Linda felt as though the sun had set on her life. Days turned into weeks as she grappled with grief, moving through the motions of routine but feeling an emptiness inside. One evening, while cleaning out a drawer, she found an old photo of them laughing together. As she held the image close, a flicker of warmth spread through her heart. Suddenly, she remembered the dreams they had shared and wondered if perhaps there was still hope for new ones, even without him. Slowly, she began to reconnect with friends and hobbies, allowing herself to envision a brighter tomorrow.

Hope can begin with a single step forward, reminding you that the love you shared can still light the path ahead.

DAILY REFLECTION

What dreams or desires have you tucked away since your loss, and how might you begin to nurture them once again?

PRAYER

Dear Lord, as I navigate these uncertain days, grant me the strength to hold onto the hope for tomorrow and to embrace each moment with love and gratitude. Amen.

"Hope is a gentle whisper that reminds us even in our grief, tomorrow can hold joy."

More Devotionals from Anchored Grace

If this devotional encouraged your heart, you may also enjoy these devotionals from Anchored Grace.

- 365 Day Devotional for Women
- 90 Day Devotional for Women Seeking Peace
- 90 Day Devotional for Women Facing Anxiety and Stress
- 90 Day Devotional for Women 50+
- Guided Prayer Journal for Women

Search **"Anchored Grace Devotional"** on Amazon to discover more devotionals designed to support your journey of faith.

Thank You
for Walking This Journey

Thank you for spending this devotional journey with Anchored Grace.

If this devotional encouraged your heart, strengthened your faith, or brought peace to your daily routine, would you consider leaving a short review on Amazon?

devo.anchoredgraces.com/grief

Reviews help other women discover devotionals that may support them through their own seasons of life.

Even a single sentence about your experience can make a difference.

We are grateful you chose Anchored Grace.

www.ingramcontent.com/pod-product-compliance
Lightning Source LLC
Chambersburg PA
CBHW071738120626
46550CB00002B/564